AMERICA, THE BAND

AMERICA, THE BAND

An Authorized Biography

Jude Warne

Foreword by Billy Bob Thornton

ROWMAN & LITTLEFIELD
Lanham • Boulder • New York • London

Rowman & Littlefield
Bloomsbury Publishing Inc, 1385 Broadway, New York, NY 10018, USA
Bloomsbury Publishing Plc, 50 Bedford Square, London, WC1B 3DP, UK
Bloomsbury Publishing Ireland, 29 Earlsfort Terrace, Dublin 2, D02 AY28, Ireland
www.bloomsbury.com

First published in the United States of America 2020
Paperback edition published 2025

Copyright © 2020 by Jude Warne

All rights reserved. No part of this publication may be: i) reproduced or transmitted in any form, electronic or mechanical, including photocopying, recording or by means of any information storage or retrieval system without prior permission in writing from the publishers; or ii) used or reproduced in any way for the training, development or operation of artificial intelligence (AI) technologies, including generative AI technologies. The rights holders expressly reserve this publication from the text and data mining exception as per Article 4(3) of the Digital Single Market Directive (EU) 2019/790.

British Library Cataloguing in Publication Information available

Library of Congress Cataloging-in-Publication Data
Name: Warne, Jude, author.
Title: America, the band : an authorized biography / Jude Warne.
Description: Lanham : Rowman & Littlefield Publishing Group, 2020. | Includes bibliographical references and index. | Summary: "Celebrating the band's fiftieth anniversary, Gerry Beckley and Dewey Bunnell share stories of growing up, growing together, and growing older. Journalist Jude Warne weaves original interviews with Beckley, Bunnell, and many others into a dynamic cultural history of America, the band, and America, the nation"—Provided by publisher.
Identifiers: LCCN 2019044066 (print) | LCCN 2019044067 (ebook) | ISBN 9781538120958 (cloth) | ISBN 9798216197423 (paper) | ISBN 9781538120965 (epub)
Subjects: LCSH: America (Musical group) | Musicians—United States—Biography.
Classification: LCC ML421.A457 W37 2020 (print) | LCC ML421.A457 (ebook) | DDC 782.42166092/2 [B]—dc23
LC record available at https://lccn.loc.gov/2019044066
LC ebook record available at https://lccn.loc.gov/2019044067
For product safety related questions contact productsafety@bloomsbury.com.

∞™ The paper used in this publication meets the minimum requirements of American National Standard for Information Sciences—Permanence of Paper for Printed Library Materials, ANSI/NISO Z39.48-1992.

CONTENTS

Foreword vii
   Billy Bob Thornton

Acknowledgments ix

Introduction: Peace, Love, and Success in the Seventies xi

PART I: THE FIRST PART OF THE JOURNEY

1 The Song 3
2 The Roots 11
3 The Beatles and the Beach Boys 21
4 The Trio 33
5 The Dawn 39
6 The Manor 47
7 The Album 57
8 The Climb 65
9 The Move 71

PART II: IN HOLLYWOOD

10 The Arrival 83
11 The California Songs 91
12 The Polarizer 101
13 The Producer 111
14 The Identity 119

15 The Freezing and the Fifty-Five Thousand	129
16 The Beast	139
17 The Split	149

PART III: YOU CAN DO MAGIC

18 The Duo	159
19 The Reasonless Rejection	167
20 The Comeback	175
21 The Friend	183
22 The Video	191
23 The Corporation	197
24 The Bowling Alley	205
25 The Farm(house) and the Home Studio	213
26 The Work	223
27 The Relevance	229
28 The Tour	237
29 The New	243
Notes	251
Bibliography	255
Index	257

FOREWORD

Billy Bob Thornton

Jude Warne has written a very articulate, informative, and entertaining biography of the band America. It tells you all you'll want or need to know about these magical cats. If you're a longtime fan, or even someone who is only casually acquainted with their music, this book will be a great read. So my job is not to blather on about my nerdy fascination with and knowledge of America's history or its music. That is what this book is for, and it does a much better job than I could ever do. My only contribution is to impart my personal experience with them as people, and my feelings of how the music and songwriting have affected me.

My pals and I as teenagers, like many others, became aware of America upon hearing "A Horse with No Name" and on the first listening thinking, "Wow, Neil Young has written a very different kind of song." But we very quickly realized that, even though Dewey cops to admiring and being influenced by Neil, it wasn't Neil but a new, beautiful sound. Spooky, mystical, breezy, and just downright mysterious. The radio DJ informed us this was a band formed in England called America. Pretty clever. Then of course we went about finding everything we could on them. Stuff you'll read in this book. Of course we saved our pennies, and before you knew it we purchased the record and wore it completely out.

Gerry Beckley, Dewey Bunnell, and Dan Peek burst on the music scene with a chemistry that just worked. The singing, the playing, everything about the songs seemed so effortless that they just breathed their own special thing. They had the beautiful harmonies, three distinctly different voices as lead vocalists, but a beautiful blend together. Gerry had the youthful voice, singing pop songs but with a melancholy and sometimes a darkness in the subject matter. Dewey had the trippy lyrics that we all tried to figure out . . . and that lonely, faraway voice. Dan Peek, gone too soon, contributed songs such as "Lonely People" and "Woman Tonight" in his own beautiful, haunting way. They were, and are, unique in their sound and writing, and yet you still hear their idols in there: the Beatles, the Beach Boys, Neil Young, etc.

Okay, here's the thing about America—there's air around the songs. You feel it. The desert, Ventura Highway, the late night, Memphis, "Sister Golden Hair." The songs take you there and put you in the same air with them. And though formed in England, we can claim them here in Southern California. They're a Southern Cali band through and through. You put the top down and drive the 101 from L.A. to Pismo Beach someday, and pop in an America record. You'll see. It's perfect.

These days music has been compartmentalized like almost everything else. Bands like America, Bread, and many others are considered "soft" rock. In my days as a teenager and in my twenties, you had Black Sabbath and James Taylor and America and Yes all on the same station. It was all just rock 'n' roll. It still is. Labels have just been put on. America has a high place in rock history as a magical combination of singing, songwriting, and sound.

When I got to know Gerry and Dewey years ago, we became fast friends, and I finally realized there's no mystery. I know who they are: great guys who love music and know how to make it. Now read the book and find out how it all happened.

ACKNOWLEDGMENTS

Thank you first and foremost to Gerry Beckley, Dewey Bunnell, and Dan Peek, who created a world-changing legacy that I was honored to try to articulate and analyze. Thank you to Gerry and Dewey for their time, candor, insight, and grace. Thank you to my agent, Alice Speilburg, in particular for her editing throughout the project. Thank you to the Rowman & Littlefield team: Natalie Mandziuk, John Cerullo, Michael Tan, Kellie Hagan, Garrett Bond, and Megan Manzano. Thank you to Jim Morey and Kyle Whitney at Morey Management Group and Peter Raleigh at Raleigh Music Group. Thank you to everyone in the America story who sat for interviews during this project: Jimmy Webb, Timothy B. Schmit, Al Jardine, Bill Mumy, Willie Leacox, Michael "Wood-z" Woods, Jimmy Calire, Tom Walsh, John Hartmann, Phil Galdston, Jim Morey, Rich Campbell, Ryland Steen, Steve Fekete, Jeff Larson, David Peek, and Matt Beckley. Thank you to Henry Diltz, Gary Strobl, Eric Halvorsen, and Lew Walker—as well as the Bunnell, Beckley, and Peek families—for contributing photographs. Thank you to Billy Bob Thornton for his beautiful and thoughtful foreword. Thank you to Robert Lamm. Thank you to Greil Marcus and Lester Bangs for inspiring me. And thank you to my parents, Mary Jane and Stephen Warne, two of the most rock 'n' roll people I've ever met.

INTRODUCTION

Peace, Love, and Success in the Seventies

"They're such nice guys."—Everyone interviewed about America the band

By the end of the 1960s, nearly every American was exhausted. The far reach of changes made—political, societal, artistic—had left all affected. The 1970s arrived just in time, a feel-good remedy ready-made. The country wondered—what would happen to the work and progress of the previous decade? Where would it go? What would its torchbearers do with it? Would it all be forgotten?

And what would happen to the music?

In late 1971, a strange and spooky single began to rise to the forefront of the radio airwaves. It sounded like Neil Young and was sometimes accidentally credited to him by radio DJs—but it wasn't his song. It belonged to a new rock group, a mostly acoustic trio of teenage guys, called America. They came out of London, but they weren't British. They were American, more or less: each of them had lived in dozens of different cities and countries during their childhoods due to the frequent relocations of their Air Force families. In the coming years the band would be known as a quintessential California band and hold onto that identity for its entire career. America's debut single "A Horse with No Name" told the story of a man who had abandoned society because it had failed him and his ideals. He was a man who had been forced to retreat into nature. It told a true story, summing up the sentiment and desire of the youth of the United States and much of the world: disgusted and disappointed.

America released their single with high hopes. They had no idea of the level of success that they were to reach, or how quick their rise to fame would be. In the early months of 1972, "Horse" and the album *America*, on which it was included, became monster hits. The achievement defined the level of success that America the band was forced to pursue from its incarnation onward, through the rest of the 1970s and '80s, into the '90s, and through the new millennium. Following the success of "Horse," the tunes "Ventura Highway," "Tin Man," and "Sister Golden Hair" were just a few of the notable chart-topping hits that America produced during the first few years of its recording career.

They had been three American teenagers from Air Force families, living in London at the tail end of the Beatle years when rock music reigned supreme. They began by playing music in the style of CSNY—acoustic, harmony-driven, guitar-heavy tunes that ultimately encapsulated the sound of laid-back California rock. Gerry Beckley, Dewey Bunnell, and Dan Peek's artistic catalogue from the very earliest disregarded the disappointment that had accompanied the end of the 1960s; to their music, it was unimportant, irrelevant. They pulled out what the era's ideological essence had been and insisted upon its truth—not by relating it to social issues or politics, but instead to the human spirit. Thus, they understood how to run their career in the 1970s as it progressed forward—with a firm grasp on what listeners would respond to.

America's articulation of the hippie ethos included the natural and straighter sides of it, and sidestepped many of the wacky and drugged-out sides. In the first few years of the band's career, during its nonstop touring and hundreds of concert performances, the trio insisted upon having live plants on every one of their stages. In lieu of elaborate stage production, America preferred to showcase its identification with the natural world, an identification that had been part of the hippies' creed. The band was also nonjudgmental of performance spaces, often agreeing to perform for "straight" crowds unironically, like those in military schools.

Because America has remained a recording artist for decades and never strayed too far from its ideological love-and-nature path, America's musical work stands as a tremendous articulation of the era's sentiments, while managing to keep them eternal, as John Lennon had said of peace and love. Since its origins in London, America seemed to embody what the 1960s were supposed to be. But the band itself was always a bit under the radar. The trio was less interesting than crazy-wild 1970s rock 'n' roll bands like the Rolling Stones and Led Zeppelin. The problem is not that America the band is unknown or forgotten now; in fact, it is one of the most in-demand classic rock acts, still touring two hundred days out of each year after fifty years in the music business. The problem is what the band is known and remembered for—in that the major and lasting success of its hits, and their cultural impact, has often overshadowed the vastness of the band's musical output. The band is so much more than its greatest hits. America was consistently true to its sound as a band, never overly involved in ever-changing trends but always aware of them.

There is the ongoing and career-long theme of the band's issue with anonymity. No front man, and a band name that suggests an entire—and freedom-preaching—nation, the "land of the free." A band name that suggests a whole country of people rather than just three individuals. This issue was also addressed in Cameron Crowe's 1975 *L.A. Times* article in which the band members expressed frustration with America the band being known, but with no one knowing who the individual members were. This was exactly what the hippie ethos had been seeking: equality, anonymity. It was communal, representing the everyman's emotions, which could be applied to anyone—dropping out of society, dropping out of ego—forgetting one's own name. America did have a recognizable logo for its members to hide behind, much like their fellow bands Chicago and the Steve Miller Band. These groups released massively successful albums in the 1970s, albums that most young people bought. With America and other logo bands, the emphasis was always placed on the music, never on a cult figure with a wild personal life.

Despite its slightly anonymous image, America achieved extreme commercial success articulating the love mission that had begun with the music of the 1960s. The movement had fallen a bit out of favor by the '70s—people had become disappointed and jaded about the scene—but masses still identified with it and related to it. This ongoing popularity was largely ignored by critics, who viewed commercial success as an indication of anti-coolness. Too straight, mellow, or sober. Too shiny. Too successful.

In 2004 Dan Peek, who had left the band in 1977, published his first memoir, *An American Band*, about his childhood and years in America. Other than that, no other biography on the band existed. As a music journalist, I had been searching for a band from the classic era of the 1970s to write about in long form. My 2015 master's thesis had been the longest nonfiction piece I'd written before; it presented a deep dive into Bruce Springsteen's 1978 album *Darkness on the Edge of Town*, comparing the album's disappointed American characters to those in Sherwood Anderson's 1919 short story cycle *Winesburg, Ohio*. I was inspired by the writings of the great rock writer and cultural critic Greil Marcus, who proved that rock 'n' roll could share paragraphs with great American literature and history. This was my motivation when analyzing Bruce's *Darkness*, and it was my same motivation when writing *America, the Band: An Authorized Biography*.

I had been captivated by America's catalogue for quite some time, when I had the opportunity to interview Gerry Beckley on his 2016 solo release *Carousel*. When I met him and Dewey Bunnell that autumn, prior to a performance of theirs at the now-defunct B. B. King Blues Club in New York, I first discussed my idea for a long-form authorized biography on their decades-long career. I wished to tell the story of America, drawing from interviews with Gerry and Dewey themselves and others in the wide America orbit. Thus began the journey that led to the publication of this book in conjunction with the band's 2020 fiftieth anniversary.

In this book, I have intended to impress upon readers and fans the longevity of America, and its vast catalogue of albums that ran much further than its Top Ten singles from the 1970s. Having been born after the group's golden era, I can attest to a general lack of nostalgia in this book. Instead, the band's tale is told via its albums, with a selection of songs from each one being analyzed. I wanted to do a deep dive into each one of the band's albums.

Utilizing the hours of interview material with Dewey and Gerry that ended up on the cutting room floor, I could write a second book on America. Both men gave so much of their time over a period of eighteen months, agreeing to sit for interviews that covered their entire lives and careers. Both of their voices take leading roles in this book, as they should. (Except where noted, all Dewey and Gerry quotes come from these interviews.)

As I had suspected at the start of my book's journey, and as every supporting player I interviewed more often than not volunteered to confirm, Dewey and Gerry are two of the nicest people I have ever met. Their personalities, to me, truly match the colors of their songs. But they are so much more than that: sublimely intelligent about the worlds of art in all forms of media, candid and clear in the recounting of their memories, and extremely easy to work with. They still possess an aura of *the golden-age rock star*, and yet they are more than that, almost seeming strained by the cool confines of that title.

I hope readers take away a realization of the depth of the band America, in both their musical output and their commitment to living truthfully, as well as their live performance. That they are a rock group with an extensive discography of well-crafted records worthy of listeners' time and reflection. That they are, with full echoes to the masterpiece of Lowell George, "Willin'." Which at times, especially as young men in the rock industry, perhaps detracted from their coolness levels here and there. America wants to be there—they want to be on your stereo, your radio, your local performance venue stage. They are authentic to their desire to play music, to perform their slew of timeless songs—made more timeless by their human themes of love, joy, and celebration of the natural world. They see no point in feigning indifference. They're pretty tough that way, and they deserve to be.

Part I

The First Part of the Journey

I

THE SONG

Dewey: "Now we're not sure of the procedure—whether we just keep goin' or we redo somethin' that we don't like?" *Gerry:* "We want to redo that song. Can we redo that one?" *Disembodied voice:* "Just keep goin'."—America on episode of *Musikladen*, Radio Bremen, 1974

The single wasn't right; that much was clear. Warner Brothers had listened to the final version of America's self-titled debut album and its proposed first single. "I Need You" was a ballad by Gerry Beckley, who, as a pop composer and unrelenting romantic, was on the path to becoming Uncle Sam's Paul McCartney. The song encapsulated the nineteen-year-old's delicate dance between innocence and experience, acknowledging the earnestness of romantic curiosity, with an unmistakable undertone of sex appeal. "I Need You" was set indoors, where Gerry's writerly character would reside for the majority of his artistic life.

The song's theme was what Lennon and McCartney had dubbed "The Word" in their 1965 song on *Rubber Soul* and in 1967 had declared to be all you need. A generation of young people had recently seized the word in their quest to redefine what mattered for society and for culture, what was important—and just how far and in how many different directions it could fly. It was something that the cumulative youth ideology of the recently closed decade had assumed for its main tenet. It was something thought to have been the answer: *love*.

But it was 1971 now. The Beatles had broken up. The '60s were literally—and in many ways figuratively—over. The year 1969 had witnessed the manifestation of the decade's full potential in the freedom-laden beauty of Woodstock. But it had also witnessed its seeming demise in the heinous murders by the Manson Family, as well as the ill-fated Altamont Free Concert on what *Rolling Stone* would call "rock 'n' roll's all-time worst day." Disappointment was palpable. Malaise and indifference threatened. A widespread sense of trust in freedom had been violated. What would happen to love? Where would it go? Who would reclaim it?

Gerry Beckley would, at least for his own band, America. "I Need You" was Beatlesque, simple and beautifully melodic, a slow song, a pop standard. It immediately established Gerry's musical character as having one foot in the past—the tradition and history of the songwriting craft—and the other in the future—the ever-evolving technological possibilities of the recording studio. Gerry was a born music producer who felt at home in the studio and was intellectually curious about its creative opportunities. He was a big-picture man, able to consider the totality of a song and understand what made it work—and what could make it better.

Dan Peek's guitar playing usually could. As a musician, he possessed an innate rock 'n' roll sensibility founded on instrumental acumen. Just what rock 'n' roll would become over the course of the '70s for the moment remained to be seen. In the previous decade the genre had expanded and defined popular music, allowing for the self-expression of unapologetic attitudes. It had been driven by the guitar. Jimi Hendrix, Eric Clapton, Jimmy Page, Jeff Beck, Keith Richards, Peter Green, Pete Townshend, Mike Bloomfield, Robbie Robertson, Duane Allman, Jorma Kaukonen, Johnny Winter, Steve Miller, Stephen Stills, and Neil Young had all come forth to wail. Still tasting strongly of the '60s, rock 'n' roll in 1971 held an uncertain future.

For America the band, rock was manifested most ardently through Dan Peek. Like Gerry, Dan felt comfortable in the recording studio. He was a naturally gifted lead guitarist, able to craft melodic lines that would define the group's sound. And his hauntingly beautiful voice, impeccably suited to high harmonies, made America famous for its three-part vocals. Dan's character enabled him to dress his actions, words, and musical performing in a coat of nonchalance. Intelligence and wry wit exaggerated his natural charisma and allowed him to instantly connect with America's young audiences—especially during stage banter with his bandmates. Like the genre he matched so closely, Dan would flirt now and then with self-destruction, but his talent for songwriting that transcended the genre nuances of country rock, hard rock, and mellow introspectives would survive it all. Dan's band membership would not make the transition into the 1980s. Before the new decade was over, he would leave America for good, never to return—just as rock 'n' roll as everyone knew it was becoming more and more infiltrated by disco, new wave, and punk.

In 1971, those terms didn't yet mean much to Warner Brothers. When considering "I Need You" for America's first single, the label knew what it wanted—and what it didn't. Though emotively stellar, productively genuine, and a traditional songwriter's song, Beckley's love-dove number wasn't enough for Warner Brothers. The label wanted its newest band to grab listeners by their collars, to wow them, to hit them in the face with its uniqueness. It wanted more. Warner Brothers dubbed the track "too British" in sound. The label was determined to release a single with wide-ranging appeal and would not be satisfied with the endorsement of British crowds alone—it wanted American kids to go crazy over America too. But what did young Americans dig in 1971? What would work? What was "in"? Acoustic, Southern California–based rock; singer-songwriter, bare-bones, emotionally real stuff was. Neil Young was.

Dewey Bunnell couldn't help who he sounded like when he sang. His influences ran deep—and having been trained as an actor, he was a studied interpreter of characters who inherently absorbed inspirations. As a songwriter he composed from musical moods and penned lyrics that sounded stolen from wild image–heavy dreams. Not overly concerned with tradition or restriction, or with the past or future, Dewey was naturally creative and a man of the present moment. His songs were journeys about people—much like the characters of Jack Kerouac's *On the Road*—who were on their way to or from something. They were about people utilizing their own freedom. And they would always be heavily dosed with nature. If Gerry wrote his songs indoors, Dewey most certainly wrote them out under the stars.

While Beckley channeled pop idol McCartney, walking the path of a traditional songwriter, Bunnell was edgier. As a composer, he veered toward songwriting's subtle, jazzy elements, with seventh chords—the sonic equivalents of awe and mystery. He went in for mood and atmosphere, and as far as form was concerned, Dewey didn't obsess over the typical verse-chorus-verse-chorus-bridge structure. He placed few restrictions on himself as a writer. In contrast to the cerebral and methodical Beckley, Bunnell relied on instincts, on channeling the capricious yet powerful elements of the universe at large. All three bandmates, children of the '60s, had lived and witnessed the volatile progression of the decade and its musical output. They inherited the cosmic residue. But while Dan was artistically captivated by rock 'n' roll and Gerry by love, Dewey, perhaps the most sociologically concerned, went in for peace.

America's first recording sessions at London's Trident Studios—during which "I Need You" was cut—had gone well, and the band was sitting on a quality debut album. Produced by Ian Samwell and co-produced by Jeff Dexter, who would soon become the band's manager, the album *America* included such tracks as the intoxicating opener "Riverside," the romantic and atmospheric Beckley tune "Here," and Bunnell's classic "Three Roses," among others. *America* was released in Europe during the last week of 1971, but with the absence of a single, the album stalled on the charts.

For the past several months, Bunnell had been working on a mercurial and distinctive tune that he called "Desert Song." Its lyrics told the story of a man who wanted to drop out of society and retreat into nature, where he could detach himself from his material possessions and realize his innate identity. Now, there was no reason for Warner Brothers to worry that the single could sound "too British," as "I Need You" had. Its narrative tasted strongly of the great American West, of anonymity and solitude. The song, which would eventually become the band's smash hit "A Horse with No Name," spoke on behalf of the youth of the world, many of whom were disgusted and disappointed with society. They wished to follow that man, to live out the idealized dream that thrived on a fundamental principle much like the one that the United States' founders had established their nation upon: the birthright of human freedom. It was through this freedom that individuals could reach new heights, allowing for the betterment of society and its future generations. This generation knew that peace was not just a passing trend or a substance-induced invention of hippies. Lasting peace was real. It was possible.

"A Horse with No Name" encapsulated this hope in its hypnotic and repetitive, guitar-laden, musical tones. The song's story and mood perfectly articulated the 1960s and '70s counterculture dissatisfaction with government and mainstream society and the concurrent inclination to retreat—to tune in, turn on, and drop out. Communes were in vogue, with their organized living off the land. Dennis Hopper's 1969 immense hit film *Easy Rider* had been on the same wavelength as "Horse." Its central theme involved the individual's quest for freedom amid a universe of societal restrictions—a fitting tale for the end of the 1960s. And so was "Horse." "The story told by the river that flowed" was reminiscent of the river in the final scene of *Easy Rider*: God's road, the river, and man's road, the highway. This was how nearly every young person felt once the '60s had ended. "It felt good to be out of the rain"—good to be away from the turmoil of the '60s, and into what would partly become the "Take It Easy" feel-good '70s.

The last verse of "A Horse with No Name" is the narrative climax, presenting its rawest truth: "Under the cities lies a heart made of ground, but the humans will give no love." Manmade cities, built right over and in ignorance of sacred and natural soil beneath. Impurity on top of purity: bulldozed-over, plentiful, earthbound elements meant to sustain human generations. People had lived off the land for years and it had been enough. The land had loved them for years, but now the humans had turned their backs on Mother Nature; they had placed their trust in chrome, metallic cities instead. Some humans, like Bunnell's narrator in "Horse," sought to "get back to the garden," to return to an awareness of their source. Nature seemed the quickest route home. Here, it is the desert, on a natural animal that has not been tarnished by human language. The horse has not been given a name, but its value and worth have not lessened because of it: an achievement that post-hippie, early '70s youth, discouraged and frightened by the era-ending Manson murders of '69 but not destroyed by them, still sought for themselves. These youths had been waiting for a rearticulation of their generation's ethos, but one that sidestepped specific political and societal issues that seemed impossible to resolve. They had been waiting for a version that was simpler, more human, more difficult to argue with. They had been waiting for "A Horse with No Name."

Some of the song's lyrics seem awkwardly worded, and almost grammatically incorrect. Some of them seem redundant, with words serving as placeholders only. "There were plants and birds and rocks and things . . . the heat was hot . . . 'cause there ain't no one for to give you no pain." Yet none of these intellectually cringeworthy moments detracts from the song's power. Dewey's narrator is an expert storyteller; he reveals each piece of his message bit by bit. The earnest message of an entire generation was the primacy of nature over machinery, community over isolation, and love over hate. Bunnell's laid-back Gary Cooper–esque cowboy quality matched perfectly with his song's lead vocals. His beautifully dark eyes suggested that they saw nothing but simple and pure nature as it was—not in a judgmental or critical way, but in an enlightened and tuned-in one. His primal view communicated an inherent distrust of organized society, a distrust that ran rampant in the ideology of American youth of the time.

Fittingly, in Dewey's song, such unwinding from societal ties can take time. Days, one after the other, must pass in order to shed the talismans, the chains of city life, and the connections to organizations, corporations, institutions. But the song itself is in no rush; "A Horse with No Name" has time. Its tempo is confident, steady, knowing. This is reminiscent of the Beach Boys' "Do It Again" (1968), a song that maintains a steady, almost slow pace, that nearly disarms the listener by refusing to speed up at any point. It knows itself, it is relaxed, it feels good in its own skin. The musical progression is hypnotic, cyclical, and formally unique, suggesting the ongoing and unrelenting power of the desert. In many ways, "A Horse with No Name" is about the search for relief. Relief from torment, baggage, oppression, and chains of all kinds.

"Dewey had some interesting, great, different, ways of playing the bridge and the breakdown," Gerry reminisced. "I remember thinking that it was kind of the same thing from start to finish. 'It's the storyline. So what we can do is build up the harmonies each time it comes around again. For the second time we'll add two-part harmony. Now the next time it comes around, let's add three-part harmony. And for the build, we'll add 'oo-ooh.'' These are, frankly, somewhat simplistic building blocks . . . but it was custom-made for that, because it was just linear."

Gerry felt that the song simultaneously possessed both a universally appealing simplicity and a lyrics-based elusive complexity: "There's all this cryptic, surreal stuff—'plants and birds and rocks and things,' combined with the 'la la' chorus that everybody can sing. So it's got that trick of 'everybody can sing it,' in any language. Some songs have all of the mystery, but without the part that everyone can sing."

At the time of its composition, Dewey planned to insert lyrics in place of the "la-la" chorus, once he'd thought of some. But eventually as they worked the song out together, the trio realized that lyrics there were not needed. The la-la's, with that catchy melody, were enough.

When Warner Brothers asked for more material, the group demoed "Horse" at the home studio of "Fire" singer Arthur Brown. Eventually,

"Submarine Ladies," "Everyone I Meet Is from California," and "Don't Cross the River" would be recorded there and released first on a maxi-single with "Horse," then on the second album, called *Homecoming*. Upon hearing America's new demo tape, the label selected "Horse" for the single.

A new recording session was booked to master the track. Morgan Studios, in a remote northwest section of London known as Willesden, was chosen. It was a place that Gerry was very familiar with, having spent many hours as a tape-op there. There was nothing much remarkable about the building, and there was nothing much remarkable about the session either. It went smoothly: vocal tracks were laid, instrumentalists brought in to provide percussion. Then it was over, and they all left.

2

THE ROOTS

Dewey was born twenty years before "A Horse with No Name" became a number-one record and sent America soaring to the heights of rock stardom. He came into the world as Lee Merton Bunnell on January 19, 1952, in Harrogate, a town in the Yorkshire region of England. "Longing for You," a pleasant, waltzy number recorded by popular American singer Teresa Brewer, had just made it to number one in the UK. In April of the following year, a teenage Elvis Presley would sing in public for the first time, performing Teresa Brewer's hit "Till I Waltz Again with You" at Humes High School's annual talent show in Memphis, Tennessee. The summer of 1956 would find him with his fourth number-one record, "Hound Dog"—the song that a young Dewey Bunnell would perform in his first public appearances, when his parents would trot him out to perform for their guests at parties. For a while, it was four-year-old Dewey's favorite song. In the early 1970s, Joni Mitchell would urge Dewey to join her in seeing Elvis perform in Las Vegas. Dewey would turn the invite down, no longer interested in seeing "old hat" musicians play live. He would later regret it.

London Central High School was a dependents school run by the U.S. Department of Defense. In 1968, it was located in Bushey Hall, a suburban area twenty miles from the city's center. In the fall of 1968, Gerry, Dewey, and Dan were all students there. The decade had been a "swinging" one for London, but this year in particular was a standout. March had spawned anti–Vietnam War protests in Grosvenor Square and Trafalgar Square, in which cultural icons Vanessa Redgrave and Mick Jagger—

who would pen "Street Fighting Man" for the Stones' newest record, *Beggars Banquet*—participated. September witnessed the Doors and Jefferson Airplane perform their landmark sets at the Roundhouse rock club, and in October Tim Buckley performed at Queen Elizabeth Hall—resulting in a stellar live album (released in 1990).

Dan and Dewey rode the school bus together every day. They built a friendship on discussions of music and sports, as well as an agreement to steal cigarettes for each other from their respective parents. Dan was drawn to Dewey's laid-back, affable nature and a unique quality that seemed to set him apart from the other students—what Dan referred to as a "British sensibility."

Dewey's British mother, Patricia Wells, had met his father, William Bunnell, an Air Force serviceman from Alaska, in 1950. William was stationed at RAF Menwith Hill in South Ruislip; he met Patricia when she worked at her uncle Eric's pub, called the King William, in the town of Ripon, Yorkshire. Decades later, following William's retirement from the Air Force, he and Patricia would move back to Yorkshire and manage their own pub, called the Union, in the town of Knaresborough.

After Dewey was born, Patricia and William would have two more children—a son, Christopher, eighteen months after Dewey, and three years after that a daughter named Trina. Dewey had been born in England to an American father—so he was considered an American citizen and a British subject. Like the band that he would come to found, he would always have roots in the United Kingdom and the United States.

Dewey would always be Mother Nature's son, too; his earliest memories were of his time as a toddler in Yorkshire. His grandfather took him for walks in the wild fields there, taught him to love trees, wildflowers, crows, goats, and horses—and the seaside's cold and windy shores. Raising puppies as a hobby, Dewey's mother possessed a natural reverence for animals, which she passed down to her son. Martin Denny's records, which featured exotic, animal-ridden soundscapes, were frequently played on the family stereo. Other albums blasted were jazz heavy; William preferred Fats Waller while Patricia went for Della Reese. And Patsy Cline. Now and then the couple would go in for Top 40 material, with Gene Vincent's "Be Bop a Lula" becoming an instant favorite to sing around the house. Johnny Mathis, as far as vocalists went, made up a large portion of young Dewey's vocal inspiration. Johnny's melodic

Left: father William, brother Chris, Dewey, and mother Patricia. Right: baby sister Trina, William, Patricia, Dewey, and Chris. *Courtesy of the Bunnell family.*

crooning, and sensitivity to lyrics, would have a lasting effect on Dewey and how he approached each song he sang.

As the family moved from home to home, William would try and convert each basement—when there was one—into a rec room, where he and Patricia would host parties for their friends. They would dance a newly popular dance, the twist; on one occasion, the Bunnells held a beatnik-themed party, in which everyone donned berets. Mr. and Mrs. Bunnell were not practicing artists themselves, but they were art enthusiasts. Prints of works by modern painters like Picasso and Pollock adorned the walls of their home.

In 1956, when William returned from serving in the Korean War, the Bunnells moved to the U.S. Like Gerry and Dan during their transatlantic relocations, Dewey would travel by ocean liner—on the impressive vessel the *Queen Elizabeth I*. First to Long Island, New York, and then to Westover, an area near Springfield, Massachusetts. Their time in Westover would give Dewey some of his earliest detailed memories; these would be steeped in nature, too—and stories. Learning to read would be one of Dewey's favorite experiences: "I have this vivid memory of first learning to read, the spark of putting letters, then words together." There he would also learn how to fish and develop a fondness for collecting natural items found in the woods, like acorns, leaves, and bugs. It was the germination of what would remain true for Dewey's whole life: a love for natural, land-tied experiences—for going out into the woods or desert, and just being.

* * *

As a student at London Central High, Gerry and his shining musicality would catch Dewey's eye and ear: "I remember seeing Gerry for the first time when he played that Beatle bass, at a battle of the bands—at the Columbia Club downtown."

"It was this really lovely huge Georgian building on Bayswater Road," Gerry reminisced. "It's now a hotel, but in the '60s it was a U.S. service facility, for all of the officers and dignitaries." It was during school track team meets, however, that Gerry and Dewey developed their camaraderie and got to know one another.

Gerald Linford Beckley was born on September 12, 1952, on Carswell Air Force Base in Fort Worth, Texas. His parents, British-born Sheila and American Air Force captain Raymond, had been married since 1944. The captain was involved in Korean War efforts in late 1951, but he managed to make it home to his family for the Christmas holidays. It was during this time that Gerry was most likely conceived. He would be Raymond and Sheila's third and youngest child; Michael had been born in 1946 and Suzanne in '49. Though too young to retain memories of living in Fort Worth as an infant, Gerry would spend his first year and a half on earth there. He would be too young, too, to ever recall his first nanny in Texas. Decades later he would learn that her name had been Daisy.

By 1953, the Beckleys had accepted the fact that life in an Air Force family demanded constant relocation. They traveled by ship to establish domestic life in England. Later, as a man in his early forties, Gerry would have a vivid dream that he was a small boy on an ocean liner, separated from his father and in desperate desire to reunite with his family. Sheila would later confirm that when the Beckleys had first relocated to England from Texas, they had indeed done so on an ocean liner. And during the trip, Captain Beckley had been in charge of a platoon of troops, on a remote part of the ship, far from Gerry and the rest of the family. Even though this memory did not reside in Gerry's conscious mind, it had taken up residence in his dreamworld.

"The earliest memories I truly have are of a place called Kenton, in Middlesex, England. I was three years old by then. We lived in a house on Northwick Circle, a residential roundabout with tennis courts in the center. I started school when we were there. I have very clear memories of that time, going to school in my little English uniform."

As was common for transient military families, the Beckleys had sought a prefurnished rental home. But the one in Kenton included an item that not all furnished homes did: a piano. Three-year-old Gerry began to play around with the keys.

Sheila Beckley, a theater and classical music fanatic, had raised the Beckley children on recordings of the Russian Romantics: Rachmaninoff, Tchaikovsky, Prokofiev. Her large Grundig stereo hi-fi console, complete with radio, turntable, and reel-to-reel tape recorder (which would prove pivotal for Gerry years later), dominated the aurality of the family's

Young Gerry Beckley. *Courtesy of the Beckley family.*

home. And when Gerry first discovered the piano, it was the compositions of his mother's Russians that ran through his mind's soundscape. He found that he possessed a good ear and began to play that way, determined to re-create the melodic and passionate leitmotifs that he had heard—the theme from *Swan Lake* becoming an instant favorite. Sheila and Raymond enrolled Gerry in proper piano lessons too, but he was frequently frustrated by them. The speed at which he could comprehend a piece of music and begin to re-create it by ear surpassed the patience required for sight-reading and for repeatedly practicing each phrase of music with exactitude. Gerry did learn to read musical notation, but he was sometimes scolded by piano instructors for going rogue, for not reproducing the sounds that were presented on the pages.

"I can't remember any of my piano teachers, to tell you the truth," Gerry recalled. "I do remember lesson moments when I hadn't done my piano homework and would just try to play it by ear. The teacher would of course say, 'That's not what's written there. . . . You know that, right?' I also remember periods of time when I was supposed to learn Gilbert and Sullivan—*H.M.S. Pinafore* shit that I just hated. I thought, 'Okay well, *this* is losing me. So eventually the lessons just disappeared."

* * *

Gerry caught Dan's attention during art class, where Gerry constantly worked on his printing class projects. "I was in the print shop," Gerry remembered, "and there was a really great teacher, one of the only aesthetic teachers there, Howard Abramowitz—a very cool teacher." The shop would print fliers for the school, as well as the official diplomas, "so you had to learn how to set type. There was an embossing machine—certain kinds of ink you would emboss and heat up." To Dan, Gerry possessed a unique quality, as Dewey did—but it was of a different color: confidence, self-assuredness, and the determination to succeed at his chosen vocation of "pop star." While other teens may have undersold their career intentions to their peers in order to assume an attractive indifference, Gerry did no such thing. He saw little point in watering down articulations of his ambitions, especially when he had the intelligence and self-esteem to acknowledge what they were.

Dan, inherently understated, was simultaneously taken aback and captivated by Gerry's forthrightness and belief in his own set of dreams. And he saw that they were very similar to his own. Both boys were obsessed with devouring the pop music of the day.

Circumstance and fortune had called Gerry's inner resilience to the forefront of his character at an early age. By the time he was fifteen years old and reached London Central High School in 1967, Gerry had lived in seven different locations and in three countries.

"When you start to move every two or three years, as a child, you start to build certain defensive layers," Gerry recalled. "You're probably quite hurt the first time or two. You make friends, and you have to say goodbye to them—and you'd have to become somewhat hardened to that. You either become the type where you look around at your new surroundings and ask, 'How will I fit in here? What do they wear here?' Or the other, where you become the rebel, because you know you're out in a year or two. They're both pretty defensive positions."

Reflecting back, Gerry considered that even though this nomadic environment was the only thing he knew, the constant pattern of being uprooted every year or two was traumatic. He had no clear sense of place or belonging.

"If you consider in Western culture how important to identity are things like hometown, your accent, things like 'Where are you from?' and your lifetime friends and next-door neighbors—all of these elements that we simplify into the *Leave It to Beaver*–esque part of our culture—we [Air Force children] don't have any of these things. And so I think those things colored me from the very earliest."

Gerry made friends in musical circles very easily. He formed quick and communicative bonds with his fellow band members in all of his musical groups. But his nomadic lifestyle had instructed him on the pointlessness—and potential pain—of forming attachments. In the end, someone would leave. His romantic nature would often lead him toward romantic interests. In his teen years there was usually a girlfriend of some kind, but when Gerry and the Beckleys relocated, the relationship didn't.

"I think to a certain extent most of us—I call it the Bleeding Hearts Club: songwriters, like Jimmy Webb and Stephen Bishop who use the fulcrum of the heart—I think in general we are relationships kind of people. It doesn't mean that they go well; in fact, heartbreak is the greatest inspiration I think. It's part and parcel of what we all ended up doing. You write about the loves of your life."

* * *

Daniel Milton Peek was born on November 1, 1950, in Panama City, Florida. Like Gerry's and Dewey's, Dan's family would always be an Air

Force family. After two years in Florida, the Peeks would pull stints in Greenland and South Carolina. In 1957 Dan's father, Colonel Milton Peek, was transferred to the Japanese island of Kyushu. The family chose to live in a home off the military base for the first year and a half, and Dan, along with his siblings Tom and Debbie, began to take piano lessons there. Unlike Gerry with his teachers, Dan would always remember Kagiwagisan—who believed in hand-whacking as a fitting response to students' wrong notes. This was just one of the reasons Dan hated his piano lessons. Three years later Dan's mother, Gerri Peek, allowed him to quit. Although he later wouldn't remember how to read music, Dan would always be able to apply his tactility to a keyboard, finding tunes fairly easily when needed. Piano knowledge was handy for an aspiring musician to possess. But Dan would always be a guitar man.

Colonel Peek was a musically interested man himself, which made for an inspiring home life for his musically inclined children. During their Japan era, the Peeks were the first family in the neighborhood to buy a stereo, and the colonel played records of every genre on it constantly. This allowed for the Peek kids to receive a well-rounded sonic education.

After Japan, the Peeks followed Colonel Peek to Syracuse, New York, and Dan, along with brother Tom, wanted nothing more than a guitar to play. Colonel and Mrs. Peek bought the boys an inexpensive Kay acoustic; it was for them to share, but it was difficult, because both boys were

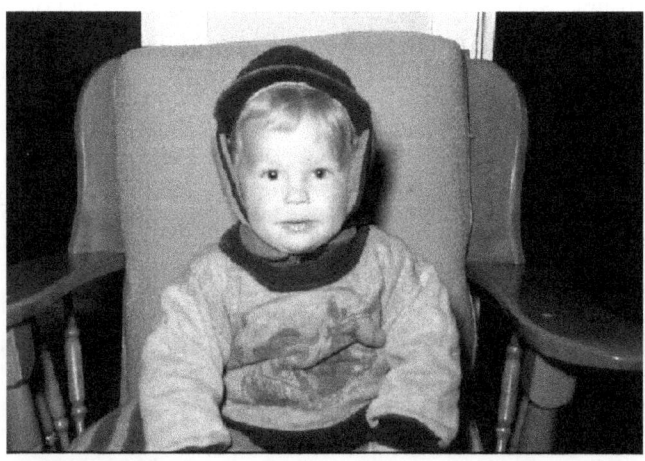

Young Dan Peek. *Courtesy of the Peek family.*

obsessed with it. They taught themselves to play the Kay by studying radio hits "Pipeline" and "Apache."

Back in 1955, when the Peeks were living in South Carolina, five-year-old Dan had mistakenly drunk a house cleaning product. His vocal cords had been damaged, but he was alright. It wasn't until five years later, when the family lived in Syracuse, that Dan's health began to show signs of strain. Suddenly he always seemed to be ill, often with record-high fevers, and suffered through all sorts of untested, untried, and sometime traumatic medical treatments and operations. He was diagnosed with rheumatoid arthritis.

"Dan was very, very sick growing up as a child," his younger brother David recalled. "He had spent so much time in the hospital. So he was also very well-read, and I think his IQ was off the charts . . . very smart. I think to combat, sometimes, a bit of the pain and trauma of being sick, he developed a really good sense of humor. There was something special about him, he could really light up a room when he walked into it, and you just kind of wanted to be around him. He was engaging and funny. Dan really did have that kind of a special temperament."

Soon Colonel Peek was transferred to Peshawar, Pakistan—a far cry from upstate New York—but Dan was glad to go. The Peeks passed a leisurely summer there, getting acquainted with their new environment. Transitioning away from upstate New York's freezing cold climate into the intense heat of Peshawar proved a restorative experience for Dan. Living in the new desert climate allowed for his arthritic condition to improve and, eventually, with a good deal of exercise, it went away altogether. Peshawar's intense heat forced the school to shorten its days of courses too, all of which allowed Dan, and Tom, to delve further into "Guitarland."

3

THE BEATLES AND THE BEACH BOYS

The surf scene of the early sixties introduced the American populace to the nontraditional lifestyle possibilities that paradise offered. Americans didn't even have to go far: the paradise was in their own backyard. Surfing had been developed by ancient Polynesians, but by 1963, it was a completely modern m.o.—largely among teenagers and young people—in Southern California. The sport itself involved riding a board out on the ocean in search of a perfect wave. Its associated lifestyle was much more than that. Surfing suggested a way of being that revolved around easy and relaxed living, time spent on or near the beach, and nature worship. Of course it was an ideal match for Dewey's persona.

Surf culture in turn inspired surf music, a guitar-driven rock genre that was becoming increasingly popular among young people. Brian Wilson and the Beach Boys of Hawthorne, California, took surf music to new heights by writing and performing original material that articulated the SoCal, beach-based living they knew so well. Their first hit single, "Surfin' Safari," reached number fourteen on the *Billboard* Hot 100 in 1962, followed by "Surfin' USA" in '63—which reached number three on the charts. The Beach Boys were the musical equivalent of American surf culture, and their early hits were just the beginning of what would become a decades-spanning contribution to rock and pop music. Rock 'n' roll, though, was about to get a whole lot bigger.

On February 9, 1964, the Beatles appeared on the *Ed Sullivan Show*, performing five tracks off their debut record that had been produced in 1963 by George Martin: "All My Loving," "Till There Was You," "She

Young Dewey Bunnell. *Courtesy of the Bunnell family.*

Loves You," "I Saw Her Standing There," and "I Want to Hold Your Hand," over the show's two sets. The world—including Dewey, Gerry, and Dan—would never be the same.

Generationally it was a pivotal time. President John F. Kennedy had been assassinated just a few weeks before the performance. As a country, America was still in mourning, and looking for direction. For the boys who would become the band America, it was a turning point in their musical careers.

"I vividly recall seeing the Beatles on *Ed Sullivan*," said Bunnell, who was living at Vandenburg Air Force Base in California at the time. "Adding to that the other incredible events of the times, from the Kennedy assassination to the Ali-Liston fight, my life became an intense experience!" In August of that year, when the Beatles' film *A Hard Day's Night* was released, Dewey went to see it in the local movie theater. He was impressed by the cinematic prowess of the Beatles, as well as the overwhelmingly positive reactions of the audience. "That's when I first picked up the guitar. I got into surf music and played on a neighbor's guitar I borrowed, self-teaching, from picking out notes and playing surf instrumentals by the likes of Dick Dale and the Ventures and people like that."

The events and experiences that Dewey went through during the years 1963 through 1966 had a dramatic impact on the evolution of his character. His family's relocation from Omaha to California in 1963 had been "an eye-opening change. Between the cornfields we played in by our house in Omaha, to the beaches and mountains and deserts of Southern California, and the fact that I was going through puberty, I was transformed. I remember becoming socially aware and self-conscious in the seventh grade."

It was during this time that Dewey adopted his nickname. Up until the seventh grade, he had always been Lee Bunnell, but now he was in Southern California. He was increasingly fascinated by the raging surf scene there. A cultural surf icon of the day was Dewey Weber, and his

Dick Dale (left) with Dewey in 2009. *Courtesy of the Bunnell family.*

name—including his line of surfboards and gear—had permeated the public consciousness. Dewey tried getting involved in the local surf scene himself—and he was singled out for it.

"I'd be on the beach, rent a surfboard, wax it—and I would look a bit surfer-guy. I remember one time, someone called after me, 'Look, there's Dewey!' Meaning—it was a put-down! Kind of like if you were a crappy baseball player, and someone called you Mickey Mantle sarcastically."

He fully understood that he had been called the name in a teasing way—but it clicked. Feeling it possessed more originality and notoriety than "Lee," he adopted the name as his own—and he's been Dewey ever since.

The culture was changing; the music had gotten louder. Beatle boots were in, and so were all things British. Canoe and Jade East colognes were popular, but English Leather was a standout. The hair had grown longer too—especially Dewey's. As a young boy, his haircuts were always done by his father. But by the mid-1960s, Dewey grew it long. Soon he had some of the longest hair in school, which attracted attention from the local girls. For a time in the ninth grade, Dewey had a girlfriend—but the romance was ill-fated: "I remember the nail in the coffin—timing is everything—I got a haircut shorter than it had been in awhile. I came to school with the haircut, and by the end of the school day, she'd broken up with me. I blamed it on the haircut."

The family's years at Southern California's Vandenberg Air Force Base coincided with a high point of William's career. He was involved with a small team that launched missiles at the base. Many nights Dewey and his siblings fell asleep to the distant rumble of the launches.

During his eighth-grade year, at a short stint in Biloxi, Mississippi, before returning to California, Dewey purchased his first electric guitar. There, he joined the Renegades—a local band—where he played current hits of the era like the Animals' "House of the Rising Sun." "The group was a very stripped-down little thing," Dewey said. "We played in the talent show, a couple of living rooms, and I think that was about it. But it was the beginning of my first formal step into realizing it was fun being a performer."

When the band was reviewed by the school newspaper, Dewey was dubbed "Leader of the Pack." He couldn't have felt further from that label. "'Leader of the Pack'—I'd always liked the *ensemble*! I liked being part of a unit that fit together; I didn't like being the leader of it. And it was too many decisions. Even at an early age."

In the eternal Beatles vs. Stones debate that frequently found its way into young people's conversations, Dewey—like Gerry and Dan—always sided with the Beatles. It seemed like a person had to be in one camp or the other and, at the time, Mick Jagger's in-your-face front man–ness was not quite Dewey's style. Later he would turn into quite a Stones fan, possessing enormous respect for the showmanship and songwriting of Jagger and Keith Richards.

"I was always trying to fit in, because I was moving to different places. So it never would have crossed my mind to do something outrageous or outlandish that would put the spotlight on me. I just wanted to blend in, get in the middle of the pack, and not stick out. So that I could move freely within my world. No sharp edges."

While the Bunnells were in Biloxi, British Invasion music had been overtaking the American airwaves, with new bands rising and coming to the cultural forefront every week. Popular musical variety television programs such as *Where the Action Is*, *Hullabaloo*, and *Shindig* seemed to push the cleaner-cut *American Bandstand* aside. "I really enjoyed Mississippi for the new Gulf Coast experiences like fishing and exploring the swamps with my brother Chris," remembered Dewey, "but I also experienced new social situations that I did not fully understand in the Deep South, as the Civil Rights Movement in the U.S. was gathering strength."

Dewey spent his freshman year of high school in San Jose, California, when his father was restationed, and the Bunnells relocated there. "I spent most of the year listening to new bands around San Jose—like the Beau Brummels, Syndicate of Sound, and the Count Five, with their great song 'Psychotic Reaction' . . . while waiting for the next Beatles or Beach Boys album. The Beatles played the Cow Palace and ultimately their final concert at Candlestick Park while I lived there, but I never saw them perform live. The release of *Rubber Soul* and *Revolver*, my favorite Beatles album, along with the Beach Boys' 'Good Vibrations' and *Pet Sounds*, changed the way I listened to music."

After a year in San Jose, William put in a request to be stationed in the United Kingdom again. Patricia had more or less talked him into it, desiring to return to her homeland, and knowing that the recently promoted William now possessed more clout in the Air Force hierarchy. She had "schlepped around all over the U.S. with her family."

The Bunnells were enthused about the prospect of returning to the United Kingdom, where they had family ties and lovely memories on which to build. Dewey regretted the loss of his connection to nature, a link that he had established during his stints across the diverse American terrain. It was a bit of a culture shock for all the Bunnell children; they barely remembered England from their toddler years. In 1967, after a transitional year at the Lakenheath base, Sergeant Bunnell was transferred to RAF South Ruislip right outside London, where the Swinging Sixties scene was raging. Dewey and his siblings began attending London Central High School, where Dewey was to meet his future bandmates Gerry and Dan.

* * *

In 1964, Dan was still living in Peshawar, where his father was stationed, but having learned about the Beatles via a *Time* article, he and his brother Tom were quick to snatch up the "I Want to Hold Your Hand" single once it arrived at Peshawar's base supply store, the Post Exchange (PX). But Dan would find that he preferred the rockier B-side of the single, "I Saw Her Standing There."

"The raw thumping pulse of the electrics and bass and the scorching lead guitar in the middle break galvanized me. Paul's soaring lead vocal completed the tour-de-force [*sic*] performance. Color me instant Beatlemaniac," Peek reflected in his 2004 memoir *An American Band*.[1]

Dan and Tom built quite an impressive record collection by shopping at the PX, garnering latest hit single releases from the Dave Clark Five, the Searchers, the Ventures, and even the Beach Boys, a group that Dan and America would collaborate with in the coming decade.

When Dan and his brother shipped off to Pakistan, they made do with the Kay acoustic they'd brought with them, but it was only a matter of time before they sought out Silvertone electric guitars from the popular Sears catalog. Tom and Dan had to wait weeks for the guitars to arrive in Peshawar, which nearly drove them crazy—but it was worth it.

Once the Silvertones arrived, the brothers knew there was no turning back. They fell faster and further down the rabbit hole of rock. Dan and Tom borrowed an amp from a nearby guitar-playing pal and began to practice. They had always been close, but their increasing co-interest in guitaring made for an open-ended partnership through which they could share cumulative musical knowledge. Learning together enabled them to quickly and easily exchange any new riffs and chords they had picked up or figured out.

Dan and Tom would play at least four hours every day, quickly implementing into their skill set new techniques that they learned from other musicians. The music community on-base was extremely tight-knit and included a vast array of notable musical aptitude among the GIs.

There were three clubs for different officers, and Dan and Tom, along with their pal John, would do their best to sneak in and listen to the live bands and jukebox singles. Soon the three boys added a drummer, Eddie McAllister, and formed a band called the Cyclones. The base's Airmen's Club was short on live acts, and the Cyclones served as the house band every Friday and Saturday night. It was rough stuff: the Cyclones were playing at peak hours for hundreds of young alcohol-influenced servicemen. During the first gig, a raucous fight got started amid the patrons. Twelve-year-old Dan was stunned—but he and his bandmates soon began to play the popular surf instrumental tune "Pipeline" and immediately stole the club's attention. It worked to the Cyclones' advantage that many of the club's attendees were only teenagers—like them—so they all shared topical musical tastes.

Since acquiring their Silvertone electrics, Dan and Tom had worked to learn specific guitar parts of their favorite pop recordings. They would play a selected record at half-speed to get a better understanding of each sound they were after, such as the intro to the Beatles' Chuck Berry cover "Roll Over Beethoven." As aspiring guitar stars, Dan and Tom were well suited to one another, with complementary playing styles. While Dan played lead on wild-and-crazy and offbeat songs, Tom played rhythm, and while Tom played lead on melodic numbers, Dan played rhythm.

Increasingly, Tom had expressed wanting to learn how to compose songs of his own, an idea that made Dan nervous. Dan just wanted to be the best guitar man he could. "His guitar playing was really unique," brother David (also a guitarist) recalled. "I think from a very young age he really took guitar playing seriously; he was very talented. He had a gift for being able to play by ear very quickly and was gifted with arrangements and things like that. I thought his guitar playing was superb." As far as guitar repairs and gear went, Dan and Tom had developed self-reliance in Pakistan, where there was no music store nearby. They learned how to make their own guitar strings and picks to replace broken ones, sometimes even boiling strings to lengthen their lifespan. When the Peeks left Peshawar, Dan and his guitar had nearly become one entity.

From Peshawar, Dan and his brother Tom had relocated to Doe Run, a small town in the Ozark Mountains of southeast Missouri where their grandparents lived on a farm. It took a bit of an adjustment for the brothers to settle into their new life. Grandpa Archie was eccentric, and he was not a fan of long hair or rock 'n' roll. Things improved when Dan and Tom formed a band with some musicians from Farmington, and they played live whenever and wherever they were able. The world of music became the only enclave in which the brothers felt comfortable. Tom and Dan were now able to play more than a hundred different pop songs, and they bought new-and-improved Gibson and Fender amplifiers.

As winter rolled around, their father was restationed to San Angelo, Texas. The colonel, the pregnant Mrs. Peek, and daughters Debbie and young Becky picked Dan and Tom up from Archie's. Tightly packed into one car, the clan drove to Texas. "My family's kind of like the Brady Bunch," youngest brother David Peek explained, "with three girls and three boys." Angela would be the youngest Peek sister. When Dan and Tom began a band in Texas with three other students, calling themselves the Centrics, things all around improved. They performed all the time at a variety of venues: house parties, dance halls, rock clubs, and town events, making quite a name for themselves in the local scene. Soon they traveled around to gigs beyond San Angelo, throughout the Texas Panhandle. Dan was just fifteen years old.

Snake Atkinson, of '60s group J. Frank Wilson and the Cavaliers (who'd released the eternally stellar "Last Kiss" in 1964), came to see one of Dan's downtown shows. Ultimately the band was offered a recording deal with a company out of Dallas. This recording arrangement required that Dan and the band compose original and new material. They did, and they demoed it, too—but Colonel Peek soon got orders to relocate, along with the whole Peek family.

Dan felt paranoid that his break with Snake Atkinson, and the recent recording deal opportunity, were his one and only chance. He feared that by leaving Texas, he would be leaving his musical future behind too. He'd gotten a recording opportunity once, yes—but what were the chances of garnering another one? He had become an immaculate imitator, able to reproduce guitar licks by Jimi Hendrix, Jimmy Page, and Jeff

Beck. He still wished, though—more than anything—to be a songwriter. To be a guitarist, a musician—who penned his own songs.

Dan soon had a horrific attack of his rheumatoid arthritis, leading to a ten-week hospital stint. He suffered from terrible fevers, during which he would lose his hair and remain in near unbearable pain. He ultimately failed the school year due to his inability to participate in gym class. Dan was forced to repeat the entire eleventh-grade year. It may have felt redundant, but—next he was set to complete senior year at Central High School in London; there, he would meet Gerry and Dewey.

The overarching experience was meant to be, down to the letter. The trip from the U.S. to London would be via ship for the Peeks, where Dan and Tom met Lew Walker, a fellow music-obsessed guitarist who also played bass. Once at London Central, Dan and Lew Walker would join to form the band they would dub Genesis—entirely unrelated to the future group of the same name that would feature Phil Collins and Peter Gabriel.

* * *

When the Beatles performed on the *Ed Sullivan Show*, Gerry's family was living in Virginia and he witnessed the live broadcast: "For me, that was a pivotal moment. For virtually anyone of my generation, it was a turning point. The only thing that I can add to that is I know that I was

Young Gerry (left) in the Weags. *Courtesy of the Beckley family.*

nowhere near as shocked as most people." In part due to Sheila's British roots, the Beckley family was accustomed to spending summers in England, regardless of where Colonel Beckley was stationed. Michael, Suzanne, and Gerry were already well acquainted with the Fab Four, having been exposed to the increasing buzz of importance that had yet to reach the States.

Soon, the Beatles played a concert at the Armory in Washington, DC. Gerry was too young to attend; plus, tickets were instantly sold out. The performance, however, had been filmed and was screened the following week in the same venue. "It was a very cobbled-together black-and-white film of the show, and all the girls, screaming at the screen! Pretty far out." He would forever be obsessed with the Beatles' musical output and cultural capital. Young Gerry had also been following the career of the Beach Boys. *Surfin' Safari* was the first record album that Gerry ever bought. He had no idea then, but within ten years, Gerry would himself be making music with both George Martin and the Beach Boys.

Gerry had already been playing guitar for a few years when the Beatles made their American debut. When folk music became popular in the early 1960s, his brother Michael purchased an acoustic guitar, only to cut off its top two strings and saw off the top of its tuning head. The goal was to create an easier-to-play four-string tenor guitar, much like that used in the Kingston Trio's recordings. It wasn't long before Gerry was borrowing the instrument to practice strumming—but he still wanted his own. Talking Raymond and Sheila into the idea, Gerry found a beginner Sears Silvertone guitar to buy.

By the time he was in the seventh grade, in 1963, Gerry was a talented enough player to join a Virginia-based instrumental surf music band, the Vanguards. Modeled after the popular beach band the Safaris, they would perform known tunes of the day, like "Pipeline" and "Wipeout." For young Gerry, it was all a learning experience. He was cutting his musical teeth.

From that point on, Gerry sought out the local music scene. In 1966, after Colonel Beckley was stationed in Ramstein, Germany, Gerry entered his tenth-grade year at Kaiserslautern High School. There he joined an existing group of senior students in their oddly dubbed rock group the Weags: "The story there," Gerry recalled, "is they went to pick a name, so said, 'Let's pick two vowels, two consonants randomly, and add an s.'"

A fellow Weags member, Tom Williams, had a connection in the United States who would routinely mail him cassette tapes of Casey Kasem's *Top 20 Countdown* radio shows. Gerry would take the tapes, listen to them relentlessly, and figure out the entirety of each song's instrumental parts. He would then go back to the Weags during rehearsal and instruct each member on what to play. "I was this little guy—but a bit strongheaded," said Gerry. Rather than undersell his talents and abilities, Gerry demonstrated them to others. The essence of his artistic vision, in every incarnation, culminated not in "the self," but "the song." Gerry lived for the music, and he knew that he was good at it. When the Weags won a local Battle of the Bands contest, it was Gerry who took the first prize trophy home. As years passed, it would assume a welcome place on Gerry's home shelves, next to his Grammy award. A reminder of where he had come from, of where he had been.

4

THE TRIO

Within months, Colonel Beckley was promoted to base commander of Ruislip Air Force Base, west of London. Once again, the whole family packed up and relocated to England. Though he was leaving behind the Weags, Gerry was not abandoning his musical aspirations; these were so much a part of himself that to do so would have been impossible.

When Gerry had first arrived at London Central High as a junior in 1967, he'd joined a local soul band in dire need of a bass player, the Corporation. "I'd never played bass regularly, but I knew how to—and I had the Beatle bass," Gerry said. "We played all covers, in the vein of 'Knock on Wood.'" Gerry's junior year passed quickly amid a constant series of successful live performances, academic requirements, and rock music ingestion.

In 1968, the West Ruislip military base was never short of top-tier musical entertainment. Teen club dances, multilayered variety shows—and occasional concerts with desirable live acts of the day. Engelbert Humperdinck, Thelonious Monk, and Sammy Davis Jr. all made appearances on the air force base. This provided for a welcome and high-quality supplement to the artistic education of Gerry, Dewey, and Dan—as if 1968's world of recorded music wasn't enough.

When the Corporation's senior student members graduated London Central that year, Gerry sought out new musicians to play with, transitioning into a role with the Daze. A Captain Merrill had recently been appointed the base chaplain; his sons Bob, a drummer, and Mike, a guitarist, were clearly talented. "They became what was the gist of this group called the Daze," Gerry recalled. When a bass player was called for, Gerry stepped in. Mike would sing most of the group's repertoire, but now and then Gerry would perform lead vocals on a few songs per set. The Moody Blues' "Nights in White Satin," Gerry and the Pacemakers' "Don't Let the Sun Catch You Crying," and Jimmy Webb's "By the Time I Get to Phoenix" were three of his hallmark tunes.

Gerry possessed an ardent, natural way of singing and had a penchant for romantic ballads. He'd always had vocal talent—back in the States he had been headhunted and invited to join the Washington Episcopal Choir, where he was paid a monthly stipend. Bespectacled and golden haired as a young boy, he grew into good looks ideal for a troubadour.

"Whenever I started singing," Gerry recalled, "the room would kind of stop the dancing, and people would gather round. It felt like 'a moment,' and I thought, 'Okay, this is pretty good.'"

While Gerry was a part of the Daze, Dan belonged to Genesis—the band he had started with friends Pete Reuther and Lew Walker.

The Hootenanny, a talent show held by London Central, was where Dan's guitaring talents were singled out, during Genesis's performance of "Purple Haze." Gerry performed his version of "Ferry Cross the Mersey." Just before the show was over, Genesis took its moment—complete with Dan channeling Hendrix in his showman's guitar antics. The school audience was receptive, wildly enthusiastic even. Gerry took notice of Dan and of the response his performance had generated. At once, the two boys began to talk at length about rock 'n' roll records—about the information

Dan (left) in Genesis. *Courtesy of Lew Walker and the Peek family.*

they had gathered, the skills they had learned, and their plans for their futures. They proved kindred spirits, who noticed the potential value in forming musical connections with each other.

West Ruislip's Teen Club soon held a Battle of the Bands, in which the Daze and Genesis vied for top prize. It was Dan's band that won out—and using the Daze's top-notch PA system to do it. Gerry and his band had been generous, and now that they had been beaten, they wanted a bit of what—and who—had beaten them. Namely, the musical talents of Dan Peek and his guitar.

The timing was perfect. Genesis was headed for a breakup as several members' families planned for an air force–style regular relocation. Dan and his guitar needed a place to go—and the Daze seemed a logical destination.

The Daze was largely a covers act, with setlists curated from Top 40 radio. But rather than merely reproduce what was heard on original recordings of each tune, Gerry—and now Dan—sought to use their creativity and aural curiosity by reinterpreting each cover song. They became obsessed with creating complete reworks of their favorite tunes, almost to the point of making them sound like different songs entirely. It was the dawn of their foray into songwriting. If Gerry and Dan could completely change songs like the Mamas and the Papas' "California Dreamin'" and Ike and Tina Turner's "River Deep—Mountain High" to sound new, they could most certainly craft songs of their own from scratch. It was during this time that Gerry and Dan forged the musical partnership that would form the crux of America.

Talented artists always seem to possess a knack for discovering other talented artists amid masses of individuals. Dan was quite content to work alongside perfectionistic Gerry, whose musical prowess he held in high regard and very much related to.

Meanwhile, Dewey became increasingly intrigued by the idea of studying dramatic arts. Since the seventh grade, he had been involved intermittently with various school plays. "The concept of inhabiting another person, a character, appealed to me," he recalled. During the summer following ninth grade, Dewey participated in a summer workshop for young actors at San Jose State. There he first took note of playwright heavyweights like Eugene O'Neill and Arthur Miller.

At London Central High, Dewey appeared in the senior class play, a production of Shakespeare's *As You Like It*. He had always liked sports as well—too small in stature to succeed in football, he'd been drawn to baseball, but had the most success as a runner. As a senior, Dewey struggled to juggle his interests in and commitments to athletics and theater. When he qualified to represent London Central in the military base high school Euro finals, he was forced to decide. Observing fellow athletes jumping well over six feet in the high jump and practicing shot put, Dewey determined in which area his future successes lay: "I had some moment of destiny and decided. I was never going to make it as a professional athlete. I would go for it in 'showbiz'—which was, at the time, in drama." Dewey auditioned for and was accepted into London's Corona Academy for the upcoming fall semester.

The Daze, which now featured both Gerry and Dan, became successful performing at various military bases in England, including a dance during which Dan and Catherine Maberry, his future wife, would first come together. As things between Dan and Cathie quickly became serious, Cathie soon discovered her family was being relocated back home, to Virginia. This strongly influenced Dan's impending plans for college.

It was 1969 and senior year at London Central High was coming to an end. To be close to Cathie's new home of Virginia Beach, Dan once more went stateside, deciding to attend college at Old Dominion University in Norfolk, Virginia. Along with their parents, Gerry and Dewey chose to stay on in England.

The majority of London Central's graduating seniors' musical groups disbanded, including the Daze. With graduation behind them and the summer ahead of them, Gerry and Dewey obtained jobs working in the air force base warehouse. "We worked in different sheds," recalled Gerry, "but you had to drive around, forklift, and load supplies. Cans. Frankly, for both of us, the only real jobs we've had in our lives were these. We quickly learned that if you also became the tea boy—tea was 10 to 10:20 in the morning or so—you could leave about 9:15, go around the warehouse, and ask what sandwiches everyone wanted. You could stretch it till about a quarter to eleven. So if you worked it right, you could get a two-hour fuck-off time."

It was around this period that Gerry began to spend his spare time playing music around London and working at various studio sessions, at which he was frequently the youngest participant. London Central High's diploma system was based upon a total required number of course credits, rather than years of schooling completed. Gerry was just sixteen years old when he graduated London Central with Dan and Dewey in '69. He was mainly a bass guitar and keyboards player, and had a lot of skill and creative ambition to offer in the recording studio. Every free second he had was spent studying record albums and their liner notes on his own.

When freshman year of college ended in '70, Dan returned to his family's home in London for the summer. The first thing he did on British soil was to phone Dewey.

Since Dan had been away at college, Dewey had joined—and left— the Daze. Dan was surprised to discover this, having been ignorant of Dewey's musical interests before. Dewey had gone on to devote himself to songwriting—and the results of a year were astounding. Dan was taken aback by the sonic samples of "Three Roses," "Riverside," and "Children" that Dewey played for him. Seventh chords galore with wildly imaginative lyrics set to them, the high and radio-worthy quality of which were impossible to ignore. When Dan performed his own "Rainy Day" for Dewey, both of them realized what was up: over the past year, they had developed into top-marks writers and players with unique musical points of view. The potential was palpable.

Egged on by the promising development of Dewey's musical output, Dan contacted Gerry. The Daze was now defunct in totality—and he was working as a tape operator at London's Morgan Studios, through which he intended to make inroads in the music industry. This role was first given responsibility of menial housekeeping tasks, with the goal of learning how to tape splice, edit, and operate the sound and mixing boards in the studio: "I did tape-op," Gerry reflected. "I wasn't ever someone who needed to clean up, but I played on a bunch of sessions. I remember Chris Neal, who had been one of the main tape-ops for years at Abbey Road. He got thrown out for being hammered always, and ended up at Morgan. He was a frustrated songwriter, so I used to do sessions for him."

As the studio's tape-op, Gerry was able to use the studio for himself during off-hours. Dan and Dewey were not the only ones who had written a song or two over the preceding year: Gerry had been hard at work composing too. He quickly asked Dan to play guitar on a recording session for one of his new songs. The musical camaraderie that had been established a year earlier during their time in the Daze proved to hold true. Feeling fortune's currents, Dan was keen to bring Dewey into the mix of creative talent.

Over the past year Dewey had been journeying through the British theater scene of the day and attending—at least most of the time—acting classes at Corona Academy of the Dramatic Arts. "I was bonding a lot with the British people. Starting to take on some elements of British people, going to parties, drinking gin and tonics with the cerebral crowd. Taking the tube to Chiswick. At this point I was ditching a class or two." More and more, he got the sense that the confines and analytical leanings of the other drama students, as well as the world of acting, weres not what he wanted for himself. They no longer rang true. Fellow students, some of whom were recognizable child actors from screen and stage—like *Oliver!*'s Mark Lester, Susan George, and *To Sir, with Love*'s Judy Geeson—were consumed with the craft of acting. They were also into fencing, ballet, and Noel Coward. Dewey was a real-deal guy, a nature-first individual; he was uninterested in pretense or superficiality, which he perceived as such a large part of the actor's world.

Dan, Dewey, and Gerry first sang together a week or two following Dan's suggestion of meeting up. A London Central pal, Daphne Brennan—who would prove to be for America what Mama Cass was to Crosby, Stills & Nash during their first sing—held a casual party at her parents' home. Snatching Daphne's nylon-string guitar, the trio that was to become America rehearsed and arranged Dewey's song "Children." Within moments, Dan, Dewey, and Gerry knew that they had the makings of a top-notch musical group. And they decided to move ahead as one, intent upon making a success of it. They knew that together, they were a talent that could not be denied.

5

THE DAWN

On their earliest songs, America worked in any available space they could find. Which more often than not was Dewey's car. He had recently saved up enough money to buy an old Morris Minor, a classic—and tiny—British automobile, whose interior provided excellent acoustics for the harmonizing trio. With only room for one acoustic guitar (or two at best) in the Minor, practice sessions were a tight squeeze. "We thought we could make a go of it," Dewey reminisced. "We really believed in ourselves, and then we got into a pattern of, 'let's keep writing.'"

Gerry, Dan, and Dewey were three unique songwriters, each with their own individual styles. But their songs became songs of the group—America songs—in the vocal arrangements. Gerry in particular was adept at this. He and Dan would arrange the three interlacing and interstrumming guitar parts too. Dan, with his higher-pitched vocal register, easily sang the third above Dewey, whose distinctive and charismatic voice was ideal for singing leads and melodies. Gerry, with his impeccable producer's ear, was naturally suited to the lowest vocal, frequently singing a fifth below the main melodic line. He was consistently able to locate his part and maneuver it during the length of a song. Gerry was also a perfectionist, knowing that the trio's potential vocal power lay in the exactness of their harmonies and the precision of their execution in live performance and recording. Their three voices were well matched to each other, in both tonal quality and harmonic need.

Occasionally the trio would practice at the Peek family's West Drayton home. "I'll never forget our path that went up to the main road where the bus stop was," David Peek remembered. "I was standing out there playing, and I remember seeing this guy walking toward me, silhouetted against the light; there may have even been a little fog. And I remember thinking, 'Wow, who *is* this cool guy?' I didn't know who he was. It turned out he was Dewey, coming to see Dan. And a little while later Gerry shows up. I remember hearing them a couple of times, playing their guitars and practicing in the house, before they got famous. If they stayed the night, Dewey and Gerry would crash out on this rattan couch my parents had in the living room. Gerry would be laying his head on the left side of the couch arm, and Dewey would be on the other end laying his head on the right side. They would have their legs propped up on the couch crossways. In the morning I would come toddling out as a little boy, probably waking them up. And then my mother would get annoyed at Dan, because he never gave up his room for them to sleep in.

"Not long after that, they came back with these two-track, reel-to-reel tapes . . . of their first album, playing them on my dad's stereo. The guys were really excited about what they were hearing. Then after that they were off and running."

Dewey, Dan, and Gerry, who had always been avid rock music listeners, quickly became even more serious about and deliberate with their popular music intake. They constantly attended rock shows in the London area, witnessing performances by Jimi Hendrix, the Rolling Stones, Led Zeppelin, King Crimson, Sly and the Family Stone, and the acts in 1970's famed Bath Festival of Blues and Progressive Music. The Beckley family home in the London suburb of Carpenders Park still housed a stellar stereo system. "I remember going to Gerry's house," recalled Dewey. "I'd lay on the floor, put on headphones, and we'd listen to CSN. Osmosis. I remember feeling that music was so much more than just one guitar, one voice. The trio spent a lot of time with more conceptual albums of the day too, in which musical production was prominent. The Steve Miller Band's early works—*Children of the Future* and *Sailor* (1968)—and the Moody Blues' classic *Days of Future Passed* (1967) were all favorites. "This was a formidable time," reflected Gerry. "Those records were very different and incredibly creative, kind of ethereal. Real headphone music. I learned so much listening to *Bookends* [Simon and Garfunkle, 1968] and things, about the positioning of instruments in the stereo spectrum. The amount of importance the EQ of instruments had. From my earlier days—wondering, 'Why does that record sound so big? Oh, everything is in echo.' So when we would listen, I would think, 'Interesting—the high hat's on the left. That's right, if you were drumming, it would be on your left.' But if you're not a drummer, and you're watching the group, the high hat would be on the right, because you're looking at him. So whoever's mixing that is thinking of himself as the drummer, when he's mixing. So those kinds of technical things—'I see, they've got the acoustic guitars wide left and right—that's why you can hear them, they're not sitting in the middle with all the other instruments.' It was a real education, because we ended up producing ourselves. It's the little things you learn."

During his stint as a tape-op the past year, Gerry had met a number of key figures in London's pop music scene. One of them was Phil Reed, half of the musical duo known as Ratfields. A lead guitar contribution to a single cut by this band would prove the most fortuitous for America. This group was managed by a man named Dave Howson, who had founded the short-lived label Middle Earth Records—which was distributed in the United States by blues label Chess Records.

Before his establishment of the record label in 1969, Howson had created the identically titled London club called Middle Earth, in the basement of a Covent Garden warehouse. London music scener Jeff Dexter, who could be seen introducing Jimi Hendrix at the 1970 Isle of Wight Festival, and who would soon be America's first real manager, would sometimes DJ there. T-Rex, Yes, Pink Floyd, and David Bowie had performed there in the mid- to late '60s, as well as American groups the Byrds and Captain Beefheart. The club was moved to the Roundhouse in Chalk Farm in 1968 following a drug bust. In the new location, American groups Jefferson Airplane and the Doors would soon hold their sole London-based live performances.

Howson's greatest claim to fame was his organization of London's 1967 massive benefit concert, the 14-Hour Technicolor Dream. It took place at North London's Alexandra Palace, and featured sets by the Move, Pink Floyd, and the Crazy World of Arthur Brown, among other groups. These sets would be remembered as some of the participating bands' greatest gigs ever—albeit acid infused. The 14-Hour Technicolor Dream was heavily influenced, on all sides, by the ingestion of acid, which in the spring of '67 had just reached a peak of popularity.

In 1970, in an attempt to drive up some industry interest, Howson invited London music industry vet Ian (Sammy) Samwell to listen to Ratfields, which had by now been renamed Follow the Buffalo, in action.

Sammy was a man with an interesting and musically valuable slew of credits to his resume at this time. In 1958, he had joined instrumental rock group Cliff Richard and the Drifters (later Cliff Richards and the Shadows) as guitarist. It was during this time that he had composed and played rhythm guitar on the group's hit song "Move It," which hit the number two slot on the U.K. *Billboard* charts. Sammy ceased playing with the group when new members joined, but he continued to write songs for Richard and other groups like the Isley Brothers, for whom he penned "Say You Love Me Too" in 1959—historically significant for its being the first occasion on which a British songwriter wrote for an American rhythm and blues act.

Sammy remained an influential member of London's burgeoning pop music scene. An eternal music fan himself, he took his own record collection to spin songs at London's Lyceum Ballroom for its lunch-hour dance sets in 1961. Sammy was soon named official DJ for twice-weekly sessions there and began to garner a loyal following of locals, many of whom were devoted to the surging mod craze. Two thousand teenagers would show up to dance—one of whom was a small, sprightly, hipper-than-hip kid named Jeff Dexter.

Dexter had, in his own right, played a large role in the development of London's youth music scene. Always small for his age, he had frequented youth clubs as a preteen, where he'd made good and fast friends with the girls there, who respected his interest in fashionable clothing. Girls motivated Jeff to dance well—romantic by nature, he found that his interest in music well accented his interest in women. After attending a summer camp in Surrey, where he'd befriended several of the girls there, young Jeff was urged to attend the Lyceum Ballroom dances with them.

While at the Lyceum, Jeff first encountered Sammy—via the cardboard cutout of his image displayed in the ballroom's lobby. He took an instant interest in his character and easily identified the real Sammy once on the dance floor. Sammy looked to be of an older generation, well and neatly dressed, in a fine suit with hair slicked back—a far cry from the long-haired youths who came to hear him DJ.[1]

Jeff developed quite a reputation for knowing how to dance the twist, and other club-goers at the Lyceum would study his moves to improve their own. Sammy noticed Jeff too and soon had him come up onstage during a DJ session to dance for the crowd. The two became fast friends, and Jeff would occasionally join Sammy as DJ, demonstrating his wealth of popular music knowledge. In the early 1960s, Sammy and Jeff became roommates, with a few other friends, occupying a house in north London on Hampstead Way. The home would become a musical hangout for artists.

By 1970, Sammy had found a more permanent corporate gig in the music industry, as the talent seeker of Warner Brothers' London team.

When Howson asked Sammy to listen to Follow the Buffalo's music, Sammy remained more or less unimpressed with the material. Except for the lead guitar work. *That* was good—superlatively so. Well, that had been done by a session player, Gerry Beckley—who had his own band, Howson informed him. "Then, bring me *his* band," Sammy insisted. Dave Howson contacted Gerry, telling him that he wished to meet with *his* band—the one that would soon be known as America.

Gerry, Dewey, and Dan came over to Dave's Middle Earth Records office and auditioned. Howson's hipness and pop music know-how impressed the band. They, in turn, performed for him a few of their songs. Howson was impressed. He was in.

"Howson was instrumental in getting us some gigs," Dewey recalled. "'He had a network of these various clubs and pubs." Soon Howson organized and scheduled a series of auditions for the band, with the top record label offices in London. America prepared demo tapes for delivery to every record label office in London, and they performed a live audition for the A&R representatives at Warner Brothers' office. The young trio felt the vulnerability of setting up their material to be judged by objective others. They had performed in multiple places, with their past respective rock groups, but it had never been as intimate as this was. And it had never felt this crucial or critical.

Warner Brothers exec Martin Wyatt, along with staff producer Ian Samwell, were in the room. Martin couldn't believe his ears. America was the talent that he had been waiting for, but he tried his best to affect an air of nonchalance, conserving his power as a dealmaker. He wanted to sign America midway through their audition; he wanted to draw up the necessary papers and close the whole thing up. Martin was so sure, but being the expert businessman that he was, he opted for reserved composure. It was one of the most difficult performances of his professional career. The moment America's audition had ended, Martin was quick to notify label manager Ian Ralfini that he—and Warner—were sitting on the next big act.

* * *

Sammy liked what he heard but knew America needed more experience playing for live audiences. Warner Brothers had promised the band that they would soon offer them a seven-album, seven-year contract, with Sammy serving as producer. The manager slot remained open. There was only one other person Sammy thought of who would be just as interested in America as he was: his roommate Jeff Dexter. Jeff, with his vast network of music industry connections, was the obvious recruit to help organize such an initiative. Jeff would become the trio's de facto manager, though official contracts were never signed.

"Ian Samwell invited us over to his place in Hampstead," Gerry recalled, "a lovely little old home where he lived with Jeff Dexter. It was a hippie commune, basically. Two or three people were about, including Robert Wyatt from the Soft Machine. So that took it up a notch. Eventually we had a contract from Warner Brothers. We made that decision; we signed and agreed to co-produce with Ian Samwell."

Following the Warner's audition, Howson kept up his deal-scouting routine for the band, negotiating and scheduling demo sessions with several other record labels in London. "There was a buzz about us," Gerry remembered. "In fact, there was a story where the head of Atlantic [Records] was having drinks with the head of Warners in London, Phil Carson and Ian Ralfini. 'We've got this great band called America.' 'No, *we've* got them.' We didn't realize you weren't supposed to do the same thing for every label. But Warner Reprise had Joni Mitchell and James Taylor, and we figured that was where we should be." Howson, amid negotiations with Warner, had also presented America and their music to London's other major and minor record labels—a general faux pas.

Soon, America decided to sever ties with Howson, as his vision for its career did not match up with the trio's own. "I don't remember any break, any animosity," Dewey explained. "Suddenly Howson was out, and Jeff Dexter and Ian Samwell were guiding us at that point."

By this time, Jeff had made quite a name for himself in the British music scene—he more or less knew everyone worth knowing. He had first risen to acclaim while dancing the most American of dances—the twist. So he had a fateful affinity for all things American where rock was concerned. Pub owners, club owners, promoters, booking agents, record producers, recording engineers. He had the perfect set of ingredients to manage a brand-new rock 'n' roll band, a band that needed a knowledgeable guiding hand, and who was in tune with what the youth of the moment was listening to. As of late, it had been a lot of American acoustic music—a lot of CSNY. Dewey, Gerry, and Dan were well aware of the cultural and musical power that the city of London possessed. But they sensed that a new artistic core was defining itself in Southern California—and that the trio themselves possessed timely beneficial qualities. They were American in nationality, and their blue-jeans-and-long-hair donning was right out of the Woodstock look. Their musical identity happened to follow suit, proving them to have arrived on to the musical scene at the exact, ideal time to be relevant. "We were simply members of our own generation expressing ourselves as such," reflected Dewey. "I personally felt very much a part of the 'Woodstock generation.' Along with smoking hash and tie-dying our own clothes, we had been to many festival-seating concerts around London and several festivals, including the 1970 Bath Festival—where everyone was sharing a common experience—sleeping in the mud and being a part of the 'group consciousness' of the age. Young people we were in contact with in England and all over Europe (especially in Holland, where America toured) seemed to embrace the common lifestyle of peace and freedom that was happening in the U.S.—in synchronicity." Even electric-guitar-mad Dan put his guitar amp up for sale. He wouldn't need it anymore: America was an acoustic act. For the band's earliest shows and label tryouts, acoustic guitars had to be borrowed from friends and acquaintances.

When the trio first met Jeff, they were enthused and intrigued by his over-the-top colorful way of dressing. He was a rare character, standing out even amid swarms of London hippies and cool kids. Jeff was very small in stature, not much taller than five feet and nimbly skinny. He had sleek and straight, light-colored, long hair, a ghostly pallor, and wore granny eyeglasses.

With all of Jeff Dexter's social and artistic connections in London's music scene, Gerry, Dewey, and Dan now had an ideal opening into the world they desired to inhabit. Jeff took them under his wing, befriending them and sharing music with them—including a valuable recording of the Beatles' Hollywood Bowl concert—which he used to offer pointers on the art of performing live. Jeff's high status in the world of London music made it easy for him to garner membership for the trio at the Speakeasy Club, known as "The Speak." It was a thrill for the three boys, who were not yet famous, who had not yet recorded their album—to spend time in a locale of such stature. There they ran into well-known actors and rock 'n' rollers of the day, and even got to see some sold-out shows held there—like one of Dan's and Dewey's favorite live performances of all time, by the minimalistic Seals and Crofts. "We called it 'The Speak,' but it was actually the Speakeasy," Gerry explained. "And we got in because all of the Warner reps were members, so that they could bring their artists in. Let's say Alice Cooper was in town for a tour or show or something. The Warner Brother guys would want to squire them all around town, so they were members of most of these types of clubs. And the Speak just happened to be the place where most of them went at this time. It varied throughout the '70s; it became Tramp's for a while. Always amazing celebrity sightings there. It was more of a band place, but Tramp's, which showed up on our radar later, was as much acting and stuff as it was musicians. The Speak was more musicians." In December 1970, America played its biggest gig yet, which Dexter had helped to secure. The band participated in a multiact performance at the Roundhouse in Chalk Farm called Implosion. It was a holiday charity event and included big name groups like the Who and Elton John.

When Gerry, Dewey, and Dan signed with Warner Brothers UK in March '71, technically through its Kinney Records section, they had the opportunity to redefine their working and living situations. Dewey and Dan had held down grunge-ridden part-time jobs at the Air Force base's cafeteria, forced to scrub dirty dishes on repeat, under the reign of a domineering supervisor. They couldn't wait to quit—even though Dan's father believed doing so would be a terrible decision. The music industry was too unpredictable, too unreliable. America was put on retainer by the Warner Brothers label, a luxury that afforded them to quit their interim day jobs and focus their time on rehearsing and performing live. They would move into a joint home all together, too, with the record label covering rent and some incidental costs. And of course, pocket money.

6

THE MANOR

"The only good memory of our years of bondage in the cafeteria was the day we came up with the name AMERICA. Gerry had stopped by again to chat and we were sitting next to the jukebox, an AMERICANA. . . . [A]t that point we were beginning to function as a unit and things just kind of happened. I do remember at one point discussing AMERICANA as a name, but it just seemed too cute. AMERICA said it all. We were Americans, American music was 'in,' and we wanted people to know we were the real deal," Dan remembered in his memoir.[1] "I think we'd been considering that name—what about America? Because we knew about the group the United States of America," Gerry recalled. "There was a CBS compilation album called *Rock Machine Turns You On*. One of these to expose all the great music on CBS, a Clive Davis thing, a sampler. That group didn't last very long, the United States of America. There was also Chicago Transit Authority, which was the name of their first album, and then they shortened it to Chicago for the second one. So there was already Chicago, and the group United States of America that we thought had broken up. And I think we kind of thought, 'Well, what about America? Because we're American.' And then we saw the Americana jukebox—it was a sign." And so Dewey Bunnell, Dan Peek, and Gerry Beckley officially became America.

With their newfound Warners funds, Gerry and Dan, who had been living in their families' homes, and Dewey, who had been living with the family of his high school buddy John Alcazar, could afford to rent their own place. It would be a tiny cowman's shed in the countryside village of quaint Chipperfield, just under thirty miles from London's city center. "The village was minute," recalled Dan, "with a church, a greengrocer, a butcher, a baker, and a pub loosely arranged around a large wooden common. Our tiny little woodframe house was actually a converted cowman's shed. Cosmetically it was fine, but there was virtually no hot water, no insulation from the bitter English cold, and the whole place was less than 700 square feet."[2]

America affectionately labeled their new home Dirtpit Manor. It held two bedrooms—one large, which Dan and Gerry shared, and one small, which was Dewey's, though he was frequently at the home of his wife-to-be, Vivien. Pete Reuther, a close high school pal of the band and a musician himself, moved into Dirtpit Manor also. While America began its early touring, he would take care of the house in their absence.

Though they were forced to live meagerly, Gerry, Dewey, and Dan enjoyed their newfound, self-supporting freedom. They spent their days rehearsing and writing songs. "We really had no money," Dewey remembered. "We were living pretty hand-to-mouth in that little shack." Fairly regularly, the trio would scale down to eating one meal a day—many of which were taken at the newly opened Hard Rock Café near Green Park. Each of the boys owned or had access to a car, which made Dirtpit Manor's out-of-the-way location more bearable.

Where Crosby, Stills, Nash & Young was formed by four pre-established musical artists, with pre-established and full-sized egos in tow, America was composed of high school grads, as yet nobodies. On the group's earliest recordings, and on the entirety of its debut EP, the trio's desire to blend its voices is impossible to deny. Listeners in 1971 and 1972 would not be able to pick out the singers' voices by a familiarity with their sound just yet. The group had not dubbed itself Beckley, Bunnell, & Peek, after all, but America.

America on tour was a new experience for everyone. It was a small operation at first. Minimal crew, cheaply bought instruments. Not much invested—not much tried or gambled with yet. It was an under-the-radar operation with three teenagers. The group had purchased a Ford transit van with most of the advance from Warner Brothers Records, roughly $2,500; new Yamaha FG-180 guitars ate up the remainder. They were the first new instruments America would buy for itself as a group.

The M1 motorway in England is a well-worn highway, a main artery that runs through Manchester and Leicester. When America and its crew began to travel it, there had been many other bands who'd started out performing live in just the same way. "We were basically doing a thirty-minute opening—with 'Riverside' and other songs—but you'd go up and down the M1 and there was a truck stop called the Blue Boar. All these vans would pull into the Blue Boar around one in the morning, they'd been performing up in Manchester or Newcastle. Everybody would stop there for greasy sausage, egg, and chips. 'Where had you played?' we'd ask. And so there was this lovely network," Gerry recalled. Jeff Dexter, a newly hired roadie named Claude, and the trio would make up America's minimal troupe at first. "The Ford transit van was customized," Dewey remembered. "I always thought that it was Howson's office we got the three airplane seats from—we had them installed in the back of the van. And we had this funky little PA system."

Soon, America was opening for bands like Family, the Band, Brinsley Schwarz—and Pink Floyd: "They had a ninety-piece orchestra and choir at the Roundhouse in London," Gerry reminisced. "And they were doing *Atom Heart Mother*. And Dewey, Dan, and I stumbled on out there, ripped on hash. On our stools, played our thirty minutes. It was pretty far out. Years later, I was flying with Roger Waters on a plane, and I asked, 'Do you remember that?' And he said, 'I remember it very well.' And you would, you know." When America opened for Steve Winwood's Traffic in London, guitar hero Johnny Winter jumped up onstage to jam with them. And when the trio and the Band were on the same concert bill at Amsterdam's Concertgebouw hall, Brinsley Schwarz asked America to make note of the Band's amp settings—they were intense fans and wanted to know everything about their musical habits in order to emulate their sound. It would not be the last time America would cross paths with the Band; in 1977 Gerry would provide background vocals and guitar on some of Rick Danko's eponymous solo album.

Gerry, Dewey, and Dan were paying their touring dues. Over the course of 1970 and 1971, America would complete several mini-tours of Europe, most of which ran from ten days to two weeks in total. A couple of these were based largely in Holland and its surrounding areas. "Holland had a whole other musical scene in fact; clubs, the Paradiso in Amsterdam," Dewey reminisced. "Every town had a little club. Our van: we had our three musketeers and our gang, and it was almost like Jeff Dexter was finding gigs *while* we were on the road. We were in youth hostels. 'I'll call ahead to that pub over there in Rotterdam,' he'd say, 'and see if we can get you in a show there.'" When Cat Stevens toured Europe in 1971 with his newest masterpiece *Teaser and the Firecat*, America was paired as his opening act. "I had these boots—the cover of *Teaser* is of a kid sitting on a curb with these boots," Dewey remembered. "And Steve'd say, 'Oh, you've got *Teaser* boots on!'"

In 1971, Warners set America up to record its debut self-titled album, with a release date in late fall. The whole initial experience, mixing included, took about two weeks at London's Trident Studios. Some months later, the record would be released "single-less" in the U.K., and it wouldn't make all that much noise.

Soon America played its first London-based gig as a band, at one of the city's country clubs. And then Bob Harris, the host of the popular BBC music program *The Old Grey Whistle Test*, saw the performance. He was impressed and asked America to make an appearance on his television show. On September 21, 1971, the band made one of its first television appearances, performing "Riverside" and "Children." America's radio and television opportunities slowly began to pick up steam. So Warner would ask for more tunes, and America would record four extras—one of which was to be the group's success-maker—Dewey's "Horse with No Name."

"'Have you got anything else?' Warner asked us. Now that would *never* happen nowadays. You would put all your energy into making the album, and prep on 'these are the singles,' all that focus. But for the label to say, within a month of releasing, 'have you got anything else?' Well we did, we were writing every day. We had three or four new tunes," recalled Gerry. America traveled out to Puddletown, Dorset, to the home of "Fire" singer Arthur Brown. There, they recorded demos of "Submarine Ladies," "Everyone I Meet Is from California," "Don't Cross the River," and "Desert Song." It was an interesting recording experience for the band; Brown's home studio was a wild and wacky place, full of hippie-charged atmosphere—brown rice, incense, and acid. When Warner received the tapes, they chose "Desert Song"—whose name would be changed to "A Horse with No Name"—for the single.

With Trident Studios being unavailable, America went to Gerry's home base at Morgan Studios instead; there, they mastered "Horse" and "Everyone I Meet Is from California," which would eventually be re-recorded electric-style and dubbed "California Revisited" for America's second album, *Homecoming*. America's maxi-single, including those two tracks and "Sandman," would be released in the U.K. on November 12, 1971. The cover featured a black-and-white snapshot of the trio, in their teenage clothes, posing in front of Piccadilly Circus.

In no time at all, the single "A Horse with No Name" reached number three on the U.K. *Billboard* charts. The hit brought America the opportunity to perform live on the BBC's music show *Top of the Pops*, sharing a bill with the Bee Gees. "Backstage at the BBC's 'Top of the Pops' was a madhouse," Dan remembered. "The show aired 'live' and a raucous audience cheered each act with fervor. Lighting and scenery were being moved, chorus girls and boys leaping about, fog machines billowing, camera angles being shouted at gaffers scudding between heavy cables and lithely limbed go-fers and cue card holders danced around all of it. It was a three-ring circus. Compared to the incredibly well-groomed Bee Gees we looked like street urchins."[3]

America continued to perform around Europe while their single continued to do well in England. "Now we had had an album, which had been a minor hit on the charts," recalled Gerry. "None of this had come out anywhere other than England. We had this maxi-single that had been a pretty big hit—so this shows up on Warner's Burbank radar." Taking note of the new group's success, Warner offered America the chance to play dates across the United States.

The band jumped at the chance to tour North America, eager to return to the U.S. in any capacity. For Dewey, it had been six years since his family left San Jose, California, for William's assignment in Norfolk, England, in '66. Warner Brothers U.S. headquarters printed up tens of thousands of copies of America's debut record to sell in stores. But there was only one problem—it didn't include the hit single, the single that all young record-buyers wanted to hear. It was the original pressing. It didn't include "A Horse with No Name." This batch of copies would soon become collectors' items. Warner corrected its mistake and printed the proper version of "record-with-hit."

By paying dues on the Euro road, opening for rock 'n' roll headliners, America had accrued quite a concertgoer following there. With a single and album on the chart-rise, and as promised to Warner, the trio embarked upon their first American tour. Dewey, Gerry, and Dan could now afford slightly improved guitars. Dan went with a twelve-string Fender Shenandoah, while Gerry and Dewey purchased six-string Yamahas. Together Dan and Gerry chose a clear lucite Dan Armstrong bass. America began the tour in Canadian college towns, kicking it off with a performance in a college lunchroom in Kitchener, Ontario. Then the band worked its way toward the major cities of the U.S. northeast. They played well-known clubs like the Cellar Door in Washington, DC, the Main Point in Philadelphia—and the Bitter End in New York City, where America got to open for popular comedian Robert Klein. The trio was also invited to appear on *The Dick Cavett Show* to be interviewed and perform "Horse." Fellow guests were Reverend Bill Graham and Pat Boone, making for a fascinating coming together of young hippies and conservative Christians. Years later Dan Peek would release solo albums of Christian music through Pat Boone's record label Lamb & Lion Records.

Lennie's on the Turnpike just outside Boston, however, proved somewhat tricky. America's week at DC's Cellar Door had been as the opening act for rock legends the Everly Brothers, whose backing band at the moment included L.A. wonders Warren Zevon and Waddy Wachtel. Years later Waddy would play on an America record—as a sideman. But the nightly shows had been stolen by America's up-and-coming appeal; most concertgoers were there to see Gerry, Dewey, and Dan, not the less relevant Everlys. By the time the troupe got to Lennie's, the Everly Brothers had canceled, on account of "sickness"—though Phil showed up to do several songs solo out of courtesy. The Everly Brothers knew the fans in block-long lines each night were not waiting to see them. "We were moved to the headline position," Gerry remembered, "and we said, 'We don't really have a whole show. Maybe forty minutes tops.' We were told, 'It's okay, we've hired this comic to do twenty minutes: Jay Leno.' So we had Jay Leno opening for us in February of '72, at Lennie's on the Turnpike."

The American tour culminated in a week of sold-out performances at the Whisky a Go Go, the famed rock club in Los Angeles. "We didn't play the Troub," Gerry remembered, "because Jeff Dexter, . . . in trying to negotiate the Troubadour, the owner Doug Weston always insisted on options. 'I'll put you at the Troub, but you've got to agree to two more appearances.' We didn't want that, so we asked if there was anywhere else we could play. The Troub was the place for the singer-songwriter. But it was, 'Well, you could play the Whisky.' We agreed. The Whisky was more of a rock club, but regardless, 'Horse' was the biggest selling

Left to right: Gerry, Dewey, Ian Ralfini, Claudie, Jeff Dexter, and Dan at the Whisky, 1972. *Photographer unknown.*

record at the time, and the album was heading to number one. We sold the place out for a week. Lines around the block."

Backstage at the Whisky after each show was wild. Hollywood musicians and actors all hung around, some even stopping by to praise America for their hit song and stellar new album. Brian Wilson, Greg Allman, Arlo Guthrie, Bill Mumy, and Three Dog Night's Danny Hutton were just some of the notables among the crowd. By night, America was holed up at the world-famous Continental Hyatt House, known colloquially as the Riot House, on West Hollywood's Sunset Strip. There, rock 'n' roll antics were in full swing all around them. "We followed Led Zeppelin in," Dewey remembered, "so there were still Led Zeppelin hanger-oners near our rooms—and people in the lobby and [on] many of the floors."

By day, the band was able to meet the staff of Warners' office, in the North Hollywood section of Los Angeles. All the while, America bore witness to its documented sales success, hearing themselves on the radio daily—sometimes misintroduced by DJs as Neil Young. "When we got to the States," Gerry remembered, "there were hundreds of stations. And we were being limoed and so on. All this was new; we weren't exactly used to all of that. From that van with the three airplane seats, to being picked up by chauffeurs. But—switch the station! There's 'Horse.' Switch the station! There's 'Horse.'" The trio also read about their chart positions in the industry trade rags. America's single and album had gone to number one in the U.S.A.—and everywhere else. During their sold-out run at Whisky a Go Go, mainstream and underground, print and television journalists demanded interviews with the new stars. The immensity and suddenness of America's newfound global success meant a fast learning curve for the young band. It struck them as a wild and hallucinatory mega dream.

When the trio and their entourage arrived home in London after Los Angeles, they faced customs difficulties because of new instruments purchased in the U.S. Jeff Dexter quickly suggested they insist their guitars were British and say they had bought everything from London music store Top Gear, to avoid having to pay tax—but Dan didn't get the memo. They were stopped at customs and immigration, and Dan was honest, saying that everything was from Manny's Music Store in New York. The band was charged several thousand dollars at customs, and was forced to buy back their own instruments from the government.

"You could see through the glass in the waiting area, where people were waiting for their loved ones to come through customs," Dewey remembered. "And we could see all the Warner Brothers people and our friends and family that were there to greet us back from our successful tour, with banners and balloons and everything else. As everybody else was going through the doors, we were being marched off to separate little interrogation rooms. In retrospect it was so funny."

All in all, it was a lovely homecoming for the world's top pop act.

7

THE ALBUM

The general idea was to keep the sound exactly the same. During America's auditions at each point in its journey—for Ian Samwell, for Jeff Dexter, for Warner Brothers in London—the band's basic acoustic guitars and youthfully ardent three-part harmonies were what defined the group.

The trio toyed with the idea of modeling their debut album on the conceptual style of *Sgt. Pepper's*, with a great deal of production, sound effects, and numerous instruments. As nearly all other fellow artists of the day, America was consistently driven by its admiration for the Beatles. Beckley, Bunnell, and Peek wanted to move in that sonic direction; now that they were being handed studio time and a record contract, they hesitated to waste an opportunity to realize their aural dream.

But Sammy knew that America's topmost quality at the moment was not its songwriting or stage prowess. It was the interrelations between three acoustic guitars and three human voices, as they were live. America didn't need studio gadgets to showcase its musicality. In 1971, Crosby, Stills & Nash—and Neil Young—(CSNY) were lords of the musical manor in the United States. For all intents and purposes, and presumably in the eyes of Warner Brothers' businessmen, America's marketability had already been tested and tried via CSNY. It was more or less a sure thing. America did possess a characteristic that CSNY lacked, however: a total, all-encompassing groupness. Many listeners of the era would have already been familiar with the careers of CSNY's prior bands like Buffalo Springfield, the Byrds, and the Hollies. The combination of CSNY would be new, but its individual voices would be recognizable to rock fans. In 1971 Beckley, Bunnell, and Peek were three unknown teenagers, and under the general label of "America," they achieved an instant and intriguing mystique. Such a mystique coupled with a megahit like "Horse" intensified the effect of success that much more. America had achieved both a number one single and number one album on their first release, a phenomenon that few other artists have ever experienced. "We were certainly launched into a new life in short order at that point," Dewey remembered. This same mystique would prove to plague America with an ongoing identity crisis of its own throughout its career evolution.

"I always say that Ian Samwell was very, very important," Gerry said. "He was in a position to make sure it didn't go off the rails, just keep 'this' (the trio) right where it is. And we didn't really know the engineer Ken Scott, but Ian picked Ken Scott, and we booked Trident Studios. Scott had been the Beatles' engineer for the *White Album*, he was in the middle of two Bowies—he had just done *The Man Who Sold the World* and *Hunky Dory*. And *All Things Must Pass*, with Harrison. So these were great credentials." This production request of the group via Samwell, to keep America's sound where it already was, would carry through during the band's entire career. This request suggested an inherent authenticity, that would eventually serve as a calling card of the group's performative quality. They weren't ones to amend their sound or image to fit the shifting trends of the pop music world. The suggestion was also well aligned with the hippies' creed of the 1960s: come as you are. Don't change, tinker, adjust, or dress up—just be. America would spend part of its decades-long career in performative dialogue with this concern.

Trident Studios was located just off Wardour Street in London. The band felt that it was highly modern, complete with the latest recording technology. Dan found it to be a bit overly clean and tidy for an ideal rock 'n' roll environment and was not a fan of the studio's floor plan. The studio and control room were on different levels of the building, requiring an elevator to travel between them. Dave Atwood, an old buddy of Gerry's from London Central, was brought in to play the album's drum parts. The percussion track was kept intentionally low, to avoid its interference with the already established America sound. "Ian Samwell brought in two people," Gerry recalled, "Ray Cooper to play percussion, which became more the drums than anything else. And David Lindley, who was living in London. Before Jackson Browne, David was playing with Terry Reid.

He played lap steel. So those two additions were just priceless if you go back to that album and think, 'What, other than us, was there?'"

Following the Warners audition, Sammy had instructed America to, when the time came to record the first album, virtually reproduce the acoustic, natural sound they'd just made—to not overly tinker with studio production elements or add too many overdubs and effects. The band listened to Sammy during the album recording process. But, for Dan, his studio manner took some getting used to. While he appreciated Sammy's genius for musical hunches during production, he didn't go in for his tough-love guidance style, feeling that it made for unnecessary discomfort. Dan, Gerry, and Dewey were young and inexperienced, not yet having developed the tough skins required for musicians in the big leagues where the stakes for everyone were high. Sammy had no time for coddling; neither did Warner Brothers.

As an observer, Ken Scott felt that Sammy and Jeff Dexter were "a very strange pairing. Most of the time, they got on very well, and they obviously had the same idea. The combination of these producers and this almost folk-ish type trio was different, but it worked."[1] The credits on the album would state that it had been produced by Sammy, Jeff Dexter, and America, though Dan felt that Sammy was the biggest contributor, production-wise. The recording experience was a learning one for the band, and it would drive them to produce their follow-up album, *Homecoming*, on their own. Ken Scott reflected:

> They had their harmonies all worked out. They stood together in the room to do their vocals. I think I had them on three 67s—each one on his own—and then I'd get the EQ and blend them upstairs [in the mix room] if I remember correctly. I don't think they were quite at a point where they could do it, or we even wanted it, where the three of them were round one mic. We separated them and got the blend upstairs.
>
> I know that later on in their existence, they refused to sing choruses more than once, so they had to fly in the rest of the choruses. I have to state for the record that on that album they sang everything. These days, that's common practice with computers, but it wasn't quite so easy to do it back then.[2]

"Gerry brought in 'I Need You' as a complete, great song, it seemed like out of whole cloth," Dewey recalled. "That was another thing about it—as young as we were, there was a lot of experience in there somehow, lyrically. Chord progressions of Gerry's. It wasn't just some fluff thing, or some blues riffs thrown together." The song was a mature, singer-songwriter's song. It sounded standard, as though it had always existed. And, like much of Frank Sinatra's and other standards singers' material, it sounded as though anyone else would be able to interpret it. Compositionally, Gerry had been inspired by the Bee Gees' "First of May," with its personally nostalgic lyrics and melodic progression: "When I was small, and Christmas trees were tall, we used to love while others used to play." Inspirationally this led to Gerry's "We used to laugh, we used to cry, we used to bow our heads then wonder why."

"You take these little bits and glue them all together," said Gerry, "and in theory, you become a supergroup of all the people you used to listen to." In America's live shows, they would frequently segue cover songs in and out of their originals, a related process to Gerry's inspirational one as a songwriter. Midset, the start of the Bee Gees' "New York Mining Disaster 1941"—slow and steady guitar strumming amid "In the event of something happening to me"—would transition into Dewey's "Ain't it foggy outside?" from "Sandman."

America would soon make friends with the great Harry Nilsson. Upon hearing "I Need You" for the first time, Harry fell head over heels in love with the tune. When Warners chose "Horse" as America's debut single, Harry told Gerry he intended to record his song "I Need You" as his next single. This was on the tails of Harry's immense success covering the Badfinger (Hamm and Evans) song "Without You," which had been produced by Richard Perry—whom Harry intended to use in recording the America cover. But within weeks of releasing "Horse," Warner Brothers decided on America's rendition of "I Need You" for its follow-up single.

Every time Harry Nilsson got together with America from that moment on, he insisted upon hearing a live performance of the song "I Need You," to which he would always sing along. And he would finally cut a studio recording of the track in 1976, for his Trevor Lawrence–produced album *That's the Way It Is*. It was after the voice-destroying, John Lennon–companioning *Pussycats* period by that time, so the result was not an ideal one. "I have very few regrets over our fifty years," Gerry Beckley reflected, "and I couldn't be prouder of our version [of "I Need You"] and the success we had with it. But to have heard Harry—with Richard producing—record it at that time, I feel, would have been something truly special."

"Here" as well would prove Gerry's precocity as a songwriter. This demonstration of composition added to the album's introduction of his writerly prowess. "I am thinkin' 'bout the days, we led ourselves astray, in more than many ways," the song went. "I Need You" and "Here," with their slow tempos and lyrical self-reflection, set the precedent for Gerry's writerly character. He seemed to harbor regrets about various love affairs, even at this young age.

The issue of time—past, present, and future—seemed to be of concern with America and its three songwriters. Gerry's romantic ballad "Clarice" dealt with it straight on, saying, "Time is coming soon, I'll find you." The track was passionate and asked a girl to follow the singer-songwriter into his next plane of experience.

"Sandman" was a real rock 'n' roll number of Dewey's, sonically and lyrically full of all the tension, fervor, and fear of the Vietnam War's ongoing disaster. "At Lakenheath Air Force Base in 1967, we had seen some soldiers traveling back from Vietnam. Maybe they were just reassigned and were now stationed at our base. But they'd been in Vietnam. 'Sandman' was loosely based on some discussions I'd heard," Dewey explained. The song would be the most militaristically charged one of the band's whole songwriting career. Their lifelong familial proximity to the American armed forces lent the song and its recording an extra dose of authenticity. Lyrically, "Sandman" is an early example of Dewey's fine talent for incorporating real-life conversation into his songwriting. Almost in the way a playwright would move plot along via brief dialogue exchanges, Dewey tells the tale of soldiers' insomnia and PTSD traces: "Ain't the years gone by fast? I suppose you have missed them. Oh, I almost forgot to ask—did you hear of my enlistment? Funny, I've been there, and you've been here, and we ain't had no time to drink that beer. 'Cause I understand you've been running from the man that goes by the name of the Sandman." This track would also establish one of Dewey's roles in the group, as supplier of at least one hard-rocking, non-ballad song to each album.

"The songs 'Children' and 'Three Roses' were formulating, but the first song I ever completed was 'Riverside,'" recalled Dewey. It would be the album's opener. The gradual intro of fast-paced guitar strumming in "Riverside" set the tone for what America's album—and America as an entity—was intended to be. Lyrically, the song conveyed a similar message to the one found in Jackson Browne's and the Eagles' classic track

"Take It Easy." Dewey's singer-narrator declares that he is "taking it all in . . . stride" and "taking life like a big long ride." He articulates his belief in universal freedom, too: "You stay on your side, and I'll stay on mine. You take what you want"—whatever that may be—"and I'll take the sunshine." The lyrics are one version of a generalized hippie vision, in which all people are free to follow their desires and allow for others to do the same. It is also an affirmation of self-responsibility in its final refrain, which is structured as a call and response echo: "The world don't owe me no livin'." Much like Gerry's songwriting precocity demonstrated in "I Need You," Dewey's mature wisdom-beyond-his-years is evident in "Riverside." The track is also a moving song; the pace moves forward steadily, its reference to a river implies flowing motion, and its intricately interwoven three guitar parts suggest a lighthearted busyness to the listener. "Riverside," along with "Horse," would also serve as Dewey's first journey song, which would prove to be one of many in his career as a songwriter.

Dewey's material would dominate most of the album's first side. "Three Roses," a beautiful, ear-pleasing love track, proved his mettle as a romantic songwriter right alongside Gerry. The song would show itself to be one of America's best examples of its catalogue's love songs. Its lyrics seemed to come straight out of Dewey's personal aesthetic, which included an ongoing reverence for nature and all of the ardent simplicity it offered: "Sitting by the fireside with a book in your hand, two lazy dogs sit watchin' your man." Then there was the relatable pondering of feelings: "I gotta stop and see what I'm on about . . . stop and feel what I want with you." He is—especially for such a young person—sensitive, intelligent, and in no rush. And he builds his song around one of the most romantic lines in the entirety of 1970s popular music: "Three roses were bought—with you in mind." The beautifully lilting guitar work of the track only serves to emphasize its lyrical ideas.

Dewey's "Riverside" would open the album—but Dewey's "Pigeon Song" would close it. The track, simply recorded with Dewey's lone voice and one acoustic guitar, is initially disarming to the listener. Right up until the last stanza, the song just seems to be detailing the antics of a destructive character who kills or ruins everything and everyone he comes into contact with. The last lines of soliloqual wondering, however, change the song's meaning: "I don't know why I done it, honest, it ain't like me. But I ain't sad now I done it, 'cause a baby boy has got to be free." The singer-narrator's acts of destruction are not acts of mindless annihilation, but desires to be free from worldly trappings. To be independent and pure—much like the 1960s counterculture's desire to "get back to the garden." Dewey's version is true to his own hippie ideology and a great concept; arguably, it takes just too long to get there, leaving the listener in a state of perplexity nearly the entire song long. His track "Children" issues similar themes, with its lyrical plea, "Come on children, get your heads back together." The words spoke to his own generation, and his fear of the 1960s ideology's fading into nothingness.

Dan's song contributions to this record were influential as well. "Rainy Day," "Never Found the Time," and "Donkey Jaw" (sung by Dewey) were his compositional attempts here. All of these were moody, romantic, and introspective to a degree. Dan was clearly stung by his failed relationship with Cathie and attempting to sort bits of it out through his songwriting. "But I know that you're gonna cry, tears are runnin' from your eyes," "Rainy Day" articulates. It continues, "The piece of my life you take is one that so often breaks." This accentuates Cathie's emotional hold over Dan. He wanted to be with her, for real—and he would, eventually. This thing between them was serious. Regrets and fears are articulated again in the refrain from "Never Found the Time": "I never found the time to see into my lady. And memories don't die but with time become hazy." For a guitar-forward and rock-heavy kind of musician, Dan's songwriting contributions to America's first record album are noticeably mild.

"Donkey Jaw" is perhaps the most bemusing track of America's debut album. "The song came out of just sitting around jamming with Dewey, and he had a little lick that the whole song became based on," Dan reminisced. "It was a throwaway, and I said, 'If you're gonna throw that away, let's write a song around it.' And we just started hammering away with the lyrics. It was a combination of a lot of things; it was a war-protest song, generally speaking. I felt like, is it going to take a whole generation of children being killed for people to wake up? I don't know why Dewey sang it—it was probably my way of saying thank you for letting me steal his riff."[3] The song's title could not be further from the narrative identity of the song.

The album's cover image seemed to say it all. Taken in Warners' London office, a space that became America's second home for a time, and in front of a Native American mural that always hung on the wall, the photo captured Gerry, Dewey, and Dan. It depicted them as the blue jeans–and–sneakers–wearing teenagers they were—hanging out, mid-conversation, enthused, and animated. Almost a divination of the awe and excitement they would feel when their very first album would shortly make it to number one. When it would make it to number one from the endorsement of thousands of teenagers, who looked very similar to how the trio looked in the album photograph.

8

THE CLIMB

"I remember the label doing an edit of 'Never Found the Time,'" Gerry recalled. "It's a lovely song, but the chorus doesn't come until the end. We thought, 'What if we edit that in earlier on?' And I remember Ian Samwell putting an edit of that song together, and the problem was back then, without click tracks or anything, the tempo ramped right up. So if you took the faster bit from the end and glued it into the middle, it would jump forward in tempo. I remember listening to it and going, 'Oh well; that doesn't work.'"

Lately, Dewey had been working on a mercurial and distinctive tune that he called "Desert Song." The rainfall level in England that year was at an all-time high, which only intensified Dewey's sense memory of his desert days spent near Southern California's Vandenberg Air Force Base. "With songwriting and me," Dewey explained, "I'd put together three or four chords, hum a melody over it, and then come up with a lyric. But this lyric was reminiscing, thinking about my time in Southern California. In the desert areas of New Mexico, where my uncle and his family lived. So it was conjuring up imagery, whatever that might be. And in this case, I was pining for the U.S. to some degree. We had been away from it for a long time. England truly is rainy and foggy."

The band worried that it sounded too corny, too strange—not the typical and reliable pop number that it was capable of producing. The band hesitated to use it as *the single*.

"I thought it was a novelty song almost," Dewey explained. "I remember sitting on my bed writing the lyrics, which came out pretty much word for word without changes, and thinking, 'I could write dozens more verses to this thing!' Songwriting's funny. You find a place in your head: if you knew what it was, or if there was a formula, you could use it. The imagery of the song was important to me. I used a weird tuning; Gerry and Dan kind of thought, 'What the hell is that dumb tuning?' It was sort of like I had found out about tunings. We became aware of that through Joni Mitchell's and David Crosby's songs."

"Dewey already had a few different tunings," Gerry reminisced. "And it was easy to say, 'Well, that's kind of an E minor, so we'll just play along with that.' Which got you these really nice—not conflicting, but combining—voices. Because not every guitar was playing the same chord, there were some overtones. There'd be a ninth in his tuning, that we weren't playing."

"A Horse with No Name" was recorded on the last session day at Morgan. Dewey sang lead and played acoustic guitar, Gerry played a twelve-string acoustic, and Dan played bass. Kim Haworth provided drums, with Ray Cooper on additional percussion. The chorus's three-part harmony was reminiscent of the work of recent and in-vogue Crosby, Stills & Nash, whose wildly popular, self-titled debut album had been released just two years earlier. "A Horse with No Name" even featured a unique tuning set-up on the players' guitars; the key of E Dorian was used. No other America song ever utilized this tuning. Dan later recalled in his memoir:

> I give full kudos to Gerry on the arrangement of the vocals, kudos to me for the driving bass line and to Sammy . . . for arranging the guitar solo in the middle (including the total cribbing of the waterfall guitar parts on "Rainy Day") and the idea for repeating the bass "hook" at just the right spot in every chorus. The extremely long, slow fade was another Sammy touch.[1]

America was released again in December 1971, this time with "Horse." It could do no wrong—it was the perfect storm of a debut record. What had been a quality debut pop-rock album quickly became an immortal masterpiece. On March 25, 1972, the single reached number one on the U.S. *Billboard* Hot 100, cheekily edging out its musical relative of a song, Neil Young's "Heart of Gold." Bunnell articulated, "I know that virtually everyone, on first hearing, assumed it was Neil. I never fully shied away from the fact that I was inspired by him. I think it's in the structure of the song as much as in the tone of his voice." "Horse" remained at number one for three straight weeks. And on the charts for fourteen weeks.

America, which now included "A Horse with No Name," went triple platinum, spending five weeks at number one. It had begun in slot 160 on February 19, 1972, climbing past and surpassing 159 albums—including classics by James Taylor, Gladys Knight, Santana, Paul Simon, and Neil Young—in just five weeks. Warners had been onto something in its demand for more material, the result of which was an undeniable success story. A radio station in Kansas City banned the single from its airwaves, reading into the potential slang of "horse" and citing it as a heroin endorsement. Several other radio stations followed suit. It only added to

First U.K. record award for "Horse." *Courtesy of the Bunnell family.*

the appeal and mystique of the new kid, America the band, whose debut single took up residence at varying slots on the 1972 *Billboard* chart for fourteen consecutive weeks.

In 2020, decades after its release and hit-making year, "A Horse with No Name" resonates with modern listeners. Its ongoing appeal mirrors the appeal of the love-and-freedom-first philosophy of the 1970s ethos. These ideas were not merely temporal, though they did connect with the era's cultural vibrations—they are eternal. Thus, America was established from its inception as an eternity-minded band. It would not be superficial or subject to one or many passing trends. It was an authentic band that a listener committed to and bought into wholeheartedly. Today, in 2020, on nearly every "Greatest Hits of the 1970s" radio program and playlist, "Horse" is included. The song is as much a part of the '70s as Vietnam and Watergate are; it helped to define the decade's essence. Being true to America's tone as a band, the song sought to reach beyond societal or specific concerns. It went all in for the humanistic, the eternal. Perhaps that was why the song's effect upon listeners in late 1971, and 1972, was so sharp: it highlighted overarching life themes like freedom, truth, and the power of nature, while communicating them with enough intoxicating power to render them immediate, palpable, current, *now*.

Beckley and Bunnell's current incarnation of America plays one hundred live (and frequently sold-out) concerts per year—none of which omit "A Horse with No Name" from their setlists. The song has been used both as diegetic and non-diegetic music for countless film and television soundtracks, including *Breaking Bad*, *The Simpsons*, and *American Hustle*. Each media usage, too, seems to directly draw attention to the song while it plays in a scene, sometimes as a spoof or as a point of discussion among the characters present. "Horse" is just too unique, too powerful, too culturally significant, to be used absentmindedly. It's a song that can't be ignored—by audiences who absorb it or by creators who borrow it for their own art—even in the twenty-first century.

In 2009, several weeks after Michael Jackson had died, his unreleased recording "A Place with No Name" was discovered and released. The song was a direct spin-off of America's "Horse." It had, in fact, used an actual sample of Dewey's original four-bar acoustic guitar intro from America's master recording. But Sony wouldn't admit that—at first.

"We heard that track years ago when Michael first did it, so it was not a surprise to us," Gerry reflected. "When it came out posthumously, everyone tried to sort out all the legal elements, because first of all, sadly, Michael's no longer with us. But there were also a million producers and a million writers, and it was quite complicated." Sony claimed that the track's producers had hired a session player to mimic the original recording's guitar riff, sidestepping the requirement to pay America a licensing fee for using their master tape, though Dewey would still receive writer's royalties. "I knew that it was the real record," said Gerry. "So at the meeting, our representatives put on the master of 'A Place with No Name' that had been released, and opened up the Shazam app, which digitally identifies songs. Immediately pops up America's *Greatest Hits*—'A Horse with No Name.' Which it wouldn't have done, had they replayed the riff; the musical footprint would have been somewhat different. And Sony's attorney just looked and said, 'That's a hell of an app.' End of argument. So it adjusted the deal."

"Who could have predicted," reflected Dewey, "that one day I would share a writing credit with Michael Jackson?! Life is full of surprises."

No matter the specifics amid which the original track is heard, for the first or thousandth time, Bunnell's tune is irresistible. The song's haunting and authentic elements speak loudly in their unapologetic truth. "Horse" is largely concerned with the plight of individuals and all the things at stake for them when living in the material world. The world changes, the materials do, too, but human beings in their essence maintain some kind of universal constancy.

The original *sound* of America consisted of Gerry, Dewey, and Dan—their perfectly blended three-part harmonies, their intertwining acoustic guitars. America the band was a trio, as far as its sonic identity was concerned. Democracy, unity, equality, and fairness were all sought-after characteristics of the band's name, its national namesake. While individual members could be singled out and lauded for their contributions, America's power remained in its togetherness, in its absolution of individuals. It didn't much matter who the members were, who sang lead on each of the album's songs, who played which instruments. The songs mattered, the music mattered. It was an admirable approach, especially given the youth and relative inexperience of America's members. It was an approach that went beyond individuals and sought to build upon the ideological aims of 1960s youth.

Dewey Bunnell had been responsible for the group's first hit, a monster hit that had rapidly propelled America into stardom. Dewey's compositional talent and originality were, in the eyes of consumers and listeners, capable of singling America out in the plethora of 1972's pop-rock bands. "A Horse with No Name" cemented this in history; Bunnell had proven himself to be a worthy and valuable band member, as far as the group's quest for artistic and material success went. One whose writerly message resonated with the youthful and record-buying masses. But the questions remained: could Beckley and Peek, as composer-performers, pull off this level of success for America, too? And could the sometimes unfriendly number three survive under the weight of talented-teenager egos?

9

THE MOVE

Following their debut North American tour, Dewey, Gerry, and Dan decided to take a recuperation break. Dewey had become engaged to his girlfriend Vivien and began to plan his wedding. Gerry and Dan took the opportunity to vacation. They went to Torremolinos, a beach resort spot in Spain. But while there, Dan had an accident that threatened to put his guitar-playing—and his life—in jeopardy.

He had been through a bad breakup with his girlfriend Cathie, whom he had followed to Virginia during his year of college. He still carried the torch for her, and with the respite in Spain, he now had time to think of it all over again. After a night out together, Gerry went back to the hotel but Dan wanted to stay out. He ruminated and got high, alone, on over-the-counter Spanish drugs. Then he punched a shop's glass window in a move of frustration, rage, and self-destruction.

"At the time we shared rooms; we didn't have the money to have our own rooms," Gerry remembered. "So I was asleep in the room and he broke through the door, kind of with his key. He fell into the bathroom—and there were not drops of blood but a line of blood. It was a massive wound; and it was like two in the morning. I had to get an ambulance and didn't speak any Spanish. And they came and got him and I rode along. They took us to a place and a doctor was awakened and looked at it, and he just shook his head and said 'No, no, no, I can't.' And I was going 'Are you crazy? Come on! He's losing so much blood.' What I didn't realize was that the doctor was saying, 'There's a lot of damage here. I couldn't do anything about that, I'm not your guy. I'm not the one you want to do this.' There were tendons and severed nerves. So we ran out of options and ended up in a convent that had a clinic in it. This is maybe four in the morning. And they just stuffed everything in the arm and wrapped it up."

Gerry made arrangements with the Warner Brothers team in London to bring Dan back and find a top surgeon—the Queen's surgeon, to be exact—to tend to the arm. The operation was a success, but Dan's fingers were still totally numb. He was told it would take a year for the feeling to come back—and that he could only hope for 70 percent functionality to return in that hand. It would always be damaged. Dan feared he would never be able to play guitar in the same way again. So he insisted upon practicing with his left hand in the meantime, to stay in musical shape. And when the cast came off the right hand, he worked hard to get his skills back up to par. But the band, who had been booked to play the United States again for a follow-up tour, was forced to cancel it, as well as its scheduled appearance at the multiday Bickershaw Festival (May 5–7, 1972) in England. Bickershaw showcased artists Country Joe, Dr. John, Captain Beefheart, the Kinks, Donovan, America's friend Brinsley Schwarz, and the Grateful Dead—one of Dewey's favorite bands and soon-to-be friends.

Dewey stopped in at the fest to witness the Dead's performance, where he met members of the band. "I have a special fond memory of sitting in a trailer with Pigpen [Ron McKernan] talking for ages," Dewey recalled. "He was very sick at the time." Pigpen tuned Dewey in to the genius of comedian W. C. Fields and showed him card tricks, even allowing Dewey to try on his well-known hat. Sadly, the following April, Pigpen would be dead—from internal hemorrhaging due to heavy drinking.

On the bright side, Gerry, Dewey, and Dan had managed to avoid being drafted into the Vietnam War, which in 1972 was still raging. Both their home nation and their adopted one were politically involved. Young men were being drafted via the lottery system, which used birth dates chosen at random to order individuals to come down to their local draft board for physical and mental evaluations. Even though the trio originated in military families, their fathers were relatively quiet about their thoughts on the war and their fears of their sons being drafted to serve. Though he did not support the war, Dewey had decided he was prepared to go if he was called, but he never was. Neither was Gerry. They had

Dan in a cast, postaccident, with Gerry's postcard home. *Courtesy of the Beckley family.*

been fortunate to receive high numbers, and therefore safe outcomes, in the lottery drawings. Dan's drawn number had been low, which demanded he report to the overseas draft board in Germany. He hoped that his medical record of a lifetime of illness would lessen his military appeal. Still, the experience was harrowing, and Dan worried he would be called to serve at any point over the coming months.

Back in London, America got to know the legendary press officer for the Beatles, Derek Taylor. In 1972, Taylor was Head of Special Projects for Warner Brothers Records. He had his own office at the London headquarters, 69 New Oxford Street. "Since Apple had folded, he was now at Warner Brothers," Gerry explained. "Anybody in their right mind would have brought Derek in because he was so connected—but his title at Warner's was Head of Special Projects—which meant that he could do whatever he wanted. He had this lovely office in the back, and we would go almost daily and hang out. Through Derek we met the Beatles, and we met Harry Nilsson. It was just incredible." The first time Gerry met his idol George Harrison, it had been on his way into 69 New Oxford as Derek was coming out. He suggested that Gerry come along, so they got into a limo waiting outside. Only once inside, did Gerry see who he had gotten in next to. "Gerry," Derek said, "meet George Harrison." Gerry took the opportunity to tell George that he had borrowed his song title for a song of his own, which had just been released on America's debut album: "I Need You." George smiled, saying only, "That's okay, Gerry. I took it from someone else!" Dan appreciated Derek's conviviality and warmth too, finding in him the guiding hand that Sammy had failed to provide. The fact that Derek's office was a nonstop hangout for America's artistic heroes and assorted celebrities—like James Taylor and Carly Simon, the Stones, and the Beatles—made it all the more appealing.

The band's career, for the moment, looked good. But the trio began to devise a plan to seek alternate management. America's massive success had caused them to outgrow Jeff Dexter. The recent tour in the U.S. made the band members realize how homesick for their native land they truly were. During their sold-out run at the Whisky in Hollywood, they had fallen in love with Los Angeles, its music history and the current scene in 1972, and California's golden promise. Compared to all that, gray and rainy England felt too small.

"The truth is, the prestige of David Geffen and Eliot Roberts was huge, and they elevated us. Had we stayed with Jeff Dexter in England, we wouldn't have gotten that kind of a lift," reflected Dewey. "We'd read the liner notes, like everybody else, of all the albums we loved. Geffen and Roberts were there." America began to quietly engage in friendly dialogues with the Geffen-Roberts team. Eliot told them of another new band he had recently begun to work with, a band America had not yet heard of. "Eliot told us, 'We've got this band we're starting to work with; they're kind of like you guys. The Eagles. They're making their first record now,'" recalled Dewey.

Dan, who disliked change in general, was hesitant about the move. He had grown somewhat attached to Jeff Dexter, Ian Samwell, and the Warners UK staff. Jeff's intelligence, boldness, likability, and determination to succeed, not to mention his numerous connections to nearly every important figure in London's rock scene, made him a valuable ally in Dan's eyes. In an attempt to provide the band with reliable representation in the United States, Jeff tried several times to secure co-management contracts with prominent American managers. But over the past year the band had noticed the lack of finance and accounting acumen displayed by Jeff, who occasionally would even ask Gerry, Dewey, and Dan to total small figures he was dealing with. Now that the figures had grown to mammoth proportions, America had doubts.

Jeff was no match for the grandeur and prestige of Geffen and Roberts' Lookout Management organization. The duo had greater industry experience and a much farther reach. The sound, feel, and style of America's music fit in right alongside their artist roster. "One of the great things about that whole group there, the Geffen-Roberts team and Lookout Management," said Gerry, "is that the California sound *is* a real thing: the West Coast sound. But—other than David Crosby, none of them were from California! There was no 'What are you guys doing here?' Glenn (Frey) was from Detroit; Don Henley was from Texas. Neil and Joni were Canadian. The whole thing was—imports." Plus the high school and related friend circle ties, which had bound the trio to London, had more or less evaporated. Even if London Central students' families stayed in the London area, most of the students went off to college elsewhere. There was not all that much of a community to leave behind.

A move to Los Angeles would also bring America closer to its record label's headquarters. "L.A. was the parent company," Dewey explained. "Warner Brothers was there. We felt like that was where it was happening, and we'd done what we could do in London. And we were young and impetuous, and L.A. looked like it had a lot more going on, more than playing pubs around England. It was just a natural progression. I know we stepped on some egos. We were pretty strong-willed ourselves. It was what we really wanted to do."

Jeff Dexter would come out of the split as the most damaged party; Ian Samwell was a staff producer at Warners UK and would be given other artists to produce. Still, the team at Warners' London office would see America's decision to leave, given that they had been successful with their current management and production teams, as a little perplexing. "I think the overriding thing was by some act of the stars aligning; they'd had a huge success out of the Warner's UK office," Gerry reflected. "And all of a sudden these young kids—us—were going to change every aspect of that. You know—'we're not gonna use the same manager, the same producer, the same studio, anything.' It was a complete, 'thank you, that was great, see you later.' So I understood their . . . concerns."

Another attractive reason for America to relocate its home base to the U.S. was the taxes issue. Dewey, Gerry, and Dan were American citizens but British residents, so they were paying taxes—on their ever-increasing incomes—to both nations. They worked the math out, only to realize that if they continued to reside in Britain, their total tax bills would soon surpass their incomes. Which was not going to work for long.

Geffen and Roberts, too, recognized the value of adding America to their list of clients. "A Horse with No Name" had gone to number one, not just on the British and American *Billboard* charts, but all over the world. The band was, for the moment, the biggest act in the universe. Soon, Dewey received a 3 a.m. phone call, which awakened him and Vivien, his wife-to-be—and her parents, whose house they were all staying in. It was from Leslie Morris, the secretary to Elliot Roberts. Having neglected to recognize the time difference, she was calling to connect Dewey with David Geffen.

"He was a commanding personality," Dewey remembered. "And in no time at all: we had only been back from that tour, barely a month. It was something like, 'You guys ought to be here, I'm gonna send you these tickets, you guys can come over here, I'll manage you; we'll take you to the next level.' He basically pinched us right then and there." When the subject of how exactly to get out of America's current management relationship came up, Geffen assured the trio not to worry about a thing, that he would take care of all that. Dan and Gerry departed London for Los

Dewey (left) with David Geffen. *Courtesy of Henry Diltz.*

Angeles; Dewey and fiancée Vivien had been planning to buy a house in England, so they needed a few extra days to tie up loose ends and back out of their arrangements. But they followed soon after.

"We told Derek Taylor, but we didn't tell Ian Samwell or Jeff Dexter," Gerry explained. "We had really bonded with Derek. So then we get to L.A. and there's a big fuss; we're not answering our phones in London. There was a big panic, and somebody said, 'Better get out to the house.' Derek, sensing the whole thing, said, 'Everybody just take a breather, I know where they are. They're with David Geffen.'"

Once America arrived in Los Angeles for good, they and Geffen began the uncomfortable legal process of getting free from their original contract setup and free from Dexter and Warners UK. "Dave Howson had slipped beneath the waves with nary a trace, but Jeff and Sammy were very much alive and kicking," Dan recalled. "We were signed to a long-term deal with them and to Warners' in the U.K. . . . This break-up had to be done face to face and with all parties present. It was excruciating. It was also very expensive."[1] Dealmaker extraordinaire Geffen dialogued with Warners in London, and then he threatened. He told Warners that if they didn't give America a new and improved contract, he would take his entire artist roster away from Warners and to other companies. Warners didn't like that idea; it meant losing CSNY, the Eagles, Joni Mitchell, Poco, Jackson Browne—in addition to America. Geffen drew up a new contract for Warners to agree to, which got America nearly three times more money than it would have gotten under the initial contract. He renegotiated America's royalty rates and album advances. And he got Sammy and Dexter to agree to a settlement as well. He got Warners UK to pay America a sum of money for having received their publishing rights. But he didn't get their publishing rights back. Those were retained by Warners, as America had agreed to it when they signed their first record contract. It was the common industry trade-off in order for an artist to get signed when that artist was still unknown and didn't yet hold many cards. And as with so many successful, uninitiated young artists over the history of published music, Dewey maintains, "It was the worst business decision ever made, basically on our behalf at that young age, as we were never told the exact ramifications of what that could mean over time. When we eventually became aware of the amount of income that we ultimately gave away over the course of our career, it was a bitter pill that continues to leave a bad taste."

David Geffen and Lookout Management didn't use contracts with the artists they managed. So the artists, which now included America, were free agents. It was through the artists' record contracts, however, that Geffen received his hefty commissions. He wrote himself into each one; and so even if he and an artist decided to part ways, Geffen would continue to receive commission royalties out of the album's sales profits. Although America eventually left Geffen and Roberts, they continued to pay them for decades.

In general, at the start of America's career, the band did not entirely understand the financial side of the recording industry. They were teenagers who had become number-one selling artists in an astonishingly short time.

Once in Los Angeles, Geffen tried to help the trio become acclimated to their new lives in the fast lane. "With all of our finances," Dewey explained, "we didn't know what we were doing. We didn't have business managers or attorneys. We were virtually green. And so Geffen was suggesting—'I'm gonna take care of all that, clean this all up. We're gonna set you up the way you should be. You're young artists.'"

When Gerry and Dan, and then Dewey and Vivien, arrived in sunny Los Angeles, they were picked up at the airport by shiny black limousines. All of them had been invited to stay at David Geffen's beautiful home in Beverly Hills. Having moved around their entire lives, moving once more wasn't anything out of the ordinary. Of all the recent changes that their success had brought them, it was the other elements that were very out of the ordinary. "It all got bundled in the same thing," Gerry remembered, "because clearly had we just been eighteen-year-old kids going from London to Southern California, [we would have experienced] culture shock. But we went from . . . we were middle-class children with parents and stuff, but we went to private planes. And if you're talking culture shock, there's really nothing quite like that."

Part II

In Hollywood

10

THE ARRIVAL

Gerry immediately found Los Angeles fascinating. "If it's the land of dreams, inevitably it's the land of broken dreams," he explained. "Because we know not all dreams come true. I had some friends in the '70s that knew L.A. a lot better than me . . . latest, greatest, best: 'This is the new club; this is the new car.' There were some people I met who would say, 'You want to go to El Cholo on Western if you want real Mexican.' Or, 'You've got to go to Musso and Frank's.' And I saw that there really *is* history here. It was fantastic and I loved it. On occasion there's a rap about L.A. being somewhat shallow, and it couldn't be further from the truth."

Dan was in awe of the city upon arrival, but ultimately he found it unsettling and strange. The nonstop comings and goings of the people there, and Los Angeles's disinclination for permanence and stillness, did not appeal to him, nor did the constant threat of a variety of natural disasters. Dewey was glad to be back in his favorite state, where he had fond memories of living in Southern California and San Jose. But eventually he would come to find the hustle and bustle of the city too much for him and his wife, and in eighteen months they would travel up north, relocating to Marin County.

The band's first several weeks were spent living in David Geffen's house. As had been America's wowing experience upon first becoming successful in the London music world, they were once again thrust into a musical community of their idols. Geffen's beautiful home and swimming pool were the setting of daily comings and goings of recognizable figures. Dan, Dewey, and Gerry spent their earliest days hanging out by Geffen's pool, getting further acquainted with the other artists—like the Eagles and Jackson Browne—who were signed to the Geffen-Roberts label. Joni Mitchell, another Geffen-managed artist, lived there as well for a time, working on her next album on the piano and occasionally sunbathing nude by the pool—which added to the culture shock that Gerry, Dewey, and Dan were experiencing. Several nights a week Geffen held get-togethers at his home, inviting two dozen or so interesting and culturally relevant guests from a wide variety of artistic fields.

"Geffen, I remember, had a 450SL Mercedes. At the time we didn't really know the premise of leasing cars," remembered Gerry. "And he'd say, 'Oh, just take the keys.' So we're like eighteen, nineteen, driving this Mercedes." The trio enjoyed getting acquainted with the different sections of Los Angeles, especially the musically rich Laurel Canyon. "That whole area, of course," Dewey explained. "We were kind of there at the tail end of the Laurel Canyon [heyday]—but it was still going on up there when we got there." Gerry, Dewey, and Dan hung out with Micky Dolenz and Davy Jones of the Monkees, Mark Volman and Howard Kaylan of the Turtles, Danny Hutton of Three Dog Night, and Alice Cooper, as well as Henry Diltz and his wife, Elizabeth. The artists were more or less welcoming, perceptive to the fact that America was a young, new, and talented band well versed in popular rock music. Gerry, Dewey, and Dan were true fans. The first time America met David Crosby, they told him how much they loved his music. To which he replied in his typical wry manner, "That's obvious." They would grow to be friends.

But it was clear—America's fellow musicians had listened to their music, they had heard their record. Which was one form of flattery. "Artists are a finicky batch anyway," Gerry reflected. "So it's not unusual—even in the art world—if it's painters, you'll see them being critical of work. So I think we shouldn't take it too personally that not everybody in that circle . . . these people were very serious. Like Jackson Browne. These people had been working on their craft for years and years, and we kind of stumbled into number one. So if there was any animosity, we didn't really take it personally."

Years later, Gerry would get to know Warren Zevon, who would recount to him the story of his and friend Waddy Wachtel's initial impressions of America. Warren and Waddy had first been exposed to America when they had opened for the Everly Brothers band during the first North American tour. Warren and Waddy would bicker about whether America was "legit" or not, as a musical group of weight, import, and promise. Waddy would say, "I don't hear it." To which Warren would reply, after thinking, "Nope—there's something there, man." Perhaps the intellectual Warren had tuned into and respected the sarcastic, intelligent cockiness that America sometimes displayed in their earliest stage banter. The Warren versus Waddy debate on America was perhaps the same one that was going on all over town, when the band first hit the Los Angeles scene. In 1980, Waddy would play guitar on America's album *Alibi*.

Some of the people America met in their first few Californian weeks would prove to be very influential in their professional and personal lives. Like photographer Henry Diltz. "We knew Henry from reading album covers," reflected Gerry. "The Doors, CSN—he also did *Sweet Baby James* for James Taylor. The guy was unavoidable, to be honest. Because he was close with a lot of those artists in the Geffen-Roberts office, when it came time to do *Homecoming*, we thought, 'Okay, we'll get Henry and his art director Gary Burden. We'll go off on one of these journeys and make an album cover.' So we met him right at the start. Still to this day, he's one of our family friends. Henry just sees the best in everybody. He's endlessly enthusiastic."

Then there was actor-musician Bill Mumy, who America had met during their initial run at the Whisky a Go Go. He had come backstage to say hello, and to tell the band how much he loved their music. They recognized him from his childhood acting roles as guest star on several *Twilight Zone* episodes, and the classic *Lost in Space*, on which he'd played the character of Will Robinson. "I remember meeting Mumy," Gerry reminisced. "I recognized the guy, but it was like—you thought you knew him from school or something. 'I know you!' He said, 'I've got a little group called Redwood.' They were an acoustic trio. 'We're recording at the Record Plant. Come on down.' So that week we went to the Record Plant; we met Mike D. Stone, the engineer. We looked around at the Record Plant and said, 'This is awesome.' So through Mumy, that's how we then picked that place for *Homecoming*. We went to the same studio, same engineer. We said, 'This will be great for us.'"

"We [Redwood] were very prolific and popular and busy—in Los Angeles and Southern California," Bill recalled. "We were not anywhere near the level of what the guys (America) were even before their hit. We were pretty much localized as a Southern California band. But we had a

Henry, Dewey, and Gary Burden in the 1990s. *Courtesy of the Bunnell family.*

good following, and we lasted from 1969 until January of 1975. So it was a pretty good run." As most of the world had, Bill had fallen in love with America's smash single "A Horse with No Name" the first time he heard it on the radio. One of Bill's close friends was fellow actor David Jolliffe, who played the beloved character of Bernie on ABC's comedy-drama series *Room 222*. And their mutual friend was Paul Markowitz, who, back in London, had hung out and played music with Gerry, Dewey, and Dan. Upon discovering that America would be playing at the Whisky, Paul contacted the band and obtained backstage passes for himself, David, and Bill. At the time, Bill lived in the Mediterranean Village apartment complex, right off West Hollywood's Sunset Strip—just down the road from the Whisky.

Bill, David, and Paul went to America's first show there, and ended up returning every night to catch the set and hang with Gerry, Dewey, and Dan. The fact that Bill and David were recognizable faces from television made it all the easier for America to feel comfortable with them. "We became really good friends very quickly," Bill reminisced, "and Redwood was recording at the Record Plant, with Mike D. Stone producing and engineering the project. He was on staff there, the staff engineer. So Dewey, Gerry, and Dan came to a couple of Redwood's sessions at the end of '72 or early '73. I know it was winter because I had my father's

1940s-era jean jacket that I had hippie-ized. A great jacket. I had this great Beach Boys *Surf's Up* patch on it, that my girlfriend who worked at Warner Brothers had given me. With these really cool hippie velvet patches on the elbows. And it got stolen at the Whisky gig! It was really heartbreaking."

After a month of living at Geffen's home, and after the band's deal negotiations had been completed, Geffen politely suggested to America that they try and find their own places to live. Immediately they decamped to the notorious Sunset Marquis Hotel in West Hollywood while they looked for a more permanent situation. Soon, Gerry, Dan, and Dewey and Vivien secured rental apartments at King's Road, a complex owned as an investment by the rock band Three Dog Night. The building housed many of the day's musicians and actors, including Bill Mumy's pal David Jolliffe. "Of Three Dog Night, Floyd Sneed the drummer and I think Mike Allsop the guitar player lived in the building," Bill recalled. "It was a modern building in West Hollywood. Gerry got this very cool three-level apartment. The guys all bought cars. And we just hung out constantly and played music together. Even though we weren't collaborating as songwriter partners at that time, we were constantly jamming together, and going to gigs and just hanging out." Gerry, Dewey, and Dan became further enmeshed in the social scene of Los Angeles, spending off time at hotspots the Roxy and Rainbow Bar and Grill.

When Dan married his long-lost love, Catherine, he and the recently married Dewey retreated a bit more into their domestic setups. Gerry, however, possessed the freedom to be more social, an interesting lifestyle experiment for the young man who preferred solitary living. In 1973, he purchased a home from filmmaker Mike Nichols, which soon became a notorious hangout for musicians and artists of the time. Located on Flicker Way, the house sat amid the famed Bird Streets of Los Angeles, high above the city. "I had lots of very good friends," Gerry remembered. "I was a somewhat more social guy at that time. And there was always something going on at my house." Having met their idol Harry Nilsson in London through Derek Taylor, America rekindled their friendship with him upon relocating to Southern California. Harry's well-known wit, charm, and charisma, in addition to his unrelenting musical talent and Beatles intimacy, made him a formidable force on the scene of 1973 Los Angeles. And an ideal friend for Gerry, Dewey, and Dan. When hanging out with the trio at Gerry's Flicker Way home, Harry would often bring with him an assortment of culturally significant artists. Actor Harry Dean Stanton and New Orleans–based genius musician Dr. John both arrived at Gerry's as guests of Harry's. Dewey, often present during his short-term stays away from his Marin County home, was a usual suspect at Gerry's endless cocktail parties.

"Ronnie Wood was living at my house for a while," Gerry recalled, "and he would bring Rod Stewart and Britt Ekland and David Bowie. So there was always stuff going on. One time I woke up and there were all these people sleeping all over the floor. It was like—wow, the Faces, man, all of them! Ronnie Lane had left, and they had this Japanese bass player, Tetsu. He was this big Japanese guy, sprawled out on the floor. Ronnie Wood said, 'That's Tetsu, our new bass player!' So it was pretty far out. There were some really great times."

Perhaps the most interesting guest at Flicker Way was none other than Brian Wilson, the Beach Boy himself, during his so-called years of recluse, living in his bedroom following his retirement from the touring band. Brian would occasionally visit Gerry and attend his social gatherings. Sometimes he would "sneak out," or venture to the get-togethers on his own, citing that he'd "stolen the Woodie"—his first wife Marilyn's Ford Country Squire station wagon with wood-sided paneling—to arrive. Now and then Brian would get lost trying to get home from the parties, requiring guidance from the Bel Air police, who were well acquainted with Brian and his complex history.

In addition to getting settled in Los Angeles, becoming familiar with the musical community there, and beginning to work on recording their next two albums, *Homecoming* and *Hat Trick*, America needed to assemble its musical personnel. "Creatively—we had to get a band," Dewey explained. "Remember, we had been three guys on stools the whole time. Now we were being booked to play in big rooms, big arenas. We had to get a rhythm section, and this was a whole other world. Technically, I always used to think, 'We're kind of a studio band; getting the details hashed out in the studio.' But the live show had to be impressive. So we began auditioning players. Geffen wanted to immediately book two-month tours, guarantees, get the money rolling in, and get his commissions. And of course we were ready to do them. That was a whole logistic thing." Fellow Geffen-Roberts musicians JD Souther and Jackson Browne, themselves already quite established in the SoCal music scene, would serve as opening acts for America's first two tours of 1973: JD for

January through March, Jackson for July and August. In the coming years, America's tour partners would include such greats as Joe Cocker, Three Dog Night, the Beach Boys, Poco, Jefferson Starship, Stephen Stills, Chicago, Kenny Loggins, Christopher Cross, Michael McDonald, and Marshall Tucker and the 38 Special. America's original drummer Dave Atwood and Pete Reuther, who served as general assistant and occasionally played keyboards, had followed the trio from London to Los Angeles. Though America would employ Wrecking Crew personnel Joe Osborn and Hal Blaine on *Homecoming*, they utilized Atwood as touring drummer for that year. Gerry and Dan would alternate re-creating Osborn's bass parts in the live show's *Homecoming* tracks. That, however, soon wore Gerry and Dan out and became less than feasible when both could have played guitar on certain songs. So they decided to officially hire a bass player. Once again, Bill Mumy would prove significant in the story of America's evolution.

Bill's pal David Jolliffe also had a band, the trio known as DD Tucker, alongside bass player David Dickey and drummer Willie Leacox. DD Tucker worked with Three Dog Night's manager, but was unable to obtain a record deal with their demo record. They spent their days rehearsing material, preparing to embark upon a small tour. But they were on the lookout for potential new musical opportunities that could take them even further—and when America sought a bass player, David Dickey quickly joined up. He was even encouraged to do so by Jolliffe, who sensed that America could provide a better musical and financial situation for his rhythm section. Dickey would play bass on *Hat Trick*, America's third album, on which Hal Blaine would once again drum. For a while, Dave Atwood remained in America's touring band alongside Dickey. Fairly soon, though, Dickey would clue Dewey, Gerry, and Dan into what he perceived as Atwood's inability to musically mesh with the group and with his own bass playing. Due to events in his personal life too, Atwood was getting ready to move on and away from America. Dickey was quick to suggest his friend and former bandmate Willie Leacox.

Dickey was a professional, having played in a show band in Las Vegas before coming to L.A. Leacox was too; he had graduated from Topeka's Washington University with a bachelor's degree in music performance. "I had migrated to L.A., and I was doing the club circuit and doing a lot of recordings," Willie remembered. "I had a two-month gig in Monterey, California, when I got the call to audition for America. They only had two albums out at that time; I was just out of music school. So I got those albums, and I transcribed the drum parts—being a music major, I knew how to do that—because I knew I would be auditioning. When I got back to Hollywood, I went over to SIR (Studio Instrument Rentals) to audition. There were four drummers there, including me. But I knew David Dickey, the bass player, so I got to go in first. It was around midnight. We did 'Ventura Highway' and they hired me, and they sent the other drummers home."

Meanwhile, in the Geffen-Roberts management office, business and personnel changes were being made. Geffen's big dream was to run his own record label. In 1971, he and Roberts founded Asylum Records. Jackson Browne and Joni Mitchell would sign to the label, and America was invited to do so as well. But the trio hesitated to leave the historic, large operation of Warner Brothers for a small, new, and independent label. Geffen was disappointed.

The more effort and time Geffen devoted to running Asylum meant less attention paid to his management duties. Soon those were completely handed over to Elliot Roberts, who found it increasingly difficult to manage the entire slew of artists on his own. Additional support was brought in and increasingly relied upon for management duties via Irving Azoff, Paul Aherne, Harlan Goodman, Bill Siddons, and John Hartmann. After all, Roberts devoted most of his energy toward the extremely in-demand Neil Young and Joni Mitchell. America, amid other Geffen-Roberts acts, were then subjected to dealing with what they termed the "Manager of the Month Club." Given that they were one of the newest acts in the Geffen-Roberts camp, America seemed to be treated with the least amount of concern.

The trio wasn't happy.

11

THE CALIFORNIA SONGS

"Full disclosure, I'm not crazy about the *Homecoming* cover," said Gerry. "At the time, big covers and big concepts were not unusual. Crosby, Stills, Nash & Young's album was covered in leatherette and gold embossed. It was of that time. But to have a triple fold—I don't think any of us thought it was silly at the time. Now looking back on it, it's got some kind of airbrushed—almost like a holocaust sunset behind it. The picture that's on the front was actually taken in the alley behind the Record Plant in Los Angeles, superimposed. Gary Burden (the album's art director) was a man of grand schemes—and we were young. Same with *Hat Trick*. We'll go out into the desert, stay up all night, there might or might not be a little peyote involved. But that's what Henry Diltz and Gary did; they tried to make an experience that the cover then would reflect. As opposed to just a photo shoot, where someone's got to throw a font on there," Gerry reflected.

America settled on Los Angeles's Record Plant Recording Studios for its second album's headquarters. The trio decided to produce themselves. It would be a classic selection of songs.

Lyrically, "To Each His Own" is a candid articulation of ongoing transience. A nomadic lifestyle that had been established as an Air Force child had now been replicated and replaced with that of the ever-traveling musician. The figures and faces would constantly change, but it didn't matter—even if it did matter, it wasn't allowed to. Gerry would alternately love and miss whoever they might be. It was a cycle he was used to. "My life is my conscience," the song declares, meaning the narrator's "life-string" of thoughts, emotions, actions, and reactions would be his own responsibility. Even though his vocation would put him in a continuous state of leaving people behind, those individuals who were being left by him—friends, acquaintances, lovers—could rest assured that he would never forget them. His sharp memory and his sense of relationship-based obligation—and the impossibility of living up to it—would forbid it.

The song's middle eight offers a reflective break in the narrative, allowing a direct question to be asked in utmost teenage ardor: "Will I make it through the summer, breaking ties with the old and new?" The reasoned answer that follows directly after—"Losing one just gains another—there is nothing I can do"—phrases a piece of learned experience beyond Gerry's years. He knows that in the end, everyone leaves. The colloquial familiarity of the idiom itself suggests a positive decision to accept the various lifestyles, choices, and preferences of other people, as well as one's own. The phrase is a worded and happily apathetic shrug of the shoulders. But Gerry's usage here colors it with irony—every person is ultimately alone—and his response to this knowing is devoid of apathy. Every time he leaves, it will always hurt. "To Each His Own" is a song about the unavoidability of loss—not via the obvious route of death, but in the smaller, subtler ways that leave silent scars.

Musically, the song is wistful in tone. Its piano introduction is mysterious and inviting, but tinged with melancholy. The trio's harmonies have particular resonance through Gerry's lyrics in this track; after all, all three of them had experienced the sadness that was a fixture of military families' wayfaring lives. All three had learned to accept it, but it did not mean they had learned to transcend its emotional implications.

"Only in Your Heart" is an expression of Gerry's writerly inclination toward matters of the heart. In this piece, a classic reassurance song, he addresses directly a romantically troubled character named Mary. Over its course, he sings to assure her not to lose faith in the institution of romantic relationships. Its tempo is moderately paced; its melodies, ear pleasing and catchy, with rhythmic, driving piano chords and echoing harmonies from Dewey and Dan. Interestingly, the song is not aimed at Mary's boyfriend, whoever he may be, but serves as a friend-to-friend "Don't worry" bit. Here Gerry talks to a girl, undoubtedly appealing to the band's female fans, relating to her on an emotional level. As a songwriter and singer, he can court a woman, but he can also console her; Gerry seems to understand women in all their nuanced complexities, refusing to treat them merely as either objects of desire or sources of betrayal and frustration.

It is on this track of *Homecoming* that listeners may really take note of the recording's studio prowess. "The song," Gerry reflected, "is obviously a Beatles-esque tune. One of the interesting things about it is that the whole outro—the reverse-backward thing—was actually done by Hal Blaine, the drummer. It's a short little song, and we finished the song with the last 'Have you seen better days?' And for whatever reason, Hal started up again, and we all came back in again! So it was just a jam at the end, that we all built on. We said, 'Oh, that's great.' And that is a great example of what Hal and Joe Osborn on bass could do; they were so creative and so lovely to work with." Gerry was very aware of the pivotal role the Wrecking Crew had played in so many of his favorite records—most notably for him, those of Brian Wilson and the Beach Boys—and now, its members would play on his record, too. It was one of many dreams come true. *Homecoming* would benefit greatly from the studio players' experience and talents.

"Till the Sun Comes Up Again" is a modern, self-aware song that seems to be writing itself as we hear it. "Think I'll write a different song," Gerry begins—and it is a different song, for him to compose. From its inception—and we hear this happening as the song progresses—Gerry decides he won't do what he's always done; he will use this opportunity to make a conscious change in direction toward the new. "Will she come to me, to keep me company?" he wonders in the piano chord–driven chorus. In response, he decides to attempt making comfortable the uncomfortable place of not knowing. She may show up, she may not. Gerry "won't know till the sun comes up again." He will have to pass the night in a state of uncertainty.

Here too, we can see Gerry's lyrical inclination to—rather than articulate intense expectation and hopefulness in answer to his "Will she ever show up?"—issue instead a factual maybe . . . won't know until the morning. Having been born into a life of transience, the trio had grown accustomed, as well, to the possibility that a person they knew, they might never see again. They were not blind to human inconsistency.

Musically, the song's accompanying harmonies of Dewey and Dan are introduced gradually. "There's a joke phrase," Gerry reflected. "I think it's from Mark [Volman] and Howie [Kaylan]. When they were with Mothers of Invention as Flo and Eddie: 'We're gonna build it like the

Supremes.' It meant, you don't fire the whole shotgun all at once. You've got all of these elements, and you want to bring them in one at a time. They're very simple things; you do one part the first time around, two-part harmony the second time, three-part harmony the third time. You don't have to listen really closely, and you're not exactly sure why each one sounds like a riff and sounds like more—sounds more fulfilling as the song goes on. Those things can be quiet and subtle, like the addition of a shaker or a tambourine. Tricks you hear if you put your headphones on. I really was very happy with my—even though they weren't singles—my stuff on *Homecoming*. 'To Each His Own,' and 'Till the Sun Comes Up Again,' two of my favorites of all time. The beginning-ish refrain of 'Till the Sun Comes Up,' I heard it in my head. I don't know where I had gotten it from, but clearly some element I had heard before, and I knew: 'Ah—this is really coming together.' They almost write themselves."

"Don't Cross the River" is the continuation of Dan Peek's preoccupation with Catherine. Like Gerry in his love songs on the album, Dan has empathy for the woman he sings to. He acknowledges her broken heart, her intelligence, her "away-from-him-ness." But unlike what Gerry does, he gives his girl direct advice: "Don't cross the river if you can't swim the tide." Don't take on what you can't handle. "Don't try denyin' livin' on the other side." Acknowledge the role you have played in your current reality. Every relationship is a two-person game, Dan insinuates here, and if a person isn't willing to accept the consequences, perhaps she should consider playing a different one. Before the last swell into the final rounds of the chorus, Dan does articulate an offer to have her join him: "If you want you can ride my train . . . you'll lose yourself and . . . maybe even save yourself some grievin'." By joining him, and buying into the relationship's ebbs and swells, perhaps the woman will see beyond herself and leave her past fears and troubles behind.

Sonically, this tune oozes country, which is primarily the result of Henry Diltz's banjo playing. The trio's harmonies, with Dan's higher-pitched melodic line driving the song's direction, create a haunting and moody insight into the lyrics' warning words. Dan and Catherine's love affair was serious and weighty and it would not be taken lightly; there would be no turning back from it for either of them. The quick train-wheel-churning tempo, kept consistent throughout, implies a destiny-mapped journey, undertaken with energetic and powerful speed.

"Saturn Nights," the album's closer, picks up the theme threads of star-crossed love and the unavoidability of the hand of fate, where "Don't Cross the River" lightly left off. It starts out with intriguing and emotionally heavy piano chords, and soon guitars and voices join in. "One more song about movin' along the highway," Dan begins, giving a nod to Carole King's "So Far Away." Moody, nearly ominous backup vocals, by the band and Dan's overdubs, segue into dramatic chordal progressions. "I've been standing on your corner, don't go away," the chorus concludes.

Dan's tenor voice, with its unique tone and intense emotion, soars on this particular track. The contemplative pace, the dreaminess of the soundscape, work together to create a compelling aural portrait. Dan was influenced by the ideas of astrology at the time he was working on the song. Saturn: the planet of expansion points, opportunities for newness, the endings that segue into new beginnings. Dan reflected, "That was a song I worked very, very diligently on. I remember sitting up in the Hollywood Hills in a little rented place that Gerry and I were in, banging away on the piano. To Gerry and Dewey's credit, a lot of it came together in the studio. I think it was the first song we recorded at the Record Plant."[1] The idea of the song narrative's relationship— the partnership between the planetary order's influence and Dan and Catherine's romance—adds an additional aura of gravitas to the recording. It is riddled with romance—the kind a girl wants to hear, to experience. It is a testament to the communicative prowess of Dan's songwriting: that he could word such an authentic emotional experience, that he could work with Gerry and Dewey to mirror this musically, and authentically so.

Dan's "California Revisited," however, is his most powerful contribution to *Homecoming*. Included on America's maxi-single from the prior year under the title "Everyone I Meet Is from California," the song managed to capture and emote the increasing popularity of California as a state of mind, as a lifestyle. Dan had never been to California when he'd penned the song in England, but he went through a period in which wherever he was, he'd run into people claiming to be from California. Whether they truly were from the state—if they had been born there, if they had grown up there, if they had gone to college there—was irrelevant. They identified with the California lifestyle of the 1970s. This identification would soon prove to have strong ties to America the band and its far-reaching cultural effects.

Dan's guitaring ability, the strongest and most versatile of the trio's, is on full display in "California." The riff around which the song is built is catchy, and the way in which it jams and then segues into the setup for the next verse is intricately done. "Everyone I Meet Is from California" is a rock song—in its attitude, composition, and overall mood. Over the course of his tenure in America, Dan Peek would prove to be the trio's rock 'n' roll guy. This truth stemmed from his innately raw guitar playing that drove the group's guitar sound and translated through his acerbic and quick wit—manifesting in his and the group's increasingly high-intensity lifestyles.

All three members had been, and would forever be, children of the 1960s and the decade's ethos. But Dewey took the philosophy very much to heart—perhaps because it activated an already present vibration ingrained in Dewey's truest character. He was a follower of Kerouac and the Beats, a believer in individual freedom, an endorser of the restorative powers of the natural world. Traces of these tenets would be found throughout Dewey's song catalogue.

The interestingly titled "Cornwall Blank" was narratively akin to "Horse" in its expression of existential wanderlust. But emotively, it was colored with greater experience. When he composed "Horse," Dewey was an anonymous teenager; with "Cornwall Blank," Dewey was a world-famous, platinum-album-bearing rock star. The inspiration for *Homecoming*'s track was Dewey's knowledge of material success, and the longing to return to simplicity. Much like that of the hippie generation's ethos. "Some time before, we had taken two little trips to Cornwall [England]. . . . We were basically venturing away from our families for the very first time, and just piling into a car and driving to Cornwall was a huge undertaking for us. That's when I thought, *Boy, it's nice to be out here and blank out—turn it all off*. It was bitter cold, so it wasn't like the tropics, but it was the feeling of getting away."[2]

Dewey's "Moon Song," too, articulated a desire to escape the present moment, to return to a simpler and more innocent time. Or at least to preserve his authentic self, amid the growing pressures of maintaining his band's worldly success. This individual desire can be seen as a stand-in for that of the era's youth culture. The 1960s teenagers, which Dewey had been, were largely insistent in their philosophies about returning to the innocence of human life. Getting away from consumerism, materialism, the increasing anonymity of modern life—and getting "back to the gar-

Dewey, Dan, and Gerry with horses in California. *Courtesy of Henry Diltz.*

den." Narratively, Dewey sets the scene to define his "dancing paradise. A case of beer, a smile, a motorcycle child. I feel the glow surround me and you." This is his American teenager's voice, the kind that is more than satisfied by a serene natural setting, some beer, and his girl. In a way, he continues the young American's narrative that the Beach Boys began in their earliest songs.

"Moon Song" has an interesting and aurally intriguing sense of musicality and showcases Dewey's gift for establishing a sonic mood. The piece begins slowly, with repetitive guitar work—and the descriptively romantic lyrics set the scene. When the components progress to the chorus—"orange funnels and snowy tunnels"—Hal Blaine's drumrolls enter to create additional sonic space, through which the trio's guitar explorations can carry out over.

Ultimately Dewey's "Moon Song" was a love song, akin to those Gerry was responsible for. But where Gerry carved his path directly, head-on into the complicated realms of love, sex, and interpersonal relations, Dewey chose to journey through the magical world of nature instead. Both songwriting approaches could only complement one another.

The trio chose to cover their friend John Martyn's "Head and Heart" on *Homecoming*, and it would set a trend of including one cover song on each of the early records. Gerry, Dewey, and Dan, in all their respective earliest bands, were covers players—and this album decision was a way of paying homage to that history.

"Head and Heart" was a unique and palpably emotional song, all about the desire and occasional frustration in an attempt to articulate the extent of the singer's want—and the potential inability of his lover to align her logical and emotional streams, as far as they concern him. "Love me like a child," the chorus pleads, serving as a philosophical match to Dewey's yearning for innocence in "Moon Song."

This cover would also allow all three guys to share equal lead vocals throughout the verses. A literal testament to America's implied vow that the band would be one artistic unit first and foremost, with its members—leads included—serving their needed functions.

"Ventura Highway," though, would steal the entirety of *Homecoming*'s appeal. Once again, as in "Horse," Dewey's compositional insight would cause a low-key musical revolution among early '70s rock audiences. The song would continue the lyrical journey that the Beach Boys had begun with their earliest hits like "Surfin' USA" and "California Girls," and even in their more introspective material like "The Warmth of the Sun." The West Coast was riddled with mythology, which Dewey felt to be true for him, as a young boy, during his time spent at Vandenberg Air Force Base and California. He sought freedom, the number one desire of the hippies' crew, and he felt that this was most easily achieved and most intensely felt through the direct experience of rawest nature. The state of California was made of the stuff.

"Ventura Highway," though, is a song about traveling, about movement. About leaving something behind, about arriving someplace new. It is a mid-moment song, a meditative song, a "being" song. Technically, Ventura Highway was California's Ventura Freeway.

Musically, most listeners would agree that the harmony-laden guitar lick drives the entire piece. It was the one bit that Dewey didn't compose himself. In a Lennon-McCartney-esque moment, Gerry and Dan sat across from one another, guitar laden, and worked out the harmonic guitar lick against Dewey's intro chords. An all-for-one approach that would prove to be one of the band's strongest go-to moves.

Like Jackson Browne and the Eagles' "Take it Easy," "Ventura Highway" was a song that defined its generation. The turmoil of the 1960s had ended—and now everyone wanted to feel fine as could be. In an authentic way, a simple and true way, a young way that would be difficult to argue with. And so it would appeal to many. "'Cause the free wind is blowin' through your hair, and the days surround your daylight there. Seasons crying no despair, alligator lizards in the air." It preached "is-ness," and it took the Beach Boys' ideology further into moodiness, into the ambiguity and modernity of 1970s America.

As though "Horse" hadn't been enough to articulate the sentiments of his generation, Dewey had offered "Ventura Highway" too. And still, there would be more.

On March 3, 1973, the Grammy Awards celebrating the achievements in music from the previous year were held in Nashville, Tennessee—a one-time location change that indicated the current trend in the music industry, which acknowledged the power of the country scene. For its debut success, America was nominated in two categories: Best Pop Performance by a Duo or Group with Vocals, for "Horse," and Best New Artist. On March 3, 1973, the band was already booked to play a big show in New Orleans; plus, upon hearing that fellow Best New Artist nominees Loggins & Messina would also be performing at the awards ceremony, America took it as a sign that they themselves wouldn't be winning. That evening their concert ended early, and so they watched the broadcast on television together.

"There was a certain element of anti-establishment-ness that we'd absorbed," Dewey recalled. It was all about abstaining from interviews, avoiding the press. "'This is all a kind of corporate stuff, and you don't want to do that,' was the tone. There was a certain trend of casting off norms of the old days. And then when we were nominated, I was very excited. But frankly at that time, everything that we did—the gold album, the gold single, platinum album, other writing awards, the ASCAP awards—we were just really taking it all as a result of this massive success that we had."

For their song "Where Is the Love," Roberta Flack and Donny Hathaway would win out over America's "Horse" in the Vocal Performance category. But when the Best New Artist was announced, Dewey, Gerry, and Dan were wowed. It was America. The band had won over John Prine, Harry Chapin, the Eagles—and Loggins & Messina.

"A few weeks later a box arrived on each of our doorsteps," Gerry remembered. "And it had the three dreaded words: 'some assembly required.' It was the Grammy; you had to put it together. It was basically assembled, but the bell of the Victrola, the big cone, was a separate spun brass ring and you had to thread that in."

The win was another indicator of America's quickly achieved mass success. But the future of the band's career was yet to be seen. "If anything, there's not much arc to it—it just started at the top," Gerry reflected. "The trouble with 'Best New Artist' is of course it implies 'Best New Career.' But the career hasn't happened yet. That's a lot of pressure. Even if you do have some success on the first go—most careers are a hit or two at most, when you put numbers behind them. Which again is an example of how fortunate we've been."

Even so, America was in good company with its category win. Three years earlier, Crosby, Stills & Nash had been anointed as Best New Artist. And in 1964, so had the Beatles.

12

THE POLARIZER

In 1972 Willis Alan Ramsey, a Texas-born, bluesy songwriter, penned the song "Muskrat Candlelight." It was a soulful recording, raw and authentic sounding, and a beautiful composition. The lyrics were intended to be a bit tongue-in-cheek, presenting a romantic plot narrative in the form of two muskrats—Susie and Sam. Via a musician like Ramsey, who was a "twangified vocalist," the song was rendered forth with an ample and equal dose of enticement and humor for the listener. The track was cute. America's new bass player, David Dickey, heard the tune, included on what would be Ramsey's only album (self-titled) release in 1972 and told Gerry, Dewey, and Dan about it. The trio liked it upon listening, hearing the possibilities for vocal arrangement and a mellow acoustic soundscape that they themselves could create in a recording.

The lyrics though, the lyrics . . . they were a bit—not cool. Lyrics like "Muskrat Susie, muskrat Sam / Do the jitterbug out in muskrat land / And they shimmy / And Sammy's so skinny." Antics like "nibblin' on bacon, chewin' on cheese" and "Rubbin' her toes, muzzle to muzzle, now anything goes as they wiggle" and "jinglin' the jango." These weren't what hip young people said or did or say that they did (at least out loud). "Muskrat Love" was an unsexy song about sex.

"I'm so over it," Gerry says now about the song, which America retitled "Muskrat Love." It is perhaps the group's most polarizing number. The group was insistent upon releasing it as *Hat Trick*'s single, even though Warner Brothers strongly advised against it. Warner's was right.

The failure of *Hat Trick*'s singles to chart would be an indicator of the album's inability to resonate with 1973 record buyers.

"On the first record," Gerry recalled, "We were a bit surprised when 'Horse' was picked for the single. They were our new tunes and stuff; we liked them all. But we thought, 'That one?' They couldn't have been more right, and we couldn't have learned a bigger lesson: there is some logic in letting 'them' pick. When we were very keen on Willis Alan Ramsey's 'Muskrat Love,' we force-fed that to them. They didn't want to put out 'Muskrat Love.' They said, 'You guys are songwriters, you've written a bunch, surely you've written something else.' We were so determined, that we felt that that, and a variety of other things, ground it and the promotion to a halt. We thought, well, that's one reason to not force-feed." In 1976 Captain and Tennille would end up cutting the song and scoring a number one hit with it, providing America with some post-traumatic vote of confidence that the song had such potential.

"*Hat Trick* wasn't so much a concept album as it was an evolution," Gerry remembered. "The obvious thing that was going to happen to that album was that we were pretty sure we were going to expand to some strings, maybe even horns. One of the things that already started very quietly on *Homecoming* was that we did that album at the Record Plant in Studio A. And in Studio B were these two amazing, iconic producers, Bob Markovitz and Malcom Cecil, and they were producing Stevie Wonder. So at the same time as we were doing *Homecoming* and *Hat Trick*, those guys were doing *Innervisions* and *Fulfillingness' First Finale*. And we got to go in all the time and see these guys—and it was all synth based. So they would come over to our studio and work with our synthesizer, to show us how to program it. By *Hat Trick*, being such Beatle and Beach Boy freaks anyway and of these other elements, there was time now to add. This would be our growing element that advanced us. The title song itself was a combination of three or four bits that we each had, and we thought, 'Well, it's kind of like a medley.' All with the best of intentions; now that we were at the back of two platinum albums, there was—I don't want to say 'pressure,' because there was a lot we really enjoyed—and there were time constraints. And it took a long time, quite a few months. Had it taken three or four months and we had another smash, another 'Ventura Highway,' everyone would have said 'golden.' But because it took a long time, and because it didn't sell, we went from two platinum albums to a record not even going gold."

With the help of Jim Ed Norman, serving as a precursor to the group's upcoming work with producer George Martin, *Hat Trick* marked the first time America used string arrangements on their album. The recording experience included a slew of interesting guest appearances by other artists and friends: Henry Diltz played banjo and Lee Kiefer harmonica on "Submarine Ladies"; Tom Scott, who went on to form LA Express and back Joni Mitchell on several albums (including a favorite of Dewey's, *Court and Spark*), played saxophone on "Rainbow Song"; Robert Margoliffe played synthesizer, and Chester McCracken contributed congas.

* * *

It would take this particular recording experience to prove that producing their own records was getting to be too much for the trio. Ultimately this realization would lead to the seeking of an outside producer for America's fourth album. Sir George Martin, legendary Beatles producer, would be the ultimate choice—and would mark the beginning of one of the most successful collaborations in the history of popular music.

"*Hat Trick*," Gerry reflected, "now that we were really becoming self-developed, took a lot longer than *Homecoming*, and as a result of pulling teeth on *Hat Trick*, and after *Hat Trick* not selling, we collectively said, 'You know what? It might be time to bring a producer back in. Who could we use?' We had George at the top of the list, and a few other names. Of course we never had to go beyond the top of the list. George said to us, 'All I'm asking is that you come over to England. I can't be gone for that long.' He had seen that *Hat Trick* had taken months to do, and we said 'Sure, we love England, we'll come over.' And when we went over to England, I had by this time bought a cottage in the country, and we rehearsed there. George said to us, I remember this quite clearly, 'I've held two months at AIR Studios. I'm not saying we have to be done by then, but let's see how we go.' And we ended up doing *Holiday*—start to finish, strings, mixing, everything—in like fifteen days. Entire album was done. And he said, 'This can't possibly be a success, nothing that easy could be a success.'"

Sir George, of course, would be proven wrong. *Holiday* would become one of his, and America's, most successful albums.

* * *

Before Sir George came on board, however, production and developmental duties fell to Gerry, Dewey, and Dan. They felt pressured. Their first two albums had been incredibly successful, and the group had risen quickly to a high level of popularity. They wanted to hold on to it; all eyes in the music industry were on them. So America decided to make more of a concept record than the first two had been—more of a flowing soundscape, in which certain songs would fade out and into their adjacent ones. In which a clear mood colored the entire record, like a poetic sound painting. *Hat Trick* was the result—and it would be one of the group's most challenging recording experiences ever.

First, it took a hell of a long time to make. The three had grown more artistically ambitious since *Homecoming* and were keen to incorporate exotic instruments, strings, and more complicated songwriting.

"As far as producing ourselves, we found that it required a lot more time, effort, booking time, paying bills, dealing with tape ops and engineers, things we just kind of bumbled into," Gerry recalled. "Because all we were worried about was what it sounded like. Guitar and mic placement. Production requires ears, and obviously being able to deal with the artists; you're the last one to know it's not working. 'This sounds great. What do you mean you don't want it on the record?' So you have to have that objectivity. And experience helps.

"What we kind of thought was, 'We'll each pick three or four of our own tunes, and we'll pick one cover. Covers were part of our show. We used to do [Arlo Guthrie's] 'Coming into Los Angeles' and '[New York] Mining Disaster [by the Bee Gees],' and all these other things. So there were lots of other tunes that we loved to jam with. We thought a way to address that was once an album, we'd pick something we all agreed would be good, divvy up the vocals. We did that for a while, through *Hat Trick*."

Gerry's own compositions on *Hat Trick* serve as prime evidence for the evolution of his singer-songwriter talent. They are stellar contributions to an outlier of an America record, and are perhaps the most understated pieces of his entire career. "She's Gonna Let You Down," "Submarine Ladies," and aptly titled album closer "Goodbye" are moody, complex, and emotionally explorative.

The first, "She's Gonna Let You Down," seems to be told from the point of view of a concerned friend speaking on behalf of a collective group. Gerry fears that his friend may be taken advantage of by the girl he loves: "We're afraid she's gonna let you down, take your money and drop you to the ground. Wouldn't want to see you messed around." He acknowledges, though, that the friend may take a while to agree, to come to terms with the situation's reality: "Love's the stubbornest game to play. Given time you might see it our way." The song's message and aim are simple, straightforward, and relatable enough for the listener. Most listeners have, at one time or another, had a friend who was in danger of being taken advantage of by a love interest who is less committed than the friend. A true friend would, as the song articulates, try to warn against potential catastrophe, while simultaneously acknowledging the potential for it still to occur. Love and desire surpass all sometimes, even a best friendship.

The musical elements of Gerry's song here are beautiful as usual: string laden, cinematic in nature. His oneness with the nature of melody, his McCartneyesque gift of the rarest kind, would never fail to appear. But it is the haunting ardor of the song's lyrics, coupled with the song's cinematic production, that resonates the strongest. Gerry's narrator here is attempting to help a friend—but what if he himself is the friend? The truth with which he conveys the lyrics hints at as much. "We're afraid she's gonna let you down," he sings. Gerry, an eternally wise child as far as relationships were concerned, sounds as though he'd been there before. As though he were trying to communicate with himself. A romantic falls again and again, no matter how much it had hurt during the last debacle. "She's Gonna Let You Down" is the source of Gerry's experienced wisdom attempting to contact his earnest and natural romantic inclinations. Yeats's "perpetual virginity of the soul" would eternally plague Gerry's compositional persona.

"Submarine Ladies" is a lighter tune. It uses a harmonica, for one, which adds to the album's overall cinematic quality, and strings. It's a confessional song of Gerry's, understated in the realest of ways. "Don't you know that I love you? I was hopin' you'd love me too" says the refrain. The song's minimalist verses try to make sense of the interactions that have gone down between him and his girl. Apathy seems to be the key concern. The aesthetic suggestion of women submerged underwater, muffled in communication, and not always available is well suited to the narrative trajectory, too.

* * *

Perhaps not since the Beatles' *White Album* had there been such a perfect closer—while they went with Ringo's lullaby "Good Night," America went with Gerry's "Goodbye." An upbeat and emotional, piano-driven number, the verses of "Goodbye" served as a series of communications between Gerry and others. Mrs. Sorrow and Uncle Freedom were anthropomorphized characters, while Sister Susie and Brother Michael were Gerry's actual siblings. "I got too many problems, they just don't understand. They think their every wish is my command," resounded the chorus. It was more than telling about Gerry's attempts to reason with the many expectations that adult life and immense artistic fame had saddled him with.

Dewey, too, showed development in his musicianship on *Hat Trick*. "Molten Love" enabled Dewey to express vocal prowess he'd not yet had the opportunity to. "There are a couple of songs in my catalogue of personal writing that are in their own little category," Dewey reflected about his song, "and that, like 'Oloololo' [on 1994's *Human Nature*], would be one. 'Molten Love' was a whole different thing, and lyrically I had to really dig into myself. . . . I wanted to stretch my voice a little bit. The melody was trying to get my voice to do something a little different, taxing my voice. The lava sounds—we had gotten the Wrecking Crew, and Hal Blaine came up with a lot of those sounds. He blew bubbles too, which is at the tail end." It's a song of atmosphere really—romantic atmosphere—that relies upon nature to be articulated. For a Dewey song, it is very produced: there are string sections and sound effects. Lyrically, and as America's album opener on *Silent Letter*'s "Only Game in Town" would as well, the verses begin with analogies between romantic courting and card games: "First she says 'Kings' / Then he says 'Aces,' / It gets pretty hard for a lady to tell / The hearts from the faces." The song utilizes a unique Dewey guitar tuning; its melody is jazzy and interesting, and like the emotions of a love affair and the elements of nature, it is unpredictable in progression. "Volcanic silver clouds fill pools and canyons around us," is the moodiest vocal line and almost leaves the listener on edge. This is in part because the song, musically, is never truly resolved—it travels through nether regions of beauty, intrigue, and mystery, never settling down. "Molten Love" rivals "Three Roses" for Dewey's—and the group's—most ardently romantic song in the oeuvre, and on *Hat Trick* it segues directly into Dewey's next song.

"Green Monkey" would prove to be one of the decade's most valuable rock 'n' roll recordings. It was originally intended to be a Santana-esque, riff-driven song; ultimately, though, Dewey built the track out from its lyrics, metering it syllabically. It was a poem put to music. Dewey and

Gerry's voices carried the harmonics through the complete set of verses and choruses—one of the first literal proofs of their success potential as a duo. The song was radio friendly. It featured another strong musical voice of the Southern California scene—the guitar prowess of Joe Walsh.

When "Muskrat Love" failed to deliver as a hit single, dying immediately upon release, Warners looked elsewhere on America's album. "'Rainbow Song' was probably one of the first of the songs on *Hat Trick* that I had written, and it used an intricate tuning," Dewey recalled. "I loved 'Rainbow Song.' Still do. That song was cemented in my life in high school, still tearing myself away from the high school vibe, and that community. And I could see that we were going to be leaving that soon, with the success, and everything we'd had: 'I am asleep on a rainbow, hoping for the rest of the ride.' It was like—wow, we've got this great good fortune."

"Wind Wave," another of Dewey's contributions to *Hat Trick*, would become one of Dewey's best-loved nature-themed songs. Its easy tempo, ear-comforting rhythms, and mellow mood made the song one of the album's most enticing. Dewey's writerly inclination to chase topics of escaping to nature would continue throughout his entire career. "Early in the morning when the sun comes up, I'm gonna grab a fishin' pole and a sleepin' bag roll," one verse detailed. As far as the simple life went, Dewey walked the walk in his day-to-day life and talked the talk in his songs.

Gerry recalled that "with *Hat Trick* it was right on the cusp of our renegotiating our deal. Geffen went in and re-signed our deal after *Homecoming*, after our two platinum albums. In addition, he didn't get our publishing back, but he convinced them to pay an additional amount for the publishing to us—which we all divvied and he commissioned."

Geffen detested everything about "Muskrat Love," and he did not feel that it could be America's next single. But he was in tune with the fact that Warner Brothers Music had just paid to try and take ownership of America's publishing—and yet America was force-feeding him a song that they didn't write and they didn't own. There was a lot of animosity. "We did some damage there around that time," Gerry recalled. "I don't want to blame it on them. I think the album was really esoteric and a bit broad."

"We really produced all that ourselves," Dewey recalled. "We spent a lot of time, late nights, I remember. Asking, 'Can you mix me a two-track, at four in the morning?' to the engineer. 'I want to take this home and listen to it—wait, it's four in the morning.'"

During the *Hat Trick* album recording sessions, America was seeking instrumentalists who would be able to support them during their touring periods. They soon gave their bass player duties to David Dickey. "David recommended this guy Willie Leacox on drums," Dewey recalled. "So that was the five-piece. David was a real good-looking guy; he had that blond hair, kind of a Norse god. But he had just been in a show band in Vegas: he was a bit campy. And we were emulating that thing, the Southern California whatever it was. Just by osmosis. I don't think we were affecting it, we were really doing it. We were members of our generation."

Dan's "It's Life" would prove to be one of the group's most enduring classic recordings. Many listeners' favorite America track, the tune would seek to articulate a person's trip through life. The piece began gradually, with slow and mellow verses, full of ambiguous lyrics. But it resulted in universally applicable revelations through the song's choruses. "The people are pretty, the flowers are too," is perhaps one of the most resonating descriptions of the hippie generation's aesthetics. The track's guitar lines are some of the album's most standout instrumental contributions.

As for cover aesthetics, America once more sought out the visual hands of Diltz and Burden. "For *Hat Trick* we went to Cahuilla Indian Reservation, a desert near Palm Springs," reflected Henry.[1] "Gary wanted to bring a big mirror so we could lay it on the ground so we could look like a hole in the ground and have the boys lean over it to look like a reflection." Dewey, Gerry, and Dan then walked along the adjacent mountain ridge, all holding the mirror. "I could see that a light kept flashing in the mirror," continued Henry. "I shouted for them to stop and we realized that the light was the moon coming up behind us. So we got a great picture of them holding the mirror with the moon coming up and then beyond them was the sun setting."

Perhaps it is *Hat Trick*'s title track that best sums up America's attempts for the album: to be more than they were, to be better, to be more complex, to be more independently musical. The song runs nearly eight-and-a-half minutes long, the longest of any America track in the group's entire catalogue. Featuring backup vocals by a slew of known talents—Carl Wilson, Bruce Johnston, and Billy Hinsche—the song was heavily dosed with a Beach Boys hue.

The term "hat trick" was mostly used in relation to hockey or soccer antics, sports dialogues. It meant three-in-a-row of a successful enterprise. A trio of chart-topping records, theoretically. Its meaning would bear more of an ironic mantle on America's career, once the third album had been released. It failed to echo its two predecessors and failed to achieve platinum status. *Hat Trick* was intended to be America's hat trick.

But it wasn't.

13

THE PRODUCER

It was time to once again enlist new production blood. America's first choice was Sir George Martin, the man who would be forever associated with and praised for his work with America's favorite band—the Beatles. The trio didn't depend on the idea of getting to work with George, but they kept their fingers crossed for the opportunity. Though America were music fans, by 1974 they were also music celebrities, with platinum-selling albums and singles to their name. And they now had plenty of studio experience under their belts. "George Martin, at that time, was in a bit of a dip," Dewey recalled. "He'd come to L.A. to go to the Oscars with Paul [McCartney] for 'Live and Let Die,' but . . . he hadn't had that much going on. When we sat down with him, it was another timing thing. He had a lull in his schedule, not much going on, and we were established young guys. He didn't have to break us [in] or anything. We do have to give George credit: everything he did, it just lifted it to a whole other level. And we like to think we helped George's career at that point as well." America requested that the Geffen-Roberts team open a dialogue with Sir George.

Elliot Roberts, right toward the end of his time with America, posed the offer to Sir George, who agreed, and then came to meet them at Elliot's office on Sunset Boulevard. The trio were overjoyed to meet, and to be produced by, the man who had shaped the classic albums of their favorite group—the Beatles. His noble and attractive manner, and will to experiment in the studio searching for innovative sounds, further appealed to America. They put their all into the new album project, demoing, arranging, editing and reediting the songs they intended to cut. The band was certain the opportunity was the breath of fresh air they had sought after the laboriousness and eventual disappointment of *Hat Trick*. And working with Sir George allowed them to once again indulge their Anglophilia. Gerry had purchased a country cottage in Sussex, England, and in the time before the recording process began, the band rehearsed all their intended songs there.

By 1974, Sir George had left EMI Studios to establish his own independent studio in London's Oxford Circus area—AIR Studios. To work on *Holiday*, he requested that America travel to London, to record at AIR. The album's engineer would be another Beatles' team member, Geoff Emerick. Sir George was aware of how long the *Hat Trick* recording process had taken and so blocked out two months at AIR for *Holiday*. He and the band had no idea the project would only take them two weeks in entirety—or that it would mark the beginning of a long and successful partnership, whose set of albums would come to define a specific and identifiable sound of their own. Years later, George's son Giles Martin would compare his earliest work with America to that of the Beatles' final album, *Abbey Road*: "Sonically, it's more like his work with [the band] America. *Abbey Road* has that precision—everything's in tune, it has the right fit, and that's how he liked things to be."[1]

America would bring along Willie Leacox to London to record *Holiday*—but not David Dickey. "After David played on *Hat Trick*, we were going over to AIR Studios in London to work with the legendary George Martin," Gerry recalled. "By this time Willie was already part of the show. Dan and I were both bass players; we had played bass on the first album. We thought, rather than all three of us (Gerry, Dewey, and Dan) going over, all playing guitars, maybe we didn't really need Dickey, and one of us could go back to playing bass. Making it a little bit tighter." Gerry played the bass lines on Dewey's hit single "Tin Man." The trio intended to call David back in to the mix and have him join them on tour, as soon as the recording process was complete. It seemed logical to them at the time, but David didn't get it. "We loved David," Dewey recalled, "but it was awkward leaving him behind as we headed off to London with Willie to work on the album with George. As I recall, beside the fact that Gerry and Dan were capable of playing the bass lines they had worked up during our arranging and demo work in Gerry's apartment in Los Angeles, there were newly learned financial and logistical elements that had to be taken into account. After *Hat Trick* we had to consider all factors involved in making a record." During the commercial failure of the group's third album, salaries, per diems, airfares, and accommodations all came out of the pockets of the America machine, which had proved more fragile than initially realized.

Following *Holiday*, when America was ready to tour with the album's material, they called Dickey back in to the mix. "By the time we flew David out to begin the European tour," Dewey explained, "he felt alienated as he stepped back into the fold, having missed a very important chapter in the band's evolution. He was having to listen to all of the stuff he didn't play, and he was beginning to feel like a fifth wheel. And frankly he did have culture shock."

The 1974 tour was about to commence, but during the night Dickey panicked, backed out, and left for home. America was forced to make a last-minute grab for a bass player who could quickly join them on tour. Dewey had recently met Calvin "Fuzzy" Samuels on a flight, and they'd exchanged numbers. Luckily, when they needed a bassist, Fuzzy signed on to tour, the itinerary of which would include the German *Musikladen* television special in late '74. He'd had a great deal of experience working with musical sibling CSN, and America was glad to bring him on. Fuzzy quickly learned their material, never even needing to know the songs' chords—only their keys.

Willie Leacox, whose background of musical training and band experience brought America's percussion up to a whole new level, made notable contributions to his debut America sessions at AIR. His calm and flexible demeanor also jibed well with the group. Willie was as thrilled as the trio was to be working with George Martin. "During recording, George just let us go with it," Willie recalled. "He didn't really tell us anything. He did some piano stuff with Gerry, but he didn't really tell us what to do or anything. He was great to work with. On the first album I did with them, we did a song called 'Hollywood.' On that song I'm playing a padded piano seat. So I'm the drummer, but I'm playing a padded leather drum seat. George hung a mic out the window—of his second-floor studio, at AIR, the studio suspended because of the subway going below—to get some traffic sounds. But that didn't work, so Dan Peek and George Martin took their Bentleys out there on the street and just sort of stopped traffic, so that the traffic would honk and all of that kind of stuff. Hanging around the studio were Joni Mitchell and her band, too."

Dewey's song "Hollywood" used some of the same moody chords that his previous material had, but this time there was an extra bit of edge. The song spoke from literal experience, and thus possessed a weighty, jaded tone. The trio was well accustomed now to the high life of 1970s Los Angeles—both its glitzy sheen and its seedy underbelly. "Stumble through the bars on forget-me-not lane / Sparkle through the glitter but don't show the pain," Dewey's lyrics acknowledged the hypocritical side of some Hollywood scenes. Situations could be superficial, and appear as fine, complete, and authentic—eventually turning out to be liars, fakers, actors. Playing a part. The entertainment industry had plenty of well-meaning folk and well-meaning art, but it also had plenty of impostors and people looking to take advantage—sometimes financially—of the talents and accolades of others. Dewey, though having moved to the more laid-back San Francisco area, spent plenty of time in Los Angeles at business meetings and working with Gerry and Dan. And he had lived in L.A. for a year and a half, at the initial height of his and the band's fame. He'd met hangers-on, friends of friends, people trying to make it into show business, trying to make it in the music industry. He'd met and befriended several established and famous fellow musicians as well. "Heartbeats echo through a cavern of love / Come to the tavern I'll meet you up above / Soaring through the heavens, what a fabulous ride / But everybody's heading for the same place to hide," spoke to the eternal conundrum of the appeal and repulsion of living life in the fast lane. Having "made it" in an industry, and having been recognized for it, brought with it a dream made real, as well as the nightmare of fame's responsibility. The musical elements of "Hollywood"—its choppy electric guitar patterns, its ambiance vocal track that included atmospheric sounds of a typical Hollywood party—all helped to make the song an "experience" song. The fact that the horn-honking was recorded on the streets of London outside AIR Studios made no difference to the Hollywood-ness of the recording.

Dewey's major hit from *Holiday* would be "Tin Man," the *Wizard of Oz*-inspired rhythmic and catchy, surrealistically worded dreamscape piece. His lyrics here also seemed to speak in the tongue of experience, describing the relationship between what one was born with and what one sought out in the material world, reminding himself and everyone that he didn't truly need anything outside of himself: "Sometimes late when things are real and people share the gift of gab between themselves / Some are quick to take the bait and catch the perfect prize that waits among the shells / But Oz never did give nothing to the Tin Man that he didn't, didn't already have." Sir George Martin even played part of the song's piano line. The single would reach number four on the U.S. *Billboard* Hot 100 charts and number one on the *Billboard* Adult Contemporary charts.

What would become Dan Peek's best-known and most loved song would also be included on *Holiday*. "Lonely People," co-composed with his wife, Catherine, was originally written for John Sebastian of the Lovin' Spoonful, at the request of mutual friend Henry Diltz. Sebastian would never record it, and so the tune would become a quintessential America track, as well as a massive hit. As Dewey's single had done, "Lonely People" would reach number four on the *Billboard* Hot 100 and number one on the *Billboard* Adult Contemporary charts. Inspired by a twenty-first-century America tour favorite, Paul McCartney's masterpiece "Eleanor Rigby," which phrased "All the lonely people, where do they all come from?" Dan's song would be dedicated to those same people. "This is for all the lonely people / thinking that life has passed them by," the lyrics opened with, instantly winning the admiration and empathy of all and any listeners who had ever, at one time or another, considered themselves lonely. It was a new kind of love song, not dedicated to one woman, but to everyone everywhere. And its lyrics were positive, and encouraging, telling people to hang in there: "You never know until you try," they insisted. This ideology went in right alongside America's catalogic tones established in the band's infancy, almost as though America picked up right where the most positive of the Beatles' material had left off upon that band's breakup. The fact that Dan had penned the song with his ladylove gave the song for the lonely all that much more truth. Dan and Catherine, once lonely people themselves, no longer were.

Sir George and Gerry together played the song's middle section on the studio's Steinway piano, with Gerry taking the bass notes and George finding the higher tune. Weeks before, George had broken both of his wrists in a sailing accident; yet, somehow, he was still able to work the piano during the session. While he got along well with all three Americans, Sir George seemed to bond particularly quickly with Gerry

Dan, Gerry, George Martin, and Dewey. *Courtesy of Henry Diltz.*

over their mutual interest in and love for production. Perhaps when Sir George had first met him, Gerry, with his penchant for writing melodic love songs and admiration for the studio process and its many moving parts, reminded Sir George of a young Paul McCartney.

Over the course of their working relationship, George would encourage the trio's musicality and willingness to try new things in the studio. Gerry recalled, "I think I already had part of the piano bit on 'Lonely People.' And George then said, 'You should do a barrel roll.' And I can't do a barrel roll. So he said, 'Move over.' And we played it together, octaves. So what you hear on the record is a duet of me and George. A lovely moment. George had the ability to make you feel comfortable. That's not a given. He would let me conduct sometimes. He would do a score, like for a section on the *Hideaway* or *Hearts* album. He would say, 'Now I give the baton to Maestro Beckley.' We had gone over every note. But I'd have to fold the book over because I hadn't been doing it page by page. I didn't want him to think I wasn't following—but I was doing it by ear, conducting. It was a wonderful feeling, to have his confidence. For example, on *Holiday*, he said, 'It would be nice to have a little something to tip off this album.' And I had been working on this instrumental 6/8 piece that I did call 'Miniature.' He right away said, 'That'll do.' And so a simple piano thing that he then scored was on the record."

Gerry's songwriting on *Holiday* had also grown and developed since his earliest days. Songs like "Baby It's Up to You" and "What Does It Matter?" were melodically captivating yet intellectually stimulating in their musical complexity. But it was his song "Another Try" that would be his standout on the album. Somewhat inspired by America's musical friend Harry Nilsson's song "One," "Another Try" details the story of an everyday family coping with an alcoholic father: "Pick up the telephone / Tell him you want him home / To sit and watch the evenings pass / And readin' the leaves of grass," yearned for a simpler more innocent and narcotics-less era, in which nature was enough to allow the father and his family to feel good. Even though Gerry's characters were fictional, the song's sentiment served to remind his own generation of young people not to get caught up in a lifestyle of partying and overindulgence, activities that the Hollywood scene was full of. Inspired by the 1920s vintage feel of Gerry's song "What Does It Matter?," America decided to base the album cover aesthetics on the concept of a Jazz Age–era picnic, a real "holiday." It rang true with record-buying audiences, and was a shinier turn away from the dusty Western desert vibes of the previous two album covers.

The album would reach the number four slot on the *Billboard* chart. But first, some handiwork would need to be done—and it would not be Geffen or Roberts who came to the rescue for America, but one of their managers of the month, John Hartmann. When *Holiday* was released in June of '74, it was noticed, but then was just as quickly forgotten. Though it hit the U.S. *Billboard* chart, it lost its "bullet." The *bullet* was an industry term for the star symbol sometimes indicated next to certain records on the chart listings. It indicated that the album had improved in some way since the previous week—in sales or radio play. In the 1970s, if an album lost its chart bullet, its attempt at big success was more or less done for.

One day not long after *Holiday*'s release, Hartmann ran into a sullen-looking Gerry at the Geffen-Roberts Hollywood offices. Gerry explained that he was depressed that America had lost its chart bullet for the new single "Tin Man." Hartmann assured them he could get the bullet back.

Displeased with how he had been treated by Elliot Roberts after he'd helped him organize a Neil Young tour, John Hartmann had decided to leave the Geffen-Roberts team. He would establish his own management company along with Harlan Goodman. They were taking Poco with them and invited America too, telling them that Roberts was not working for them. America had fallen out of favor with Geffen and Roberts, and once they lost their *Holiday* chart bullet, they jumped ship to join Hartmann and Goodman.

In a May 1975 *L.A. Times* article by Cameron Crowe, Hartmann articulated this about *Holiday*: "The album came out," he said, "went to number 50 on the charts and began to fall. *My heart stopped.* I got enraged and called Joe Smith (president of Warner Brothers Records) to find out what was going on. He politely told me we were bombing. The Souther-Hillman-Furay band—three people no one had ever heard of—was roaring up the charts and America was bombing? Joe Smith told me not to pay any attention to chart figures, that they were a hype. I said, 'Then get us a hype.' We turned it around, broke 'Tin Man' and eventually even 'Lonely People.'"[2] In an attempt to garner more attention for *Holiday* and its singles, Hartmann organized a huge and extravagant lunch party for Columbus Day 1974. On behalf of America, he invited the entire Warner Brothers staff—including every secretary, mail room attendant, and vice president—to the party, sending out elegant paper invitations to all. Upon their arrival, Hartmann instantly won favor by welcoming attendees as "Warner Brothers and Sisters," at a time when the Women's Movement was increasingly gaining traction and appeal. Hartmann gave a Columbus Day speech, verbally playing on the idea of 'discovering America,' and the band arrived to perform a stellar live set of all the new *Holiday* material. From then on, Warners was even more tuned into America's career, and all concerned parties were more than happy to give the band and its album every possible promotional push. "Tin Man" got its bullet back, the album turned into a massive hit, and America had a new management company. "We were back," remembered Gerry. "Followed by 'Lonely People.' Smash hits that could have died, had we stayed with Geffen-Roberts."

"Later in life you realize how many people were involved in this," Dewey confessed. "You realize there's a whole bunch of players involved. People working very hard."

14

THE IDENTITY

"The winning America-Martin combination continues through *Hearts*, the trio's first release under its young and ambitious new managers, Hartmann and Harlan Goodman. 'We're working hard at broadening the America audience now,' said Hartmann. Under their new direction, the band has already completed its first film score, for Universal's *The Story of a Teen-ager* ('It's a sort of teen *Midnight Cowboy*,' cracked Beckley. 'Ratso Rizzo Goes for Burgers.') 'We're going for a more middle-of-the-road audience,' explained Harlan Goodman. 'We're doing the *Smothers Brothers Show* rather than *In Concert* and a Bob Hope special rather than *The Midnight Special* or *Cher*. Ultimately, we'll do a special of our own.' And who knows? Maybe the day will come when Peek, Bunnell, and Beckley will become household names and faces as easily identifiable as their records. 'I sure hope it's soon,' opined Bunnell. 'People still think of us as 15-year-old Neil Young imitators. It's too bad that your initial image stays with you for so long.'"[1]

For America's fifth album, to be titled *Hearts*, the band would once again enlist the services of Sir George Martin and Geoff Emerick. Always game for a destination recording experience, Sir George agreed to come to Dewey's neck of the woods—the beautiful art-focused Sausalito, near San Francisco. Lee Kiefer, an engineer at the L.A. Record Plant where America had recorded its second and third albums, suggested the band spend some time at the plant's northern location for a change in atmosphere. "Once *Holiday* was a hit, big hit," Gerry recalled, "not only are we back after the hiccup with *Hat Trick*, but George Martin was back. The whole notion of George saying 'I want you to come over and work at AIR' was out the window, because it had only taken two weeks. So we immediately start to sketch out sessions for the follow-up album. And Dewey was established in San Francisco at that point. We said, 'Let's go where Dewey is. There's a lovely Record Plant there. We'll go up there.'"

At the time of the recording sessions, in January 1975, the Bay Area—Mill Valley, Sausalito, and San Francisco proper—was still very much a happening area for rock 'n' roll musicians. Bands like the Grateful Dead, Journey, Santana, Fleetwood Mac, and musicians like Van Morrison, Huey Lewis, and Mike Bloomfield, all hung around. Many of them could be found nightly at Mill Valley's nearby bar and music club Sweetwater Saloon. Some of these artists recorded at the Sausalito Record Plant too. Dewey would eventually become very close friends with Steve Perry, Phil Lesh, and Jerry Garcia. And Dewey became acquainted with the writer and boss Merry Prankster Ken Kesey, who was in the Grateful Dead orbit. "I was intrigued by and read all the Beat writers and poets, and particularly the Kesey gang because Neal Cassady drove them. Kesey's relationship with Kerouac was sort of a bridge between the Beats and hippies before Cassady died in 1968. I wished I had been there in real time, but the intensity of being around the Dead family in the early '70s was the closest I'd ever get."

In November '73 Dewey and his first wife purchased a house in Marin County, transitioning from the L.A. scene into the San Francisco one. From 1974 onward, Dewey commuted down to Los Angeles regularly—often on the fun, boutique, West Coast–based airline PSA—for recordings, overdubs, rehearsals, meetings, and any kind of television show appearances. "I would come down and get a hotel, often we'd have a week of rehearsals at a time. I'd hang out with Gerry, and Dan—sometimes separately, sometimes together. But by then we were compartmentalizing our lives more than living in each other's pockets."

Dewey also became increasingly interested in the visual arts during this time. "Early on, I became acquainted with an art gallery owner in Mill Valley by the name of Robert Green who helped me focus my interest in fine art and art history. Among others, Bob represented a young, talented abstract artist, Mark Erickson, and the three of us would go to gallery openings around the Bay Area and discuss works and movements, and express our individual feelings and opinions about the art we loved. I was able to expand on my interest in the art world with them,

Ken Kesey with Dewey. *Courtesy of the Bunnell family.*

which began with my early appreciation of mid-nineteenth-century artists associated with Impressionism, Postimpressionism, Picasso, Cubism, Dada, Surrealism . . . and all things 'Modern art' through current times. I've always been amazed by the art world."

Dewey tuned in to a local movement that had begun during the late 1940s, the Bay Area figurative movement, which had been spurred on by a reaction to the New York School of Abstract Expressionism. Dewey viewed a retrospective collection at SFMOMA and was captivated by the works of David Park, Richard Diebenkorn, Nathan Oliveira, Paul Wonner, and William Theophilus Brown. Dewey began to spend large amounts of time at San Francisco's Campbell-Thiebaud Gallery, which he described as "where Charlie Campbell represented and interacted with all those artists for decades, and I acquired a few original works. Eventually I met most of the artists and went to their shows and other galleries who represented them like the Berggruen Gallery, who had fantastic large-scale shows. They were all a generation older than me but incredibly young at heart [and] inspired. Bob and Mark and I would visit Bill Brown and Paul Wonner at their home and see their personal art collection, complete with Picasso, Giacometti, and Lucien Freud pictures, contrasted by their incredible collection of Hopi kachina dolls and ancient birdstones. And then take them to lunch and talk art for hours. I have such fond memories of those years in Marin with those guys and still love visiting art museums and galleries, looking at art books, and occasionally adding something to my own collection. I can't imagine life without the visual arts." America's *Hearts* period was suffused with multimedia artistic influences from all angles.

Musically, Dan's "Woman Tonight" was one of the most interesting tracks on *Hearts*. Willie Leacox contributed an atypical drum accompaniment, an effect dramatized by Gerry's inspiration to begin his piano part on the measure's second beat instead of the first. David Dickey's fuzzy-sounding bass, a major guitar solo by Dewey, a syncopated synthesizer part by George Martin, and alternating vocals among all three singers resulted in the reggae-inspired classic. The first take in the session was used for the album, and it would always be admired by America's fellow rock 'n' rollers for its uniqueness and mystery. "Woman" hit a mid-forties slot on the U.S. *Billboard* Hot 100 and Adult Contemporary charts as well. But it would not be the only chart maker of the album.

Gerry Beckley hit one of his songwriting peaks during the *Hearts* era. Always one for traditional songwriting and one who respected the blood-sweat-and-tears, hardworking element of the craft, Gerry would finally come up with a number-one recording of his own song, "Sister Golden Hair." With its upbeat tempo, slide guitar inspired by George Harrison's "My Sweet Lord," and somewhat more serious and morose lyrics inspired by the writings of Jackson Browne, the track would be a beautiful composite of Gerry's influences, while simultaneously bringing his unique personal vision to a further point of originality. Musically, the track was upbeat, catchy, and destined for active radio play. Lyrically, the song was remarkably authentic to some of Gerry's habits and practices as a person. The track's character-narrator is someone who has been missing in action as far as Sister Golden Hair is concerned. He uses the song to apologize, saying that he has "been one poor correspondent," but that it doesn't mean he has not been thinking about her or that he loves her any less. The sing-along-able "mmm bop shoo-op," amid slide guitar riffs during the song's closeout, played upon the song's melodic lightness. Perhaps one of the track's most significant elements is how the lyrics and melodics seem to be at odds, almost as if the singer-narrator is attempting to travel from the land of darkness toward the land of light.

Gerry's other impressive contribution to the *Hearts* album would follow in a similar train of musical thought. The album's opener would be a piano-driven ballad that would incorporate heavy amounts of orchestral string arrangements. It would be one of the most beautiful and most romantic tunes that Gerry would ever pen. Upon its release in 1975, it would also reach number twenty on the U.S. *Billboard* charts and number four on the U.S. Adult Contemporary charts.

"Daisy Jane," a wordplay on the phrase "daisy chain" and also inspired by Nick Drake's tune "Hazy Jane," seemed to speak from the same emotional place as "Sister Golden Hair." Gerry's character-narrator was dealing with a mess of conflicting emotions and was trying to sort them out. The lilting, tender melodies, and the deep, cello-driven orchestrations suggested intense and true emotional depth of feeling. The metered sound at the start of the song—which could only be heard if the stereo volume was turned up high enough—sounded as though it mimicked a heartbeat. It suggested an awareness of having a heart at all and, thus, of getting attached to other people outside of oneself—and with it the vacillating resistance to acknowledging it.

The inclusion of the metered sound was initially unintentional. "I had the octave repeating chord at the start of the song," Gerry reflected. "I think I wanted this pulse and had said to David Dickey, 'Hit that.' But to me the other little facet of that story, when you listen very closely, the thumping actually goes 'BA-dum, dum dum, dum, dum, BA-dum, dum, dum,' etcetera. We all sat there listening back, with our dog ears, listening to the intro, and we heard this little pulse. We said, 'David, don't do a rhythm hit.' And he said, 'I'm not doing a rhythm hit.' But we still heard it. Then we had to start soloing everything and [discovered] that little catch rhythm, that sixteenth-note rhythm, was *my* foot coming off and on the sustain pedal on the piano. 'Hold—chord—lift.' And it was that lift that put the little pulse you can hear. Just one of those nice little things, those happy accidents."

Though "Daisy Jane" narratively dealt with the southern United States—Memphis—Gerry was nowhere near the city when he conceived the song idea or demoed it upon its completion. "I wrote that in Sussex," he recalled. "By this time, I had a little country cottage in the south of England, and would hole up there just for some peace and quiet. Had a lovely little upright piano and wrote 'Daisy' and some other bits there."

"Bell Tree," too, would be a melodically moody piece, which would point to one of Gerry's career-long compositional topics: time. "Days, where'd you go so fast? Finally lost at last," the lyrics said. The vocal performance here would be one of Gerry's career bests, and one of his most resonant.

Dan and Gerry would share a rare writing credit on the song intended for a Don Coscarelli and Craig Mitchell 1975 film originally called *Story of a Teenager,* eventually retitled *Jim, the World's Greatest.* "I think that had something to do with Dan," Gerry recalled. "I think it came to the office, came to John Hartmann. He happened to tell it to Dan and Dan took it on. Dan wrote this ballad, and I think I wrote that bridge. I was kind of the bridge guy. I love the bridge in structure, and Dew's songs often needed bridges in structure and stuff. I take pride in that I can visualize what a bridge is and how it works, I can see it on the keyboards—both a guitar keyboard and a piano. So I like bridges." Much like Dan's "Lonely People," "Story" would lyrically be positive, encouraging, and life-affirming. "Boy, please don't throw away your life / All the joy, please don't end it with a knife / 'Cause you know there's hope for you" was direct and aimed at young people in need. Gerry's bridge articulated a stronger stance, speaking up for the teenager narrator's abuse: "Everywhere I look I see your face / Every step I take seems out of place / You got to be a man to run the race / I'm not a hopeless man / How can you say I am?"

Dan's other material on *Hearts* was more melodically diverse than Gerry's album contributions. There was the calm and reflective "Tomorrow" and the angsty, rocking "Half a Man," both of which seem to be romantic addresses. "I'm only half a man / When I'm not by your side / I try to make a plan / And I don't try to hide / So come on over closer to me / And everything will be just like it should be," Dan's lyrics in "Half a Man" called out. The constant touring that America had been subjected to, which had only increased with the success of *Holiday,* had the potential to take its toll on all the band members' emotional connections.

As Dan and Catherine had with "Lonely People," they would once again co-write a song together—this time it was "Old Virginia." The state was where they had spent college time together, when Dan had chosen to leave London and attend Old Dominion University for a year, in order to be closer to Catherine. "Reach out old Virginia / Won't you rock him close to you / The poor boy's had a hotel so long / He don't know what to do / It's time to come on home / And put your feet up for a while / So much travelin' 'round can take away your smile," seemed to perfectly encapsulate Dan's and Catherine's emotional and psychological wars with Dan being on the road.

Dewey's contributions to *Hearts* were perhaps the most nature-inspired songs he had penned since the first two records. "Midnight," "People in the Valley," and "Seasons" were all of this sort. "Seasons" was the album's closer, and it was a beautiful and lyrical poem on the power of the year's four seasons and the nuanced journey through each transitional change. Well-arranged strings spruced up the track, making it grander in sound. "Midnight" would be a songwriting team up between Gerry and Dewey, though overall the track was clearly a Dewey song—and its lead vocals were sung by him as well. The track would serve as the B side to the single release of Gerry's "Sister Golden Hair," and would be the most perfectly fitting sonic foil to side A. "Midnight" was slow, mysterious, and aurally explorative. Like Dan's material, Dewey's "Midnight" lyrically suggested a yearning for a missing romantic partner: "Midnight rolling in, sunlight / Reaching out for your return // As you were running through the tunnel of life / And soon you'll dance around the fire of fright / Tonight."

Once America began to tour with their *Hearts* material, audiences proved to be just as captivated with the band, as indicated by the albums' and singles' sales. In May of 1975, *Billboard* magazine reviewed America's show at New York's Felt Forum: "It was as if the phrase 'captive audience' was coined for America. From the moment they stepped onto the stage the crowd did nothing but cheer. The May 9 show opened with a clean, crisp rendition of 'Tin Man' and the group displayed the feature for which they are best known, fine harmony. They continued the momentum with highlights such as 'Don't Cross the River,' 'Company,' and a mighty version of 'Ventura Highway.' They have a total, complete sound, strong vocals and strong instrumentals.

"This material is a departure from the easy listening one expects from America. Dan Peek mans an electric guitar and the group transforms into a rock group. The pleasant harmonies of Dewey Bunnell and Jerry Beckley [*sic*] remain, enhancing the driving electric force. The crowd kept cheering throughout the entire 70-minute set. America, then, returned for an exciting encore of 'Sandman.' After a standing ovation, they returned again to play the second encore, 'Horse With No Name,' the tune that brought the group to fame. After some 23 songs, the audience was still eager and continued to applaud for 10 minutes. This show proves that America is a safe bet for continued success."[2]

Meanwhile, Dewey's life in Northern California had been growing increasingly more enjoyable, and increasingly more suited to his true character and lifestyle preferences. But when he was in Los Angeles working with Gerry and Dan, and went out to hang out afterward, he usually went to the band's familiar spot, the Record Plant in West Hollywood, where there always seemed to be someone Dewey knew. There he would meet and say hello to people like Frank Zappa and Captain Beefheart. It was a happening spot at all hours of every day, with a lounge, and game room showcasing the earliest forms of video games available to play. When musicians weren't recording there, they would host evening parties in the newer Studio C section of the plant. America had recorded *Homecoming* and *Hat Trick* in Studio A. Gary Kellgren, co-founder of the Record Plant, also threw wildly entertaining parties at his home, inviting many of the Record Plant's artistic crowd.

"The only time I'd been in John Lennon's presence was at a party up at Gary Kellgren's house," Dewey recalled. "Gary knew all the artists and was a key member of the scene in L.A. and had frequent gatherings at his house. That night the place was packed and I had squeezed up to the bar to get a drink for my wife. As I turned to head back, a hand reached out and grabbed the plastic cup from my hand. As I turned, saying, 'Hey, that drink's for my wife!' I saw that it was John Lennon standing there holding the bottom half of a female mannequin saying, 'Oh sorry, mate!' It was a surreal moment. He seemed to be having a great time chatting with Bill Wyman later as I made another pass around the house. My brushes with John Lennon are few, but I'll never forget them."

Later on Dewey would run into John Lennon again, during his *Pussycats* sessions at the Plant with America's close friend Harry Nilsson. "I go back in there, and the first thing I see is Mick Jagger and [his then-wife] Bianca playing air hockey on this board just outside the studio. And I go into the studio, open the door, and I see John and Harry. Harry I knew pretty well. I'd never met Ringo, who was sitting on the carpeted steps. They were listening to a playback. John and Harry were behind the board, and Harry looked over and just kind of acknowledged me, and Lennon looked at me, and said, 'Hey.' I probably was not there more than fifteen minutes, because I felt really uncomfortable. I was in awe."

Since working with Sir George Martin, America's line of connection to the ex-Beatles had become increasingly more direct. George Harrison had been present at some of the *Holiday* sessions at Air Studios in London. Dewey had been out to George and Pattie's house in London's Henley-on-Thames, where they swapped guitar stories and ate dinner together. And when Paul and Linda McCartney came to Los Angeles, the America trio was invited to their wild and grand parties, with guest lists totaling in the five-hundred-plus range.

"Those Paul McCartney parties were fantastic," Dewey recalled. "They were like some kind of a psychedelic dream. There was one on the *Queen Mary*, and I remember the first one up at the Harold Lloyd estate." The dress code was specific: white formal wear. "Everybody was there— Jack Nicholson, Chevy Chase, Steve McQueen. All the guys from Chicago. And of course, Paul and Linda. it was wild." Afterward, Dan and Catherine invited Rod Stewart and Britt Ekland back to their home, where Dan played him the latest version of "Today's the Day." Rod loved the song, and years later Dan would wonder if it had moved him to pen his own classic, "Tonight's the Night."

15

THE FREEZING AND THE FIFTY-FIVE THOUSAND

In November 1975, in accordance with their Warner Brothers contract, America released an obligatory greatest hits record. While other bands with similar multi-album deals might release their greatest hits albums as the last albums of their deals, America was already sitting on more hits than they could count after only five albums. Following the immense success of the band's recent single release from *Hearts*, "Sister Golden Hair," Warner Brothers aimed to strike while the iron was hot. *History* presented an assortment of tunes from the band's five records, and provided the opportunity for the current producer-in-residence to try his hand at mixing the first three albums' contributions. Songs like "Ventura Highway," which added bass reverb and double-tracked vocals, "Sandman," which was cut by one minute, and "Don't Cross the River," which added a fiddle part, were once again made new by the "fifth Beatle," Sir George Martin. Some tracks were also crossfaded. As decades progressed and America's familiar canon continued to receive airplay, these mixes would be used and recognized most by listeners.

History's cover would become forever recognizable to America for its unique design. It would be brilliant for its artistic achievement in representation of the band's entire career up until then—its "history"—which included traces of London, its Big Ben and red double-decker buses, and of California, its plethora of nature, lush green trees, and Golden Gate Bridge. And it would be notable for its then-unknown artist's incendiary future to come. "At Hartmann & Goodman, we had my brother Phil who was the comedy legend and so forth, but he was also a brilliant designer himself and a great creator, who had done many album covers for my artists," John Hartmann recalled. "So one day Phil comes into the office with a set of watercolors that turned out to be *History: America's Greatest Hits*. He said, 'Look, I've done this rough of the America cover!' The band said, 'That's awesome!' We showed the watercolors to the band and I remember Dan Peek said, 'That's not a rough, that's a cover!' Did another painting with the bass player and the drummer in front of the Crossroads of the World tower, which is where our Sunset Boulevard offices were. So Willie Leacox and bass player David Dickey were inserted into the watercolor that appears on the back of the album."

History was released in the U.S. on November 3, 1975, and it quickly achieved multi-platinum status, holding a number three slot on *Billboard*'s Album Chart. America—and Warner Brothers—once again had a massive hit album. The question was—where could the group go from there?

America's friendship with and connection to the band Chicago would always be an interesting one. Both acts were "logo groups" whose band members, despite immense commercial success and creative prowess, often became invisible behind their band names. Most young record buyers of the time knew of the bands, and many were ardent fans. But were they familiar with the individual players' personalities—their names, their artistic evolutions? Or did they succumb to the bands' nuanced tones of anonymity? Decades later, Chicago keyboardist and singer Robert Lamm would collaborate with Gerry, and Carl Wilson of the Beach Boys, on the *Like a Brother* album.

"My band, Chicago, had emerged in a big way, maybe two years, before America," Robert Lamm recalled. "We became friendly with Gerry and Dewey, primarily through roadies [sound technicians] in each band." Roadie Jerry Vaccarino, who would later work with the Eagles, was a mutual friend of Chicago and America. "There was no denying, when I heard the songs on the first America album, that these 'cats' could write, sing, and play, in a quite sophisticated manner, given that much of '70s mainstream pop/rock was based on blues forms. To my ear, Dewey's and Gerry's music was so unique, in much the same way as Chicago's was so hard to categorize, yet both were highly identifiable. All the albums were well crafted. Both bands had much to say about life experiences and the culture. For both bands, longevity and constant touring speaks volumes about the appeal of the music."

For their sixth studio album, America decided to record at Caribou Ranch. It was a studio owned and operated by Chicago's manager, Jim Guercio. Upon arrival, reviews of the establishment and the surrounding area were mixed. The only available period for America to block out studio time fell during the dead of winter—February 1976. The experience was collectively judged to be freezing cold. Laying down vocal tracks for the album's material was tough, given the high altitudes of the studio's location in the Rocky Mountains. "I don't have a lot of fond memories of it. To get to an altitude of 10,000 feet and then try and sing vocals, there's just no way. Things like that were an issue," Gerry recalled.

What was also tough: trumping the recent creative and commercial mega-success of *Hearts*. Gerry, Dewey, and Dan would try—and they would all feel the pressure to succeed. The band and George Martin now had a clearly defined and committed working partnership, having created two chart-topping albums in a row. The trend of recording each new album with George in destination studios, rendering each album recording experience a vacation experience as well, would continue with Caribou Ranch. Years later Gerry would wonder whether returning to London's AIR Studios or close to home base in Los Angeles would have helped the trio to feel more in their element as recording artists.

"We'd already done those five albums and we had a *Greatest Hits* out," Dewey reminisced. "So in retrospect, had I been thinking about it in a more controlled or planned way, we should most likely have said, 'Yeah hey, five records, a bunch of success, a *Greatest Hits* out there: this next album better be different in some way.' I can only say that with hindsight." As beautiful as *Hideaway* would become, the record fell right in line with America's creative trajectory. The title *Hideaway* implied an enjoyable vacation or getaway to a locale that offered privacy, comfort, and the opportunity for self-reflection.

With the addition of George Martin as producer, America's albums had become vaster in sound and utilized more complicated arrangements in songs. Gone were the days of three teenagers with acoustic guitars perched on stools. America now had bassist David Dickey and drummer Willie Leacox; the band had developed a comfortable working relationship with George and trusted him to the utmost. Decades after the release

Left to right: Gerry, Elliot Roberts, Dewey, John Hartmann, Harlan Goodman, and Dan. *Courtesy of Henry Diltz.*

of *Hideaway*, America and its fans would wonder whether the album and its follow-up *Harbor* could have benefited from starker soundscapes. The songs from both records showcased how the trio had matured as songwriters, but the increase in production elements, like string arrangements, sometimes made that harder to detect.

Gerry's romantic ballads once again form a strong presence. "She's a Liar" and "Who Loves You," though dramatically disparate musical numbers, almost seem to speak to the same woman as a courtship evolves. "Liar" is angsty, full of the narrator's confusion and frustrated attempts to figure out *just who is* the protagonist, Caroline. The underlying current, in its driving and commanding guitar notes, is one of desire. As Gerry tells it, this chick falls "in and out of love," constantly changes her mind about the people she runs around with ("First she calls them friends and then she puts them down"), wants a whole lot of everything, wants to be something that she isn't but also doesn't try hard enough to be it. Whatever "it" is. She's complicated and frenetic and Gerry dubs her to be "a liar." Nevertheless, he still plans to "try her tonight." His voice, naturally mellow, melodic, and on the softer side, is driven to rasp and crackle in this track, almost as though the emotion he feels is beyond proper articulation.

By the time "Who Loves You" rolls around, Gerry—and the narrative situation—has calmed down. The tempo is slower, the mood is softer, the narrator has succumbed to his feelings for the girl, and simultaneously acknowledges their sometime ambiguity. He knows he wants her and that she is meaningful to him—but he can only speak to the present moment-ness of these truths. "Love is falling on me," the verse begins, the only appropriate reaction to which could be surrender. "Look who loves you when you're feelin' down," he insists to her, a main selling point in the narrative argument that comes up several times. All these emotive changes in the lyrics are appropriately dramatized by exciting and cinematic stringscapes. Imagining the song without this lush sonic grandeur would render it a much more introspective, private number. Perhaps the piece's most interesting moment is when Gerry redirects his attention to himself and away from the girl. "Who's gonna trust you now, boy?" is a Van Morrison–esque repetition that comes just before the song returns to its B section and closes out. Is the narrator's trust now in question because he has succumbed to truly caring about this girl who he was hitherto only mildly distracted by, now that his mind and heart have been changed? He has shifted from the realm of the cerebral into the nether regions of emotional murk.

"Watership Down," however, would be Gerry's most notable composition on *Hideaway*. A film adaptation of the celebrated Richard Adams novel, slated to release in October '78, called for a George Martin–produced soundtrack. Naturally George asked America to put forth some song ideas, and Gerry came back with his song of the same name. But when the film shifted its producers, and ties with George were cut, there was nowhere for the beautiful track to go but onto America's next album. Ultimately the film's soundtrack selected Art Garfunkel's recording of Mike Batt's gem "Bright Eyes" for its main song, which would reach number one on the British charts.

Though the film that inspired it was a tearjerker, presenting the harsh truth of humans' environmental disregard and its inevitable destructive effects on the natural world, Gerry's song speaks the language of inspiration and hope. Even if he himself has mortal uncertainty, his song transcends this, and achieves a palpable knowing that is at once reassuring and realistic. "I can feel there's better days / Well, they're coming, they're coming / I can see them through the haze / So can you," repeats the chorus. The way in which Gerry's narrator states his feeling first, and then echoes it with "so can you," effectively brainwashes the listener into agreeing. When the message being transmitted is of such an egalitarian quality, it seems only beneficial for the universe to agree. The background vocals provided by Dewey and Dan on this track add even more fullness to the already lush recording.

Hideaway might be the most cinematic of America's discography. In addition to the film-inspired "Watership Down" and the overall increase in varied productive accoutrements, there is a two-part instrumental composition appropriately titled "Hideaway Part I" and "Hideaway Part II." Dewey penned this, with arrangement assistance from Sir George Martin. "At that point we had a real working communication—George, Gerry, Dan, and I. George had already seen how we worked, seen how we would write separately, how we had developed respective songs on various projects." During the *Hideaway* sessions, Dewey "felt comfortable enough just to say to George, 'This isn't really a song yet, but I really like these chords, these changes, and it's kind of an instrumental.' It never developed beyond that lyrically or with choruses or a melody. George thought we could do something with it and it became the instrumental parts one and two. Each had a different time signature. I always thought in the back of my mind they seemed cinematic; both of those pieces seemed like they could be used in a film of some kind—as a soundtrack for a dramatic moment. That never happened." A bit akin to "Miniature," the instrumental that begins *Holiday* and leads into "Tin Man," the *Hideaway* instrumentals evoke magic, excitement, action, and reflection. Reminiscent of a quality overture piece, "Hideaway Parts I and II" point to Dewey's compositional prowess. A master lyricist easily able to communicate ideas and their related emotions while simultaneously painting vivid scene pictures, Dewey forces the listener to just take in his musical offering in these instrumentals. The pieces possess beauty, palatable yet intriguing melodic turns, and inventive orchestrations that properly reflect a sense of drama.

"Letter," too, a Dewey contribution on *Hideaway*, points to his incredible sense of rhythm. This aligns with his Stephen Stills–esque rock 'n' roll vocal and how his composing often works off each song's rhythm rather than a traditional verse-chorus format. After all, so much of the "stellarity" of "Horse" stems from its driving acoustic guitar–fueled, chordal, rhythmic strumming. The melodic bass line of "Letter" combines with a catchy, funky, chordal strum to create the track's soundscape. Lyrically, the song highlights Dewey's aptness for empathizing with a woman's point of view. Presumably the protagonist has had her heart broken—caught her man cheating on her—and Dewey rearticulates her story in second person back to her, with the wish of "I hope you find some reason to be free." His narrator's desire is not to rail on the cheating guy, but to encourage the girl to realize her own personal power. Given the fact that Dewey is most often a propagator of peaceful philosophy, this vein of encouragement is not surprising.

While "Letter" may be slightly more of an "indoor song," "Amber Cascades" is most certainly an outdoors one. It is reminiscent of "Moon Song" in its celebration of nature, beautiful and inventive articulations of a variety of outdoor scenes, and encouragement of living an enjoyable life. However, "Amber Cascades" takes the song concept further by lacing it up with the band's shared philosophy of peace. The catchy chorus echoes the anti-war and anti-violence initiatives that the 1960s youth brought forward and that Dewey would make a recurring theme throughout his lifetime of composing. "We call to the man who walks on the water / We talk of a plan to stop all the slaughter in view / It's in view." Like Gerry in "Watership," with "I can feel there's better days," Dewey uses "Amber" to offer a ray of hope for society. He alludes to Jesus Christ but chooses to focus only on his peacemaker characteristic, steering clear of any notions of religiosity. The song's overall visual tale comes across as a gorgeous, somewhat trippy dream. Sonically, enthusiastic backup vocals from Gerry on the verses and the band's signature three-part harmonies laced throughout serve to render "Amber Cascades" as a high point of the trio's latter-day album cuts.

On *Hideaway* Dan is also concerned with the evolution of relationship complications. "Can't You See" and album single "Today's the Day" are optimistic and sonically comforting. Feeling the toll of consistent road life and all its ups and downs, Dan used his work on *Hideaway* to express his deepening connection with his wife, Catherine. He missed her, and as in his earliest songwriting era of "Rainy Day," he still drew on the feeling for creative inspiration. "Home, miles away from home / And there's no place I'd rather be. / Can't you see?" The tempo and melodics of the piece are slow, lovelorn, and wistful—as are those of "Today's the Day."

Upon its release, "Today's the Day" proved to be a minor hit for the group, reaching number twenty-three on the Singles chart and number one on the Adult Contemporary one. It is one of Dan's most romantic compositions, and is more along the lines of Gerry's romantic pieces, songs that transcend the specifics of their situations and become standards in their listener applicability. The song's instrumentation contributes enough of an upbeat swing, but at times it seems that the tempo is a hair too slow for its own good, almost dragging at certain moments. This would not detract from its hitdom, but it fell short of the *Hearts* achievements.

"I think we kind of plateaued a little bit," Dewey said. "Certainly if you look at the charts and the sales and so on, *Hideaway* was a marked downturn in the reaction. It's the old thing—when the public and the critics have gotten to know you virtually inside and out, you can't really get their attention much past that. And of course, as established as we were, there was a lot of competition. New bands were coming up. Things were changing. There were new sounds happening and we were still on our singer-songwriter sort of thing. It was doing what we did—writing these songs and arranging them. I think, in retrospect, that it was a wake-up call: the fact that everything you put out isn't necessarily going to be the next great thing." Even so, *Hideaway* would reach gold status and hit number eleven on the pop charts. It would be the last in the group's career to achieve metallic credentials.

On the bicentennial weekend of America the country's birth, America the band reached a pinnacle of live performance. July 3, 1976, found the group sharing a bill with Santana and one of their biggest musical influences, the Beach Boys, at Angel Stadium of Anaheim. "Those kinds of events always brought us together," Al Jardine of the Beach Boys explained. "It just worked. Because they [America] were so much in vogue, as we were kind of toward the end of our early career. They were just coming up, so they were a perfect act, and really nice guys—just made sense to work with them. They had so much going on, they had hit records, and we were not having hit records at the time—but we had a big career. So it kind of worked beautifully." Since Carl Wilson and Bruce Johnston's vocal appearances on *Hat Trick*, the two bands—America and the Beach Boys—had maintained a relationship of friendship and musical kinship. America looked up to them, and the Beach Boys appreciated and recognized their own artistic echoes in America's music. "They complement each other completely," Al Jardine articulated. "Gerry's voice is like fine golden thread, and Dewey has that amazingly thick, resonant voice which complements Gerry's other harmonics. Their voices are rich with tapestry." Decades later Al would ask Dewey and Gerry to contribute vocals to "San Simeon," a track on his 2010 solo album *A Postcard from California*. "There's nothing like having those two voices on a track that describes one of the most beautiful areas of California's coast," reflected Al.

In the audience at Anaheim in '76 were 55,000 people. A Henry Diltz photograph of America performing for the large crowd would forever capture the moment and would be included in the next album's poster photo collage. The weather that day was California perfect, and the immense crowd, particularly in the stadium's upper decks, would become so enthusiastic during America's performance that they would be encouraged to calm their fervor via warnings over the scoreboards. The "Horse" finale would be made all the more meaningful by the Beach Boys joining in. For America, the mega concert would be bookended by a July 2 Oakland performance and a July 5 Aloha Stadium performance in Hawaii. "Those are lifetime memories," Gerry reminisced. "It doesn't really get any bigger than that."

16

THE BEAST

America loved to conclude its national and global tours in Hawaii. They would play at the Honolulu International Center (HIC), now the Neal S. Blaisdell Center, and then, unwinding from the most recent wild tour, relax and recuperate in Maui or Kauai for a week or two. When the trio's newest album project was being planned, America figured, "What better place to record than Hawaii?" Especially after the hardships suffered during the freezing Colorado sessions, the band was ready to work in paradise. As George Martin had once again signed on to produce the latest America project, his penchant for destination recording was still in practice. Somewhere that felt good and comfortable, somewhere isolation would not become a problem.

Be careful what you wish for.

Building a recording studio and surrounding complex out of a rented property in Kauai proved to have the opposite effects on the band and its posse from those of the *Hideaway* experience. By this time in the America saga, in November 1976, the traveling troupe had grown some. Buffalo-based keyboardist and saxophonist Jimmy Calire and percussionist Tom Walsh had joined. And they were all at the compound for the recording experience, along with David Dickey, Willie Leacox, Geoff Emerick, and George Martin.

The compound on Kauai, funded by a generous Warner Brothers allowance, was paradise manifest. America rented half a dozen houses on a beautiful stretch of Poipu Beach. A mobile unit of Los Angeles' Record Plant was shipped over and a studio was constructed on the largest prop-

George Martin, America, and John Hartmann on Kauai during the *Harbor* sessions. *Courtesy of Henry Diltz.*

erty. Guitar tech and soon-to-be lead guitarist Michael Woods lived and worked out of this building; George Martin and Geoff Emerick shared another, the frequent site of celebrity visits throughout the recording process. Jimmy Webb and Art Garfunkel both made appearances. "At this point George Martin was an attraction for everybody in any field of the business. His legacy with the Beatles was always a dominant factor," explained Dewey. Henry Diltz, too, was flown in to document the *Harbor* period.

"There were so many distractions that it was very hard to just focus on making the record," Gerry recalled. "We were all chartering helicopters all over the island." Being a nature enthusiast, Dewey was enthralled at living and recording in Kauai. He had always wanted to learn scuba diving and now had the chance to. The entire band became heavily involved in the scuba diving initiative. Private instruction was held every morning at the compound's saltwater pool. "I agree that there were a lot of distractions," reflected Dewey. "While we all were dedicated to making the record, we did cut corners." Sometimes it seemed that the recording sessions for *Harbor* had to be squeezed into island activities and general revelry, rather than the other way around. It was a culmination of the high life of partying that had been steadily growing along with America's commercial success and that of many late-1970s lifestyles.

America's constant, large-scale international touring had led their operation to lease a Vickers Viscount N306 airplane to use for private band transport. It was yet another piece of proof that the band had achieved and was trying to maintain a lofty level of material success. When other rock bands toured with them, like fellow '70s-era favorite Poco, they too would occasionally join America on the plane. "We did a lot of touring together," Poco bassist and singer Timothy B. Schmit remembered. "I became so friendly with those guys. Sometimes they would headline, and sometimes we would, usually in Europe. America was bigger than us in the States, and we were kind of equal in Europe at the time. I pretty much always stayed and went up to sing on the encore with them. The Poco-America combination as a show was probably ideal. Poco never got to that level, where we could lease a plane. They invited me to fly with them if I wanted, so I spent a lot of time with them." Timothy would make appearances on many of America's '80s and '90s studio albums too. Following his long run with Poco, in 1977 he joined the Eagles, a band that in its earliest days had introduced America to a high-stakes card game, appropriately titled Eagle Poker. For a while America played

Eric Clapton, Dewey, and Chris Hillman. *Courtesy of the Bunnell family.*

rounds of it after each evening's performance. "It was a guts kind of game," percussionist Tom Walsh reflected. "So if you chose to go in, either you won the pot or matched the pot. The pots would get up to $1,000 or something. We had these little IOU sheets, bits of paper. After a while, I thought it was their [Gerry, Dan, and Dewey's] way of putting a little more money on the table (for the other band members) because they tended to lose. Then their manager [John Hartmann] said, 'You guys either have to get better at poker or quit playing.' And they started getting good at it; then it was no fun, so the game kind of petered out. We had a big game once at the Watergate Hotel. I lost three hands in a row, and I spent the whole rest of the tour just playing cards, you know, trying to win back my money. Those were the days. We were all crazy." Also at the Watergate game were Chris Hillman, who was opening the America tour for a season, along with co-Byrds Gene Clark and Roger McGuinn, and Eric Clapton, who had come to see the Byrds play. To this day, Dewey has an IOU sheet from Clapton, reading "$200, E.C.," for which he has not yet been paid.

Dewey's most intriguing composition on *Harbor* had been written on the heels of a necessary tour cancellation the group had made the year before. And it was also a personal reaction to the residue of the 1960s counterculture, which was becoming increasingly difficult to locate. Dewey, one who always identified with this philosophical camp, felt disappointed and estranged.

"Are You There" would be Dewey's callout to his fellow hippies as to whether they were still invested in the philosophy of peace and the lifestyle of love. "I was always, or thought I was, a child of the '60s. I loved the whole Woodstock generation, and I felt like I was part of that. And it was dimming a bit." He was dealing with coming-of-age realizations of the rock-star lifestyle. The canceled America tour had happened a year earlier, but the trio still felt the decision's sting. It had been the usual album support tour, this time for *Hideaway*. And it was canceled after just a few shows due to band fatigue. Dan had all but lost his voice, and all of America's members felt the toll that frequent post-show celebrations had taken. "The day we lost our voice with little choice, I can't explain / An act of agony," the lyrics went. The need to cancel a large-scale tour, and thus disappoint fans who had purchased tickets, sponsors who had put up funding, venues that had been booked, and John Sebastian of the Lovin' Spoonful, who had set aside the block of time to tour with America as a supporting act, seemed to the trio as a sign of temporary failure. Confirmation that it was not perfect and did not have a perfect career. That it was mortal and capable of falling from its lofty heights.

Dewey's song's question also went out to his fellow bandmates, asking whether their original, innocent intentions and desires to be artists, to be musicians, were still innocent. Almost like a cry out to the echo of America's initial incarnation, asking whether that character and image could still be found. So much had happened in a few short years, so much had changed. It seemed that the chinks in the band's armor were finally starting to show. And it was unclear as to what would happen next—if the status quo of albums, tours, and success could be maintained. "We made a cry to the underground / Are you there / I looked and saw that they were still around / But do you care." Dewey's heart was still in the peace, love, and rock 'n' roll ethos, and he only hoped that the hearts of his fellow hippie-minded friends and fans were too, even amid the decade's increasing malaise. This wonder and mystery are appropriately echoed in the song's moody chord changes and choppy guitar strums through the verses. As Dan's and Gerry's background vocals echo each of Dewey's Are you there?'s, the listener can't help but feel he is listening to a dialogue of three friends, trying desperately to hold on to what brought them together in the first place.

Gerry, too, at the time of *Harbor*, seemed to occupy a similar emotional room to Dewey's.

"Monster" may be the best song that Gerry Beckley ever wrote. A lifelong believer of the "write ten songs to get two good ones" composer philosophy, he would always be a songwriter's songwriter. And the somewhat dark-horse "Monster" would serve as beautiful evidence of this belief.

It was a regal and terrible dragon roaring, hoarding its gold to keep others from getting it—all fangs and fiery breaths. All of us are well acquainted with this beast. But some have many dealings with it.

His song's character took him exactly where he swore he'd never be: where his ego, more often than not, was running the show. Twenty-something rock stars, who'd become world famous as young teens and now were beginning to come to terms with the adults they had grown into, were learning massive lessons. They spent hours keeping their own personal monsters at bay, the monsters that had accompanied fame and fortune.

On an album that showcases its own near overproduction, "Monster" is a black sheep of a track. Just an acoustic guitar with some simple chords in waltz three-quarter time—a meter Gerry rarely used—with some added three-part harmonies here and there. The recording is stark, and Gerry's songwriting style, which always seemed to be open to the addition of sonic accoutrements, here resists the temptation to build up and out.

"The monster exposed himself from underground." The part of the self that Gerry's character-narrator always tried to keep hidden has been tempted forward by the sirens of success. "Heart, court and harmony just ain't the same, my black and their green playing some games." The old and familiar ways and methods of Gerry's character, of his mining the heart for song material and his group's harmonic arranging of this material, were no longer special to him. The luster had been lost. The darkness of self-loathing and the avarice of bandmates and friends and lovers took over.

"These are the things that you'll never do," instructs the chorus, seeming to detail a flashback of a self-to-self warning of pre-success Gerry: "Feeding the wife on the phone." Lying, taking advantage of trust of another and, in the process, hurting the self most of all, by disappointing. Now alone. Successful, talented, but self-feared to be a potential fraud, an impostor of good fortune, the person he'd worried he could become all along. "Running away from your home" is given as another thing that the song's narrator insists "you'll never do," but is exactly what Gerry's character has done. Being eternal Air Force children at their cores, America was well acquainted with the practice of running away. And home, always difficult to pin down as a literal place, was also becoming increasingly fuzzy as a metaphorical place for the trio.

What's most interesting about this song is how it seemed to fit the perceptions and perspectives of all three band members. Even more than the group's many love songs and nature-appreciation songs, "Monster" spoke the bright truth of what the trio had lived. And what's more, the song's resonance stemmed from far beyond its band source. It was relatable for any other rock musician in the late 1970s who struggled to cope with the threat of alienation from his own authenticity, the currency he had used to get him to his pinnacle. And perhaps, too, the song struck a chord with the listening public of 1977 who worried, on levels of varying depth, that it had wandered too far from its hippie dream of the 1960s—

that it had gone commercial, gone dark, gone robotic. That it had forgotten. Became a monster.

Years later amid periods of self-reflection, Gerry would wonder if his songs on *Harbor* would have fared better under less production. Songs like "Sarah" and "Sergeant Darkness," would be among his best and most underrated compositions. "Sarah" was right out of Gerry's "Broken Hearts Club," a lovelorn number full of grandiose emotions with grandiose orchestrations to match. Flowery string arrangements by George Martin brought to mind those of the great Gordon Jenkins on America pal Harry Nilsson's *A Little Touch of Schmilsson in the Night* (1973). Listening to Gerry's character-narrator sing "Sarah" is akin to viewing a Fred Astaire or Gene Kelly MGM musical character soliloquy—hands in pockets, singing aloud to the audience in an attempt to discover just where he went wrong with his girl. The lyrics' lingo, which includes "Golly Dad, she was the best thing that I ever had," possess a certain air of nostalgia for '50s Americana *Leave It to Beaver*–esque living, also present in Bruce Johnston's classic "Disney Girls 1957" (*Surf's Up*, 1971).

Part of the *Harbor* recording experience on Kauai included the making of a mini-documentary film. Warner Brothers contracted America's manager John Hartmann to make it. A luau, some inter-band discussions, and several live studio recordings are captured in it. George Martin and Geoff Emerick can be seen walking around the compound and working with the trio in the studio. George reflected: "The idea of recording out here struck me as a pretty adventurous one when we started out. We had recorded in remote locations before, of course, but never without a studio. I think that all in all, the results have been absolutely exceptional. I think it gave the boys a tremendous freedom, working in a location like this. It contributed something much more than we really expected.

"Critics often harp on America's so-called lack of identity, which is about the worst thing that can be said of them at any time," George continued. "But for my part, this freedom, the fact that they can do so much different material all the time is in fact a tremendous asset. This gentle ballad of Gerry's ["Sarah"] displays a tremendous emotional honesty. And I don't think there are many people who can come up with a lovely song as this."[1]

"Sergeant Darkness" finds Gerry's character-narrator in a state of light, having come from darkness, and in terrible fear of the darkness returning. The overall mood of the song is therefore tentative. The darkness in question here is twofold: it is literal, speaking to Gerry's lifelong predicament of insomnia, and it is also metaphorical, representing fear of loss and misunderstanding.

The beginning verse articulates gratitude, first seemingly to another person and then to the sun. Giving thanks to the morning that has arrived, that the night has passed, and that sleep is no longer a requirement. "Thank the morning for bringing you / Hope you never turn your head and run," indicates an insecurity toward the status quo, almost as though the speaker senses impending change. "What it [the darkness] does to me isn't good to see," mirrors the sentiments expressed in "Monster." Ego-derived elements had surfaced amid the band dynamic and decided to stay. "Start a battle, who's the first to fall / Hope it isn't me / Have to wait and see." The fate of America's future during this period seemed very up in the air. Musical times were changing, disco threatened, the '80s loomed. How long could the trio stay on top? How many more number ones were possible? "Should I live with rain and then the sky will clear?" Gerry's song concludes. It was raining in America, but how long would it last?

The song's melodics are haunting and beautiful, full of trepidation, and the recording's arrangement is packed with emotion. The opening verses are delicately presented, but as the track progresses, fullness reigns. An electric guitar solo brings the musical story to its climax.

Years later Dan would feel the song may have been directed toward him during the *Harbor* era, articulating the potential complications of their deep friendship. Interestingly enough, Gerry had composed and demoed "Sergeant" in between America's *Hat Trick* and *Holiday* albums, placing its origins timeline to long before the trio went through such a period of reevaluation and transition as they did during *Harbor*.

"Kauai is more a state of mind than a place," Dewey reflected in the *Harbor* documentary. "The beauty of it and the feeling of being present in another time, all that changes you. I can definitely feel the effects that the islands have had on me personally, and I know what it's meant to our music. It's like home, even though you've never been there before."[2] His song "Down to the Water," the album's concluding track, resonates as a more mature, yet vaguer, "Ventura Highway" in its all-is-well, "Take It Easy" message. Yet this feel-good tune is less concerned with movement, with progression, with getting somewhere else. It is self-contented: "The weather's fine / And everything's all right / So let's go down to the water tonight," are the song's recurring phrases. It seems the perfect sonic backdrop for the band's *Harbor* living experience on Kauai—its scuba diving lessons, celeb visitations, and luaus. "Down to the Water" is a party track. And its most powerful musical moment occurs when Gerry complements Dewey's verses with an easy, beautiful harmony typical of the group's sound: interesting that the verses' vocals on the album's final song are dominated by a duo sound—the same duo sound that would, from that album moment on, define America the band. "Though they swear they won't ever break up," a March 1977 *Rolling Stone* article by Leonard Lueras covering the *Harbor* sessions states, "the future of America seems as unsettled as the winter surf off the Kauai estate's lava beachfront."[3]

Harbor would be released in February 1977 and reach number twenty-one on the U.S. *Billboard* charts—a remarkable achievement in and of itself, but a let-down for the band who had established itself upon consistent hits. And it would be the group's last album with Dan Peek.

"When we finish producing an album, even in a place as beautiful as Kauai, there's both a sense of accomplishment and a sense of sadness," Gerry expressed in the *Harbor* documentary. "We are no longer part of the process, we are part of the product. Our feelings are shared with the universe."[4]

17

THE SPLIT

It was the most difficult thing.

They loved each other. They had been best friends since "teenagerdom." They had become successful, talented, famous together. They had become America together. Had they not cared about each other so much, the whole breakup thing would have been easier.

"I had reached my crossroads," Dan explained in his memoir. "I knew now that one more hit record, one more sold out tour, one more glowing review or screaming fan was not the answer. One more or a thousand more, it didn't matter. Another mansion, another sports car, another whatever, I was still a black hole looking to be filled up. No amount of money, fame, drugs, adulation, success or accomplishment could fill that void."[1]

It was difficult too because everyone was partying, enjoying themselves. Dan wasn't alone. He recalled, "Success or failure, the spectre of death seemed to hang over the industry like a storm cloud."[2] The financially abundant 1970s rock-pop scene flaunted every kind of narcotic and cocktail a person could contemplate. If you had the money, you could get it. And the industry had the money. America had the money. Drugs and alcohol were around, and the entire band and their heavyweight musical colleagues were all exposed to them. They played the same shows, they were part of the same scenes. But where Gerry and Dewey and the rest of America seemed to be able to enter and exit most scenes when and where they wished to, Dan wasn't. He could get sucked in. And for a time, for him, the high of substances reigned supreme over the high of music. Where Gerry and Dewey could socialize, then get onstage in whichever city they were and supply a quality audience-satisfying performance, Dan couldn't always. By 1977 he couldn't really do both.

Then he wasn't happy. Then because of that, Gerry and Dewey and the rest of the band weren't happy either. Then it became complicated.

Dan's contributions to the *Harbor* album had been pretty great. "Slow Down" had been a fun disco number. "Don't Cry Baby" and "These Brown Eyes" had been romantic gems and served as stellar examples of Dan's songwriting talents. "Hurricane," though, would be the most indicative of Dan's emotional state regarding his and his band's career trajectory. "How long will the wind blow? Everybody talks; nobody really knows." Dan pushed for "Hurricane," with its upbeat tempo and fun flavor, to be the album's single. But George Martin and Warner Brothers nixed it in favor of "God of the Sun."

The *Harbor* sessions were fun for America; their time in Kauai was enjoyable and sometimes therapeutic. And there was plenty of festive intake to go around. But Dan would frequently stay up all night and have to be put to bed in the morning, only to wake up at the end of the band's working day. The trio's schedules no longer jibed. "Dan would wake up at five or six in the evening as we were wrapping it up," Gerry recalled. "He'd try to get up to speed and get on board. We ended up with his catchphrase, because he always used to say, 'I really want to hear that!' If we'd said what we did that day, and he of course had missed it. It just summed up many of the things that were a part of pulling apart the fabric, which obviously was well under way by that time."

Through the history of popular art, so many success stories rode the hills and valleys of insecurity and confidence, waging the battle against the ego-dragon within. "You don't get to test the waters of that particular challenge unless you get there," reflected Gerry. So many would face difficulty in trying to make sense of their past obscurity when confronted with their present cultural recognition. For some, it was difficult to cope. And substances made it easier.

"For a while Dan was kind of in a sorry state," pal Bill Mumy reflected. "You know everybody had their '70s experiences with alcohol, drugs, and different things. I mean it was that era, everybody had their toes dipped in different waters. And I completely understand, and understood at the time, why Dan needed to take a break or leave the band. It was pretty clear to me. Because Dewey and Gerry, regardless of whatever they were imbibing, they were both always capable of getting up in front of the Greek Theater or wherever it might be—here's 6,000 people—and playing a good set and singing a good set. It never, that I ever saw, affected Dewey's or Gerry's ability to do their job. Whereas with Dan, sometimes it did."

"It was all lunacy at the time, and it was mostly drugs and alcohol—probably drugs more than alcohol," guitarist Wood-z reflected on the 1977 rock scene. "There was always one guy who was the most . . . far from reality, it seemed like. And at that point in time Dan was that guy. And it seemed like after Dan left, there was a while where that thing took over. . . . To me, it was like there was this phantom thing that kept infecting different people."

When Dan returned home after the Hawaiian *Harbor* sessions in November '76, to the luxurious Malibu property that he shared with Catherine, he wanted a fresh start for his lifestyle. He had tried several times in the past to break away from dependency on drugs and alcohol. He'd also spent two years abstaining from drinking, directly following his hepatitis C outbreak. But lately, the grandeur of his beautiful beach home and the opulent lifestyle that it suggested egged Dan on to keep his excess going. America's constant touring also did this for him, making it difficult for him to separate overindulgence from his rock 'n' roll performing. Dan tried to take advantage of the health-forward lifestyle that was also prevalent in 1970s Los Angeles, pursuing vegetarianism and exercise regimens. But it didn't quite stick.

The entire Peek family, who still remained tight-knit, also got the feeling there was trouble in paradise. "We took a family vacation out to California to visit Dan when he was still in America, about a year or so before he left the band. We could sense that he was really having some challenges. And then I remember a phone call that Dan made to my parents, the gist of which was, 'Please pray for me. . . . I'm wondering if maybe it's not a bad idea to get out of the band. Pray that I make the right decision.' I remember we were really concerned about that, and not necessarily sorry that he was considering leaving the band—although that was sad. I think the importance was for his well-being. Eventually he did leave and then went on to pursue another track."

Soon an accident would push Dan to turn his life around. After one particularly intense night of partying, he fell off a forty-foot cliff by his home and ended up in the hospital, only to join the rest of the band on tour a few days later. This near-miss, which almost cost him his life, drove him to return to his religious roots: he was moved to become a born-again Christian. Dan wanted a second chance for his life happiness, and this was the best way, in his view, to arrive there. He spent a month-long vacation with family in Missouri, acclimating to his spiritual enlightenment.

Dan had first been saved at age twelve, just as his mother had been. The family studied the gospel together. "I remember my mother, when I did get saved . . . said, 'Son, if ever at any time, you wander away from Jesus, he will always take you back. He will always take you back!'"[3] Dan recalled.

"At an early age, Dan did have a personal kind of encounter with the Lord," his brother David described. "As a young boy he had been influenced by my mother and grandmother, with their strong Midwestern-Baptist upbringing." When Dan faced addiction-related struggles during his late America years, the Peek family wondered if Dan's interest in substances was a way of seeking out pleasure and relief from the long-held, traumatic effects of his childhood illnesses. And they hoped he would find a way back to his place of light.

"I think that there was a clear history of a kind of a Baptist family upbringing," Gerry recalled. "And so as he would get a little more . . . extended in his life and emotionally frail and stuff, we would start to see these elements of 'Well, the Bible says . . . ,' but it wasn't out of the blue.

"It had been coming and going as part and parcel of his wrestling match with himself and with substance abuse. He was putting it in as a possible counterweight and a source of inspiration and then losing that battle, I think, for quite a few years. But he clearly didn't push the big button and dive in until after he left. I think that [for] him, leaving the band was the final kind of thing. And I think that's what pushed it into a far deeper relationship. And within a year or so he was starting to appear at the 700 Club and Christian shows and stuff."

When he returned to Los Angeles, America began rehearsing for its next tour. Though there was tension amid the trio and their slowly diverging paths of artistic and lifestyle intention, things remained pretty professional. The rest of the band was largely unaware that dramatic change was to come. The keeping up of appearances was a testament to the integrity of Dewey, Gerry, and Dan. "Everything was fine," Tom Walsh recalled. "Any time you have a band like that—I'm sure there was tension, but there was nothing really dramatic. Everybody was doing their job. In a lot of ways I just look at it like Dan made the choices he made to live his life the way he wanted to live it. It just became untenable for them to keep it going all together and making different choices."

The rest of the band, too, was seeking to "healthify." Nonstop touring and traveling, coupled with nonstop celebrating in between, had run the whole troupe ragged. Dan's new and dramatic spiritual outlook did not exactly fall in line with the band's modus operandi, but since everyone concerned was up for some self-improvement, it kind of meshed with the new initiative.

Rehearsals would be held in Hollywood at SIR Rehearsal Studios, and would be of the early morning variety, in sharp contrast to rock 'n' roll's usual night-owl-ness. But Dan found that the rush-hour commute from his home in Malibu took hours both ways. The predicament stressed him out intensely, and he once more retreated to drugs to cope. When he was a no-show at the following day's session, everyone got the gist.

Just like that, Dan was out of America.

It was for the best for everyone, it seemed at the time. Dan wanted to get clean, to detoxify from lifestyle poisons, to explore the possibilities that his newly connected religious focus could offer him. And, it seemed at the time, that he could not achieve this successfully while remaining a member of America the band—while remaining within the very life that had driven him into inner conflict and bodily abuse.

For a time, Dan's behavior had been "tolerated," John Hartmann recalled. "I mean, you know—this is one of the great three-part harmonies of all time. If you look at the artists that Hartmann & Goodman managed, that was our specialty. We had Poco, Peter, Paul and Mary, Crosby, Stills & Nash, America. I mean, these are the great three-part harmony bands of all time. And so we put up with a lot of Dan's stuff for a long time." The band knew that if the idea of breaking up was introduced to John, that he "would do everything humanly possible to preclude that from happening. I was not going to go along with that and blow that three-part harmony. So I didn't find out about Dan's firing until it was a fait accompli. At that point, what can you do?"

"We did have a sit down when the final thing came, when he finally left," Dewey remembered. "It was a mutual thing. We sat down up at Gerry's house, with our manager at the time, John Hartmann." Colonel Peek, who had some business background, made the trip out to LA for the transitional meetings, supporting and helping his son. "By then it had gotten out of the central core. His family knew that this was going to happen, he was going to be leaving. He wanted to. It was still a bombshell for the public, and for the record label, and we were still with Warner Brothers at that point. And we never looked back."

"In a sense it was a huge sacrifice on the part of Dewey and Gerry, to disintegrate the core of the band, and certainly the public image of the band as a trio, in essence to save Dan's life," John reflected.

Lawyers and business managers on all sides were called in to sort out the paperwork. Contracts and limited business partnerships connecting the trio all had to be sorted. Dan could have insisted on claiming usage but decided that he would no longer attach himself to or use the band's name. He wanted a new beginning for himself, and a chance to redefine his personal and musical identities. In the spirit of the trio's original intentions when they started their group, Dan's third of royalties for his work would remain the same.

"The actual day—there was physically a day when that happened, up at Gerry's house," Dewey remembered. "There was no real begging, pleading. All that had kind of happened. It had been, 'All right, I'll get it together, don't worry.' That part was done. It was a done deal kind of, and it was just a matter of formalizing it. Then there were some attorneys involved, Dan relinquished his ties to the name. All that 'who owns the names stuff,' you hear about that all the time to this day. Different artists who somehow wrangled the name of their band, and then you could go out as that person. So that was an immediate need and there was no argument there. That was kind of emotional, for me. I really do remember getting choked up. 'Gee, the three musketeers, this is it.'"

Dan and his ways that had become wild, were now gone from the band. He had come in with his impressive guitar playing that had first wowed Gerry and crowds at London Central High's Battle of the Bands. He had developed his songwriting to demonstrate a myriad of genre and subject matter compositional abilities. And he had helped to define the sound of America the band, with his easy, high harmony. Though the entire group was exposed to the substance-laden rock scene of the 1970s, Dan cleaved to it most, choosing to include substance intake in his definition of what being a rock musician meant at the time. His role's journey in America would in part resemble that of rock 'n' roll music and what happened to it during those same years, the early to mid-'70s. It had begun with an earnest love of the music, and raw talent, and a philosophical embracing of the previous decade's hippie counterculture's peace and love. And it ended with an overattachment to artificial highs and a detachment from the mission of music. By the conclusion of his time in the band, Dan had rejected Gerry's belief in "tuning in," and his respect for the recording studio, by his unavailability to participate in key *Harbor* sessions and choosing to forgo group rehearsals at SIR. And he had been driven to ruffle the feathers of Dewey's preference for peace, no longer completely on board with the group's mission of creating quality, communicative, and successful music together. When Dan left, he took a part of America's rock 'n' roll spirit with him.

When the idea of replacing Dan's position in the band was proposed, Gerry and Dewey chose not to—even with rumors of Poco's Timothy B. Schmit being a potential successor (he soon joined the Eagles). To them, America was a trio formed in ardent, youthful friendship and mutual love for music. Its essence would always be that of the original trio. "The band was such a deep thing for us," Gerry articulated. "We'd gone to high school together. To try and throw somebody into the mix or audition people. . . . There was no Bruce Johnston [of the Beach Boys] waiting around to fill the spot."

"We were not breaking up the band, that was not the deal," Dewey explained. "And we made a conscious decision to say 'we can't replace Dan. We're not going to go looking.' Because whatever that position was, Dan Peek, Gerry Beckley, and Dewey Bunnell—that was an organic relationship. That Dan seat can't be filled: that chair is pulled away now that no one's sitting in it. And Gerry and I were in the other two chairs."

Part III

You Can Do Magic

18

THE DUO

Gerry and Dewey would go on together, and America would be a duo from then on. Guitar Man Dan was now gone, so in an attempt to replace the main instrumental lines in America's songs, both Gerry and Dewey—themselves well-and-able guitar players—would alternate serving as lead guitarist for the band.

The band's contract with Warner Brothers was still outstanding. They had yet to record a live album. They set out to arrange the execution. America had a three-night-appearance scheduled for the end of July 1977 at the Greek Theatre in Los Angeles. It was determined a perfect opportunity for the live recordings. America wanted George Martin to creatively spearhead as usual—but George Martin was not available. His tax situation in 1977 was complicated. He resided in a beautiful home in the Bird Streets of Los Angeles, but for the time being, due to visa and work permit problems, he was prohibited from performing in the United States.

America had very recently been involved in the soundtrack production of *Casey's Shadow*. The film, released in 1978, was directed by Martin Ritt and starred Walter Matthau as a struggling horse trainer given a chance to make it big with his family's black sheep of a star horse. The film score was done by none other than Elmer Bernstein, who held claim to the recognizable scores of *The Ten Commandments*, *Sweet Smell of Success*, *The Magnificent Seven*, and *To Kill a Mockingbird*, among countless others. Elmer and America ultimately severed ties with Ritt's film, but they stayed in touch. When George Martin was unable to conduct America's orchestra for the live album recording, Gerry and Dewey selected Elmer Bernstein to conduct. Much of the work for America's *Live* album was already done via George Martin's current orchestral arrangements; George would serve as producer and arranger of the *Live* album and Elmer was enthusiastic. And a three-night run would allow America room for editing and mixing different sections and performances. At the time, Dan had only been gone for two months. America the duo was still finding its footing.

As their performing career proved to possess a decades-long lifespan, America would become a fan of symphony shows, choosing to include at least one in every year's concert schedule. But at first the experience of putting their own guitar-based pop songs to orchestral backings took some getting used to, particularly for the natural and effortlessly authentic performer Dewey. The band had done some orchestral shows with George Martin the year before, in a few Hollywood Bowl performances. But these Greek Theatre dates were different—minus Dan and George. "The orchestra thing was all new to me and very intimidating, it always has been," reflected Dewey. "It's gotten more comfortable over the years. It's powerful, and hard to describe having them behind you—especially hearing your own music with the orchestra, with the symphony. It's fantastic. These are schooled musicians. It's really a world away from strumming tunes on your guitar in your bedroom."

The live album concluded the band's contract with Warner Brothers Records, though it did not achieve outrageous commercial success. *Live* was released in October 1977 and hit 127 on the *Billboard* charts, the lowest of the band's numbers up until that point.

Gary Davis, head of promotions at Warner Brothers and a consistent fan of America, had recently been fired from the label. Replacement Russ Thyret was not a constant fan of America, and so John took this opportunity to take America to Capitol Records for its next recording contract. "Warner Brothers saw the act as in decline," manager John Hartmann explained. "And they didn't really care about re-signing them very much. So I made a deal with an A&R guy at Capitol Records: a Brit, Rupert Perry—who really valued the band and got them twice as much money. It's not a normal deal to leave your catalogue and go to another label, but I figured—these guys are going to be around a long time. They're gonna need to get well paid for their albums. And this is a way to ensure that they would have an enduring career." John had begun his industry career as assistant to Elvis Presley's career dictator Colonel Tom Parker, whose main management advice to John had been, "Build duration into the act." This advice had been in the back of John's mind when he negotiated America's label move to Capitol.

For the past year Gerry and Dewey had alternated between playing lead guitar parts during live performances, trying to emulate Dan's guitar sound. Both of them talented players themselves, they still felt another lead guitarist was needed for the band. "Dewey is the king of doing a lot with a little," Matt Beckley, Gerry's guitar-playing son, reflected decades later. "To me, that efficiency is the ultimate goal of anything: not trying to impress people, but to move people. Dewey has a unique right hand. He helped define the sound of an era, with those seventh chords of his. And my dad has this ability to seamlessly find the thread between chords and notes. I don't know if people realize what a gifted guitar player he is."

Dewey would never be a "gear guy" as far as guitars went, preferring the message to the medium. What he had in plentitude were unique creative ideas. His songs would come into existence regardless of their potential guitar solos and riffs. Gerry, on the other hand, thrived on the abundance of possibility that various guitar makes and brands could offer to the musician. With his producer's ear, he heard every nuance amid the change from a Gretsch to a Gibson. For years he played a heavy Gibson double neck, then the Ibanez Artwood twin, onstage—both of which helped him to reproduce certain multi-octave live renditions of America studio songs. But he would always be a Gretsch guy: "I love Gretsches. My entire collection is based on George Harrison and the Beach Boys." At least, until he found his Martin mahogany acoustic toward the end of the 2000s. From the early '90s onward, both Dewey and Gerry would be fans of Taylor guitars, Dewey favoring a pair of black 614e models.

The year 1978 saw the promotion of Michael Woods—who would always be known as Wood-z to his bandmates—from guitar tech to lead guitarist. The time had come to branch out. "They put the word out that they were going to have auditions," Wood-z recalled. "I talked to Gerry and said I wanted to audition. And then Gerry said something like, if I could get another guitar tech as good as me, then I could have the job. It was a Cinderella story for me. But it was part of their character too. They didn't want a big hassle of having a bunch of auditions and having to meet a new guy. They knew what I was like. They had been out with me on tours for a couple of years, and they knew I knew all the songs. They knew I could play and everything. So they just put me in there."

Wood-z was just what the band needed for its live performances. He was a stellar musician who could play any guitar lick ever, and he'd had plenty of experience playing for audiences during his years of bar band stints. Wood-z knew how to work a crowd, lending enthusiasm to every solo. Gerry and Dewey, who had always been fairly mellow and understated when it came to performing, appreciated this. Wood-z's love for music always showed. During his earliest days of touring with America, and beyond, he would go out of his way to find the best local bands and small clubs in every town and city they passed through—just to hear live music, absorb it, learn new things. Many times he would jam with the local players. Wood-z's guitar chops only increased.

"Dewey and I wanted to carry on," remembered Gerry. "We'd been doing a ton of shows every year, making albums. We were quite content—so we didn't have a choice—it just had to happen. But you then have to wrestle with the remains. Three people is a three legged stool; you can't have a stool with two legs. So there was a redefining of the dynamic that there was no way around."

There would be three co-writes by Gerry and Dewey on the latest album: "All Around," "Tall Treasures," and closing track "High in the City," all of which seemed to be sonic coagulations of Dewey's and Gerry's musical characters. "On *Silent Letter*, we did a lot of co-writing and tried to blur the lines so it wouldn't be quite as stark, wouldn't be a black song and a white song," Gerry explained. "High" was perhaps the most impressive in terms of complexity in composition. It sounds like a Los Angeles night-journey song, with its "Downtown"-esque excited-to-be-out-for-the-evening sentiment, but it achieves a greater grandeur via its use of two character-voices, performed by Dewey and Gerry. Dewey sings the main verses, depicting the person in motion, looking for a good time, wondering where it can be found: "Now I'm high in the city / Feel the evening air / The crowds in the city / Compete for a share / It's all so busy, a complete affair / Down here." And Gerry sings the bridges, offering another attitude in contrast to Dewey's character: "I know a place where we both can go / To set our hearts on fire / I know the city's the only show // Can I take you for a ride / I can make you satisfied / All in all it's worth your while / Change that frown back to a smile / Tonight." The melodics of Gerry's portion offer one of his warmest vocal deliveries in

Left to right: Tom Walsh, David Dickey, Dewey, Willie Leacox, Gerry, and Jimmy Calire. *Courtesy of Henry Diltz.*

terms of tone quality, complete with Beach Boys–inspired background harmonies. "High in the City" culminates in a meshing of the two vocal characters, alternating between the two and modulating musical keys to amp up the drama—with occasional interjection from a choir.

Dewey would forever refer to *Silent Letter*, released on June 15, 1979, as "Silent Record" for the neutral reception it received upon its release. George Martin had once again served as producer. Still, Dan's songwriter voice was notably missed. The band, and their loyal audience, tried to adjust to the updated sound. After all, pop music on the whole—always changing—sounded a bit different in '79 than it had in the early '70s. Punk, new wave, and disco had all carved niches for themselves—none of which were well suited to America's core harmonic, easygoing sound.

Silent Letter would come to stand as a high point in the band's discography, though they may not have been aware of it at the time. The duo's desire to confirm the fact that they—that the band—were fine as a duo resulted in a well-composed selection of songs with nuanced production. Without Dan's sometimes country-rock lilt, the new album assumed a character of utmost pop-ness, decorated here and there with a hard rock edge or jazzy accent courtesy of Dewey's "composerdom." The record would be recorded at L.A.'s Brittania Studios, and mixed in the spring of '79 at George Martin's Montserrat AIR Studios.

Silent Letter's opening track would be a cover, and it would be the opening track of the filmed 1979 concert in Central Park, becoming a classic America concert movie by Australian documentarian Peter Clifton. Showcasing Dewey's recognizable, timeless rock voice, "Only Game in Town" was a catchy track, with lyrics that served as metaphor—everyone was looking for love, and finders, keepers, losers, and weepers all ended their night with some kind of loot. The song choice, penned by Lewis Anderson, Julie Didier, and Casey Kelly, established a greater precedent for America, seeking outside songwriters for album material. Dewey would serve as lead vocalist for the track, ideally suited to the verses' image-heavy storytelling. The song's concept, one of unavoidable surrender to a lifestyle or structure already in place—"the only game in town"—was one way for America as it stood to express what it felt. A myriad of trials, complications, and mixed emotions ran rampant through the life of a musician, of a band—but it was that or nothing at all. And Gerry and Dewey were incapable of "nothing at all," of dropping out. So for them it would be the myriad.

Another performance featured in the Clifton film was that of another cover, and a quintessential West Coast pop track. "California Dreamin'"—a timeless Mamas and the Papas gem that America had recorded as part of a soundtrack project for John D. Hancock's beach party flick *California Dreaming*—had been released as the soundtrack album's single in March 1979. The B side was FDR's "See It My Way." "Dreamin'" would become a frequent live number for America's tours, with Gerry introducing it as a track the band wished it had written. After all, the composition oozed California-ness and pop ingeniousness, the two qualities that would come to dominate America's artistic identity. "Dreamin'" served as an ideal example of Gerry and Dewey's creative compatibility. It was a strength that had been present since the friendship's, and the group's, incarnation—but since Dan's departure it had become more pronounced. More impossible to ignore. The song cover featured Dewey on lead vocals, inherently "rockifying" the pop song, with Gerry on backup harmonies and piano accompaniment.

The artistic partnership of Gerry Beckley and Dewey Bunnell would prove to be one of the most successful in pop music history. America's identification, and sometime overidentification, with the concept of "the group"—their ability to work together, to compromise, to recognize the strengths and weaknesses of themselves and each other and maximize the effect of their elements to create a total product of Wow—was part of what made them great.

The song "1960" would be Gerry's standout composition on the album, an unintentional answer to his close friend, composer, and confidant Harry Nilsson's autobiographical "1941." A sensitive piano-based number, "1960" served as ardent wondering about what the future held for Gerry and his band. Its lyrics would be an early foray into nostalgia. Where "1941" would detail the story of Harry's origins and the life-altering, premature departure of his father, "1960" would articulate the idyllic memories of Gerry's youth and the uncertainties of his future. The track's bridge about Gerry's introspective thoughts at this time in his life and art is telling: "In the city of the lost and found / It's hard to get a break / Hard to stop from getting turned around / And make the same mistakes." Gerry felt that this album and moment in America's lifespan was a turning point. Dan had left the band, which was the decision of Dan alone. But Gerry and Dewey had been there the entire time; they had been exposed to the same temptations of indulgence and decay. Now that they both remained, they worried that they could fall victim to similar fates, sooner or later. And so "1960" was a declaration of Gerry's—and America's—intention to succeed as a musical act with staying power, with the ability to transcend fad, fashion, and decade. "My reputation's on the line / At the start of '79 / But like the sun, just watch me shine / Today."

* * *

Dewey's "One Morning" would seem to be a thematic continuation of earlier nature-pleasure songs like "Wind Wave," "Rainbow Song," and "Midnight." Encouraged by intricate orchestral production courtesy of George Martin, the track's chorus was a dramatic calling out to the audience along the lines of the one found in "Amber Cascades." "Are you going to see them on the mountain now / Goin' to see them trees / Goin' to watch the circles take a bow / Goin' to help agree / To be / Today," was "a cry out to the underground," another beckoning from Dewey to his like-minded friends who were also children of the '60s. "One Morning" found Dewey recognizing the magnitude and awe of nature's power, and reminding his listeners of the fact that this experience was also available to them. All was not lost. The outdoors was still magnificent and still deserved praise.

It would be one of the album's singles, Gerry's orchestrated ballad "All My Life," that proved to have the greatest staying power. Upon its release the song became a massive hit in Asia, one that would always be a setlist "must" for America's concerts there from that point onward. "All My Life" belongs in the category of Gerry's standard songs, those whose relatability and recognizable form made them easily coverable by other singers. A timeless love song, the track's lyrics articulate the sentiment of readiness to settle down after a time of searching, questioning, and sometime confusion. "There was a time, that I just thought / That I would lose my mind / You came along and then the sun did shine / We started on our way / I do recall that every moment spent / Was wasted time but then I chose to lay it on the line // I put the past away." The composition is a notable mark of maturity in Gerry's compositional lifespan, and it would be one of his most human and vulnerable expressions of love, of determination to make this relationship *The* relationship, *The One That Worked*. Like the most longevous of love songs, it is ardent and inspiring, and like the most successful of wedding songs, it makes monogamy sound appealing. "All My Life" would be a lifelong favorite of Wood-z, at whose wedding, decades later, Gerry would perform it.

One year prior to the release of *Silent Letter*, Gerry had a wedding of his own. He married Eleanor in 1978. The couple's son, Matthew Linford Beckley, was born on July 16, 1979, one month after the release of *Silent Letter*. Matthew's godfather would be Gerry and Dewey's close friend and musical colleague Jimmy Webb.

Silent Letter stalled at 110 on the *Billboard* album chart. It was the first studio album release since Dan Peek's departure. Despite the commercial disappointment, Dewey and Gerry were determined to make the new arrangement work. *Harbor*'s album cover had depicted a setting sun, an ending, a band with an identity in flux. But this latest one made it perfectly clear, with its two confident-looking faces: America had changed.

America was now Dewey and Gerry.

19

THE REASONLESS REJECTION

The opening track of America's latest album would be called "Survival." It would be a Gerry Beckley song. It would also be a true-to-life kind of thing. Like that of any pop group, the future of America—who was riding on its tenth anniversary—was uncertain. It was 1980 now. The decade had changed. The band was trying to survive.

The lyrics of "Survival" articulate a vow to succeed, to withstand any and all hardships that may arise, to survive—and though expressed through the words of Gerry's character-narrator, they could fit right in with the particulars of America's true story. "It's too late I know / to change the way we go / From this day on I want to stay on." The band's career had long ago been set in motion, in 1971, with the recording of the debut album and legacy-founding song "Horse with No Name." It had progressed and developed through the territory of successes, artistic and commercial. It had weathered management changes, record label switches, and the toils and final departure of a key member. In 1980 America was publicly declaring—via its new song—that it would not be banished from the music industry.

And it was trying to make its relationship with new label Capitol Records work—even though, commercially speaking, America had yet to reproduce its early success with Warner Brothers. It had yet to win the label over, to establish a strong rep in the new decade, to prove that it could be a successful '80s act, just as it had been a successful '70s act. *Silent Letter* had not fared extraordinarily well on the charts—its highest *Billboard* spot was 110—which only lessened the band's already diminishing commercial clout. So when America lobbied for "Survival" as their new album's new single, and Capitol didn't agree, America lost the fight. The label and band couldn't agree on *Alibi*'s sides A and B either, so they would be referred to—officially so—as "Our Side" and "Their Side." In a further attempt to break the mold of the established America machine, Gerry and Dewey would select a cover photograph taken by Henry Diltz—which featured neither Gerry nor Dewey but instead depicted an abandoned baby doll's head in Monument Valley. The band's official logo was also abandoned and replaced with a new design, done by a new art director, on the album cover.

* * *

For the single, Capitol chose one of the most intriguing America songs of its entire catalogue, a cover of a song penned by John Batdorf and Sue Sheridan. The label felt it was catchy—which it was, and that it had hit material written all over it. America had learned, through Warner Brothers' insistence in releasing "Horse" as a single and its discouragement in releasing "Muskrat Love" as a single—both of which it was completely right about—that the record company could be dead-on in selecting an album's seller song. So "You Could've Been the One," America's intriguing song, was selected.

It was intriguing mainly due to the lyrics' improbability factor. The Batdorf-Sheridan narrative, told and sung by Gerry on *Alibi*, articulated the tale of a guy who is turned down by "an angel out of place at this downtown devil's bar." He spends the rest of the song on the idea that she "could've been the one." The plot is pop song simple enough—but the way in which this girl turns down Gerry's character-narrator happens somewhat too quickly and without explanation. "Do you wanna dance girl / You said no thanks / And I watched you drift away // Well you had your chance / You could've been the one / Tonight you could've been the only one / For the rest of my life / I'll be dreamin' of you when this dance is done / Knowin' you could've been the one." The "no thanks" reply comes so soon that it almost seems the character-narrator is at a loss as to how best to respond to the rejection and move along.

The whole song is disarming and lacks narrative believability, which may in fact be the major reason for its lack of commercial or critical impact.

Alibi was the first America record, after a string of seven, that was not produced by George Martin. Everyone felt that the America–George

Martin creative journey was done. It had been pushed to its fullest potential, resulting in several top ten singles and albums, and many records sold. Even *Silent Letter* had been a bit of a push for the collaboration. Now in 1980, America wanted to change up their elements, to record more cover tunes than usual and enlist new producers.

"In general, whenever a new personality, be it a producer, a writer, has come into our story, usually it's Gerry who has reached out," Dewey explained. "That's what happened with Matt McCauley and Fred Mollin. I didn't know a lot about them. They had produced a song called 'Sometimes When We Touch,' a hit" recorded by Dan Hill in 1977. The track had reached number three on the *Billboard* Hot 100 chart.

McCauley and Mollin were essentially a tag-team of producers who worked very much as a duo. Gerry and Dewey had been in the market for a new producer setup for *Alibi* and McCauley and Mollin were present, available, and interested.

"For the most recent albums, George [Martin] was clearly in control," Gerry recalled. "Although Geoff Emerick as an engineer was vital to it, it wasn't a duo production—whereas Fred and Matt were really clearly a team."

Alibi's musicians did not include America's established touring band of Leacox, Dickey, Woods, Calire, and Walsh. Beckley and Bunnell were after a studio sound here and they intended to rely upon the wealth of Los Angeles' top studio players of 1980. The album would be recorded in several local studios.

"*Alibi* was a great and interesting record," Gerry recalled, "because it was the first time we had put together a band of L.A.'s hot session guys. Waddy Wachtel, Dean Parks, and Steve Lukather. And Lee Sklar on bass, Mike Baird on drums for most of it." *Alibi* would once again be a highlight in the songwriting careers of Gerry and Dewey, presenting ballads and rockers that would prove the band's longevity factor.

"Coastline," in both song lyric material and overall soundscape, would be the Beach Boys–iest composition that America would ever produce. Written and sung by Gerry, the song would lyrically reference specific geographical locations in Southern California ("I head down Sunset north to Santa Barbara") and musically reference late-'70s Beach Boys albums *Sunflower* and *Surf's Up* in its instrumentation and sophisticated compositional transitions. Dennis Wilson's innovative gem "All I Wanna Do," as well as Gerry's favorite Beach Boys composition of all time "'Til I Die" both received artistic echoes in "Coastline."

The track's opening introduces Gerry's character-narrator as deciding to exercise his California "car-dom" and take a leisurely drive out by the coastline. "I drive to the coastline / Looking for visual pleasures to catch my eye / The sun turns around hits me on the shoulder / I fly away." The lyrics establish an independent voice. "I could live in the walls of a prison / Where the warm summer winds would never blow / Then again, think of what I'd be missing (as to the other side) / And how some do it I'll never know, I'll never know." The song's narrator insists upon living beyond the bonds of self-imposed imprisonment. It is almost as though the love that he has—for his woman, his friends, his world, anything—acts as a tether. But the tether is worth keeping.

Gerry explained, "The Beach Boys built a lovely studio down in Santa Monica. And so when they did *15 Big Ones*, and when Dennis [Wilson] was doing *Pacific Ocean Blue* I spent a lot of time down there with them. I'm on some of those Beach Boys albums. But I just remember it starting to color my approach. You know, these kinds of four-four chords, and Brian (Wilson) would always move the bass notes around with the left hand and stuff. So 'Coastline' is clearly a kind of Beach Boy-esque thing."

Dewey's "Might Be Your Love" and Gerry's "Right Back to Me" would showcase a jangly guitar sound reminiscent of the Byrds' Roger McGuinn's work. Dewey's composer contributions to *Alibi* were at once true to character and identity expanding. "Catch That Train" is a fast-moving track along the lines of earlier piece "Ventura Highway," with movement and angst built right into it. Dewey's Kerouac influences in his lyrics were impossible to neglect. "'Catch That Train' is another in this long line of songs that when I began writing a new song, I reached into that whole sort of moving, outdoor, 'trains,' the visuals of that—going somewhere and nomads seeking. I know it's important to me, in my own bubble world when I write. A song where the lyric is expressing some drive, some need, some phrase that's . . . always in motion. It's like life: it's always in motion, it's always moving somewhere, there's a continuum."

This track, though, would be composed with assistance from Gerry. "A lot of times I would come with fully formed song lyrics and verses and choruses, and it always seemed to need a bridge," Dewey said. "A lot of the time, especially in the early days, if there was a co-write with Gerry, it usually meant he'd helped me with that middle eight—eight bars of a bridge. I was no good at that, Gerry was always good for that part. He could find a transitional chord from the end of the last chorus."

"Hangover" would be a relatable song, in its literal depiction—and catchy musical rhythmics—of the aftermath of a fun night of drinking. A trademark Dewey rocker that showcased the star quality of his voice. JD Souther, Richard Page, and Timothy Schmit would all lend background vocals to the track. Dewey would always be a talented lyrics writer, and he showcased this in "Hangover." The character-narrator expresses worry over his lack of knowledge of the night he has just spent, waking up to a headachy morning. His biggest concern is whether he can make it through the impending day.

"Valentine" would be Dewey's other rocking contribution to the album: "It is kind of a silly song; I was always trying to make sure that we had some up-tempo songs. Because Gerry writes long and intricate-based ballads—at least much more complex melodies. I made a conscious effort to counter that with something that would just give some blues progression and just rock it out. We'd been labeled initially, right from the get-go, as a sort of soft rock band. I just wanted to make sure the listener or critics knew that we were a lot more multifaceted. And they did not always work, and I don't think 'Valentine' really worked."

In fact, *Alibi* would offer a healthy dose of cover songs. Along with single "You Could've Been the One," there was Dewey's cover of "I Do Believe in You" and Gerry's of "I Don't Believe in Miracles." Gerry's "Miracles" hearkened back to the version by Colin Blunstone of the Zombies. Russ Ballard, who America would soon join forces with, had penned the tune. Russ Ballard would be responsible in part for America's major hit on its upcoming album, and its subsequent album in totality. The recording is, more or less, a piano ballad, expressing the same romantic hope that Gerry's songs always move toward, and Gerry's naturally soft voice lent itself well to the sensitivity of the words.

As for "Survival," it would both establish and cement a career-long foothold with audiences in Italy. The track and album would hit Italy's *Billboard*'s Top Ten. The U.S. charts would not allow *Alibi* to pass the 142 album slot and would completely ignore its singles.

In the prior year, toward the end of 1979, both Jimmy Calire and Tom Walsh had departed from America's touring band. And in 1980, bassist

David Dickey left, to be replaced first by Bryan Garofalo and then by Brad Palmer a year later.

"I think things kind of slowed down," Jimmy reflected on why he left, "and they wanted to reduce the band. It kind of hit its peak. We had one tour where we weren't selling the halls, and an adjustment had to be made, and that was one of the adjustments. They pared the band down, so Tom Walsh and I were out. In time things righted themselves out. Their fan base never really went away. When I was there, it was at stadium time. They needed a bigger footprint: percussion and extra keyboards. They have the right balance now. And some of it was management style; they realized by paring things down, and not having limos, and not having private planes—they were young guys, you know, they were being rock stars. . . . At one time, Crosby, Stills & Nash were touring, and America said, 'Why don't we go back out on the road?' and they did. And I remember CSN was ahead of us on one tour.

"They didn't do limos. It was a bit of an eye-opener for the guys, because—it's not about living the high life; we're here to make a living. Here to entertain the troops but also go home with some dough. They [CSN] were doing the same thing, but they weren't spending nearly as much money.

"At the time with America, there was a lot of money being made, but there was almost more being spent. And I think they caught on. Before, we would have suites in the hotels. So they stopped doing all that. They got wise. It was also part of us growing up. You're twenty, and the next thing you know you're thirty-five, and forty."

The year 1981 would mark a change of management once again for America the band. John Hartmann would transfer his mantle over to young Jim Morey of Katz-Gallin-Morey. The band wanted a change of direction that mirrored their desires for the new decade. "Our management company Hartmann & Goodman was kind of basically coming apart in front of us," Gerry recalled. "They were starting to split up as a team, and John Hartmann was trying to get more into film production. And we had a shortlist of who the hot managers were. I remember having a meeting with Roger Davies, who had been handling Olivia Newton-John and Tina Turner.

"And we took a meeting with Jim Morey, kind of as a favor to our business manager at the time, who said we should really meet the young guy over at Katz-Gallin. It was a legendary Hollywood firm that had handled Kate Smith and then went on to handle Neil Diamond and Dolly Parton and Cher. And we just felt that it sounded like a fit for us."

The first idea Jim presented to America was the concept of a world tour, something the band had not done since 1974. They immediately responded to his fresh approach. America needed some newness in its m.o.

"We interviewed a lot of different managers," Dewey remembered. "We still had some clout, but our pulling power had lost strength. It wasn't likely we could walk into an office and say, 'We're a ready-made hit band.' There was a time when you could do that. We had already had a few not-so-successful albums. When we went around the offices interviewing various managers, we did settle on Jim Morey. He was the nicest guy when we met him. He had had a lot of success. He was a little bit more middle of the road."

He was what Dewey and Gerry had been looking for. They had already experienced the wild drama and excitement of being managed by trailblazers like David Geffen in the early '70s. Now they wanted someone dependable, someone who would not turn them over to managers of the month.

"No one remains someone's manager forever," Jim Morey explained. "The fact that I have been Gerry and Dewey's personal manager for thirty-nine-plus years is pretty unusual. I managed Michael Jackson for over seven years. I think Neil Diamond for fifteen years. I was involved with Dolly Parton, it will be twenty years. But it always comes, at some point, to an end. Not necessarily because of personality or emotions but because of business kind of things. There's only so much you can do and then it ends. And you move on and they move on.

"What makes it unique with Gerry and Dewey is, I think I've kind of become the other member of the band. Although it's not onstage."

Thirty-nine years later, Jim Morey is still the manager of America.

20

THE COMEBACK

In November 1981 America embarked upon a three-city tour of South Africa, on the heels of their new manager's game plan to have the band tour internationally. Nature-enthusiast that he was, Dewey was initially very excited by the prospect of spending time in South Africa, where exotic wildlife ran rampant and safaris were possible. But in the weeks leading up to the tour, he began to tune in to the potential negative implications of his band's performing in apartheid zones.

"There was a lot of controversy, and we were very naïve," remembered Dewey.

In 1980, in an effort not to comply with the nation's decades-long apartheid regime, the United Nations issued a cultural boycott of South Africa. The initiative instructed all U.N. states to prohibit any cultural exchanges—including those of musical performance—with South Africa, as to do so would serve as an expression of tolerance of racist practices. Thus, it became even more taboo among American performers to perform there.

Sun City, in 1981, was South Africa's Las Vegas. Frank Sinatra and Linda Ronstadt had recently performed there, as had many other significant artists. It was a resort town, not properly representative of the nation's character. But America would not be stopping there during the tour. Instead, they would play a week in Cape Town, a week in Durban, and ten days in Johannesburg, all areas where, unlike Sun City, the specifics of apartheid policy were strongly enforced.

Dewey's friends and artistic colleagues urged him not to go, to respect the United Nations boycott. His longtime friend Jerry Garcia, and Jane Fonda and her husband Tom Hayden, political activist and author—who was well versed in the apartheid situation and filled Dewey in on what he needed to know at the time—all discouraged him. Hayden was a member of the so-called Chicago Seven during the 1968 Democratic National Convention protests. The more Dewey researched the racist actuality of South Africa, the more he became intent upon not going. But getting out of his touring commitment proved difficult and near impossible by that point. As Gerry and Dewey considered the pros and cons of going and not going, they saw the benefit of going through with the tour too. In a 1982 *Rolling Stone* article titled "Apartheid Rock," Gerry stated about boycotting South Africa: "I don't see how sealing it off would be anything more than sweeping the dust under the carpet. We like to think that our songs and our way of life—the fact that we're Americans having a good time—might give them hope that there is an outside world where this stuff doesn't happen."[1]

Ultimately America went forward with the tour, but with an added stipulation—in part to make a point about their feelings on apartheid—that people of all races be allowed into the America concerts, despite the cities' regulations on apartheid. "There were definitely fans there who wanted to experience the music of America," Jim Morey recalled. "I think we did the right thing. It would not have accomplished anything for America not to go."

It was an admirable aim. But at the time, most people of color subject to apartheid in Cape Town, Durban, and Johannesburg were unable to pay the venues' high ticket prices to America's performances. So the audiences were mostly white just the same. Traveling through the nation, Dewey was reminded of his days as a young boy in Biloxi, Mississippi, during the early '60s, when segregation had been rampant. As the freedom-and-equality-loving people that Dewey, Gerry, and their band members were, they felt at odds with the governmental regime. They tried to put on their usual quality performances for their audiences, as they always did. And they tried to enjoy the natural beauty of the nation, even getting to go on a safari. Dewey's naturalist character, as experienced as it was, truly appreciated the opportunity to observe such exotic wildlife. During a braai—a South African barbecue—he had a run-in with a Cape cobra. Treating it like the rattlesnakes he was familiar with handling,

Dewey used a stick to slowly approach the cobra—who proceeded to leap up and chase him right into a nearby river.

Not long after returning to California from the tour, in 1981, Dewey's second child with Vivien was born—a baby girl named Lauren. The couple's son Dylan had been born four years earlier in '77. And by 1982, Gerry and his wife Eleanor would be divorced. But little did Dewey and Gerry, who were both turning thirty, know how momentous the year of 1982 would be for them—what a turning point it would be for the band's musical career.

They began work on their next studio album, which would be titled *View from the Ground*. America had begun their musical journey more or less on the highest peak, and it had seen the glorious views from there.

Dewey with his children Lauren and Dylan. *Courtesy of the Bunnell family.*

Now, over a decade later, they still had a nice view—but it seemed that it couldn't get much lower.

It was about to climb, once again, very, very high.

At America's previous management agencies of Geffen-Roberts, and Hartmann & Goodman, most represented artists had been singer-songwriters, musicians who performed their own material almost exclusively. America included. But at Katz-Gallin-Morey, clients were often in search of other artists' songs to cover.

"At the time, it was a great idea to look for some outside material," Dewey reminisced. "We sought out demo tapes from publishers and people around us in the know. We started listening to tapes with an open mind. There was a lot of schlocky stuff, and some weird stuff—but then we found Russ Ballard. He'd written a song for Santana called 'Winning.' We liked that; he had a good track record, he'd written a lot of songs at that point. I think he actually wrote 'You Can Do Magic' with us in mind."

Ballard was a successful songwriter, producer, and musician, having sung and played guitar in Argent, and written for Three Dog Night, Rainbow, and Roger Daltrey. By the time he worked with America on "You Can Do Magic," he had not produced any tracks in four years. Ballard wrote and produced both the hit single and "Jody" for America after being recruited by Capitol's A&R V.P. Rupert Perry.

The entire *View from the Ground* project possessed an air of newness, of potential for success, right from the very beginning. Gerry and Dewey had now been a duo act for five years. They had switched managers and record labels. They were ready to be an '80s band too. Lyrically, and musically, "You Can Do Magic" was the perfect song for a comeback. Released in the U.S. on July 6, 1982, the single would breach the Top 10 on *Billboard*, peaking at number eight in mid-October. "It was really a great time," Gerry recalled. "It was 'mission accomplished' for us. All this kind of messing with the formula had finally come up with something that worked."

It worked, in part, because Russ Ballard's writing and production had emphasized the qualities of America that also fit in with what was commercially successful in '80s popular music. The sound of Gerry's melodic and mellow lead vocals, the slick overall sound of the recording, the meeting of the guitar riff with the typewriter-esque sound in the intro gelled together to create ear candy. The same kind that America had been responsible for in their earliest days of recording. They were back, having fully translated their '70s acoustic sound into an '80s produced sound. Audiences responded immediately, just as they had done upon first hearing "Horse with No Name" in '72.

This album would be the first America album to feature the songwriting prowess of the band's longtime friend Bill Mumy. Track two, the gorgeous and moody pop number complete with jangly guitars, "Never Be Lonely," was a co-write between Bill and Gerry. "Writing with Gerry, was organic," reflected Bill. "We hung out every day. We traveled together. When his first marriage was ending, Gerry and I went to his house in England together for a few weeks. When my long-term relationship, before my marriage, ended, Gerry and I went to England for a few weeks. We spent a lot of time together for a long time. So our writing and collaborating was more of, 'Hey, I just need a bridge.' Gerry is the greatest bridge writer in the world. He combusts bridge music. In five minutes you can give him a weird, complicated song that modulates keys, but it needs a bridge. In the time it takes him to sit down and play it—you'll go 'wow, that's a great bridge.' He's really good at that."

When viewed through the lens of a performer attempting to win the affections of an audience, the lyrics of "Never Be Lonely" echo the somewhat autobiographical sentiment expressed through America's cover track of "You Can Do Magic." The listening public had somewhat denied America kudos more or less since the massive success of *Hearts*, with a subtle decline through 1982. "Got you by my side, I'll never be lonely. Got you by my side, I'll never be afraid," Gerry's character-narrator expresses in the song's opening verse. "Here in the middle of now or never, Finally found where I belong. I could go on like this forever," he insists in the whimsical Beatles-ish middle-eight section. America had finally found where it could establish an identity for itself in the 1980s world of recorded music.

"I like working with Bill, he's one of my oldest friends," recalled Gerry. "I have fond memories of working on 'Never Be Lonely.' He's a great lyricist, Bill, and there's some great stuff that he helped me with lyrically on some of my solo projects over the years."

Bill would also write tunes with Dewey, who since 1974 had kept a routine of traveling to Los Angeles once a month from his home in Marin County, to work on musical projects in the L.A. area. This was mostly with Gerry and Dan in the early years, but Dewey soon focused more on writing with Bill Mumy and eventually with his artistic partner Robert Haimer. Childhood friends, the duo had made a name for themselves as Barnes & Barnes in 1970. They self-released the single "Fish Heads" in 1978, a brilliant comedic piece that was later translated into a Bill Paxton–directed music video for *Saturday Night Live* in December 1980.

"Love on the Vine" was such a track, written by Dewey and Bill, as well as Robert Haimer. "Usually what would happen is we would come down to my house, in Laurel Canyon. Robert would be here, because we were working on a Barnes & Barnes thing. And we'd go to the Pear Garden or something and have dinner in our house. And then we'd come back here to my studio, and Dewey would open his notebook, and he would say, 'I've got something,' you know he'd come up with—he'd got a few lines here. And there're eighty guitars here and basses and keyboards and drums and percussion. We knew we were writing for an America record. We weren't writing for a new band, for a Barnes & Barnes & Bunnell project or something. We were writing so that we could contribute original material to the next America record. So that was going to be all Dewey, and our role, Robert and I, would [be to] put more logs on the fire. That's actually a pretty accurate description of what we would do. By the time two days were over—it was usually two days, sometimes three—there was a really good demo of that song. Then Dewey would take it to Gerry, and [the] producers, and if it worked they would duplicate that in the studio, and it would become that song. There was a lot of them, our songs, that never did get realized."

With a simple lyrical concept and a catchy hook in its melody, "Love on the Vine" served as an homage to the doo-wop-arranged songs of the '50s and early '60s: "I know that the berry's ripe on the vine; and I know that the grapes will soon turn to wine. Yes I know I'll be there, just in time to love you." Intricate, background, four-part vocal arrangements, performed by Henry Diltz and his band the Modern Folk Quartet, heightened the productive effect of the track. "Love on the Vine" would always serve as a fine example of Dewey's talent for composing a straightforward love song, as well as his knowledge of pop music history. He had, after all, come of age in the 1950s and '60s when this sort of song was all over the radio.

While "Love" was a simple affection song of Dewey's, "Even the Score" was a very complex affection song of his, and it would close out the album. What at first seemed to be an angry song soon clearly showed itself to be an angry-because-I-love-you song. The lyrics detail a character-narrator at his wit's end with his significant other, unsure and eventually having no idea as to how to rectify the situation of their relationship. Musically, the track showcases Dewey's supreme talents as a rock vocalist, translating emotional moments of anger and annoyance in the lyrics into gruff-edged musical expression. "Starin' hard at that big front door / Is it time now to find my shoes / It ain't the loss of love no more / I'm just tryin' hard to live with you," articulates a mature stage in a romantic relationship, where Dewey's character-narrator didn't consider leaving his love. For that would not be a light or easy move for a committed couple. Everyone had gotten older, and the relationship stakes had gotten higher. Dewey's early teen romance that had ended over a haircut seemed ages ago. Musically, Dewey's song was an example of how he would always try to make sure there was a hard rock 'n' roll number or two on every America record. He was an ideal match for Gerry, who was most gifted at composing ballads, assuring that every record has a good dose of those.

"Right Before Your Eyes"—known colloquially as "Rudolph Valentino" due to the song's catchy lyrics for the chorus—was a ballad sung by Gerry. But it had not been written by him. Canadian musician Ian Thomas had penned and recorded the song in 1977 for his album *Goodnight Mrs. Calabash*. America's cover of the track would reach number forty-five on the *Billboard* charts upon its release. The song's narrative depicts a tongue-tied young man in love with a girl he sees on the Madison Avenue bus every morning on his way into work. Unable to tell her how he feels, Gerry's character-narrator imagines himself as silent film heartthrob Rudolph Valentino, who would be able to approach the girl, who in the fantasy would be Greta Garbo.

The song could be super cheesy, but instead, Gerry's vocal delivery renders it an authentic, tender, and appealing articulation of desire. As a singer, Gerry possesses a warm and melodic kind of voice, ideal for three-part harmonies and for singing intimate, piano-based ballads. It was an instrumentalist's voice, a producer's voice. A songwriter's voice. Interesting to consider how, as a young musician in some of his earliest high school bands, he had never, at least at first, intended to be a lead singer.

"Inspector Mills" was an original composition of Gerry's that would prove itself as a writerly standout on the *View from the Ground* album.

The narrative begins with a phone call by Inspector Mills, which Gerry's character-narrator answers and begins his tale of woe. The answering voice on the recording, however, isn't just anybody's but, instead, a player from America's past.

"The song is kind of like a little story, a mini film," Gerry explained. "That's actually George Martin. It wasn't produced by George. But we went back and I said I wanted the track to start with a guy calling a detective agency. So it starts with a phone, and we actually said 'George, we're gonna call you, and we're gonna record this.' So that's when it goes 'Hello?' That's George Martin answering the phone."

"Inspector Mills," the B side of the "Right Before Your Eyes" single, became a hit in Asia, especially in the Philippines. The track was rarely included in America's live performance setlist, due to its number of musical movements. Swelling string arrangements by Matthew McCauley heightened the drama of Gerry's character's impassioned attempts to locate this girl he saw at a Beverly Hills party. Gerry based the song's lyrics on a story of trying to find the girl, in sharp contrast to *Alibi*'s Batdorf-Sheridan cover of "You Could've Been the One," in which the girl in question is lost in the first couple of lines, and Gerry complains about it for the rest of the number.

The Beach Boys–influenced, complex middle-eight section of "Inspector Mills"—"Someday soon I might be in love with you"—would be one of many examples proving Bill Mumy's words true: Gerry was one of the best bridge writers around.

21

THE FRIEND

In 1982 the Rankin/Bass filmmaking team, who had been responsible for stop-action holiday classics *Rudolph the Red-Nosed Reindeer* (1964), *Santa Claus Is Comin' to Town* (1970), and the *Jackson 5ive* cartoon series (1971–1972), to name a mere few, made a new animated feature. *The Last Unicorn*, based on Peter S. Beagle's fantasy book of the same name, told the tale of a unicorn on a quest to discover where all of the other unicorns in the world have gone to, and if she really is the last unicorn. Mia Farrow, Jeff Bridges, and Alan Arkin were all enlisted to supply character voices.

Jimmy Webb was enlisted too—to pen a score for the film. He did, with some beautiful orchestral material to be recorded by the London Symphony Orchestra—as well as a few songs. Charles Bass then asked Jimmy whether he was familiar with the music group America—because he felt they would be ideal performers for the film's songs.

It was fate once again bringing America and Jimmy Webb together. Yes, he was familiar with America, Jimmy told Charles. He even considered himself a sometime honorary member of the group. They were close. Mutual friend Matthew McCauley, who had produced *Alibi*, was even on board to do the soundtrack orchestration. It would be a musical family affair. After a quick call with Jimmy, Gerry and Dewey were on board. They traveled to Wembley, England, to cut the tracks at De Lane Lea Studios, bringing their backing band of Wood-z, Willie Leacox, and Brad Palmer along with them.

The soundtrack was released on Virgin Records in November '82, becoming a huge hit in Germany along with the film. "It didn't do too well here in the U.S.," recalled Jimmy, "but it was sent to New Jersey and they used the full stereo Dolby soundtrack. They remastered everything, making it look like a real state of the art film for release in Germany. And it went to number one. It was the number one movie in Germany, and when it went to video, it came back to America and it was number one on the American video charts. So really, to be frank about it, the release of that movie was a terrible blunder in the United States. It was released in mono. It didn't have a proper distributor. It had so much more potential, and it was so sad to sort of sit on the sidelines and watch it kind of wither away. But it had this great life in spite of the very bad opening." Ever since the soundtrack release, "The Last Unicorn" title song has become a mandatory setlist inclusion for any America show in Germany.

Fate had brought America and Jimmy Webb together more than once. As a high schooler, Gerry had often sung Jimmy Webb's classic "By the Time I Get to Phoenix" in talent shows and musical reviews. They had first met in their early days with press agent Derek Taylor at the Warner Brothers London office. And in '72 when the group relocated to Los Angeles, Jimmy Webb was one of the first people they looked up, making plans to get together and talk music. They would sometimes hang out and record together at Jimmy's Valley estate, Campo de Encino.

It would take a bit of time to become clear, as America and Jimmy continued on their separate artistic trajectories, but the identity crises that each traveled through would be somewhat similar. Rock 'n' roll points. Street cred. What they lacked. Because they were slightly more cooperative, more commercially willing, less likely to destroy hotel property. Because they were clean, they were nice. At least their music was. And they had money. They had been recognized by the charts, accepted by the industry, won Grammys.

"It was diabolical," Jimmy explained, "because here you are: you're so successful. And I was successful; writing for people like Frank Sinatra and the Fifth Dimension. And Glen Campbell, who was considered, frankly—I hate to say this about someone who was so beloved to me. And such a great friend and such an ardent supporter—but Glen was considered middle of the road, if not square. He really wasn't that at all; he played on most of those Beach Boys records. On the whole album *Pet Sounds*, it was mostly Glen on guitar. He was really a very hip guy, but he couldn't get that kind of cred. And he wondered, 'what magical thing do I have to do to get this? Do I need to turn myself into something else? Because I love rock 'n' roll. I want to be a part of what's going on. But ironically my success in the commercial world is holding me back.' So I think it was a difficult problem.

"Which doesn't exist now, obviously, because commercials and rock-pop stars, and everything—and variety shows and award shows—are sort of integrated into this vast complex. And nobody cares. Nobody cares whether you've taken money for doing a commercial, which was really an uncool thing to do in the '70s. And eventually you get a song from Neil Young called 'This Note's for You.' But I took money for 'Up Up and Away.' I didn't think about it too much, but boy did I get a lot of grief over it. One of the first things that David Geffen ever said to me was 'You can't play Vegas.' You know, there were these unwritten rules, weird rules. About what you could do and what you couldn't do and still get up on the stage with Crosby, Stills & Nash. And my boss Johnny Rivers, who was the number one male vocalist in the United States for four years in a row—he couldn't get any credit to this day.

"Really it was like America kind of coming to my rescue and saying, 'Listen, I'm not going to let them totally shove you out the door of the airplane. We're gonna make you a part of our rock concerts.' And so that was right up my alley, because it was my sworn purpose to eradicate somehow that Jim Webb image. It got going, it had its own momentum, it had its own press. We don't have that anymore. Everybody does commercials. That abyss is not there, there's no decision to make."

Even with a slew of industry accolades, and the composition of countless songs that would become part of the American songbook and be covered by known and gifted recording artists, Jimmy was dissatisfied. He continued to try to make a name for himself as a solo performer, one accepted in the rock world. After some performances at the legendary Troubadour in Los Angeles failed to launch his own performing career in the way he desired, Jimmy was invited to open for America for part of its current 1977 tour. The acts that Warner Brothers often assigned to open for the band on its tours were the label's other artists it wished to give exposure to. They didn't necessarily have any further connection to Gerry and Dewey. But in the fall of 1977, with Dan having split just months earlier, the label finally asked Gerry and Dewey who they wanted to have open for them. It was an easy decision.

Jimmy Webb joined America on ten dates from September 8 through November 23, 1977. His latest album, *El Mirage* (Atlantic Records), which included original gems "The Highwayman," "If You See Me Getting Smaller," and "The Moon Is a Harsh Mistress," had been released in May. None other than George Martin had served as producer, not long after he'd completed work on *Harbor*. Touring with America in the fall of '77 satisfied some of Jimmy's long-held rock 'n' roll dreams.

"It was a wild experience," Jimmy recalled, "because I would walk out and the crowd would be, most of the time, drunk. At least warm and fuzzy. Sometimes not TOO warm and fuzzy, because (at the start of the show) a voice would say, 'Ladies and gentlemen, now Jimmy Webb.' And I would walk out, and there wouldn't be a sound. There would be a smattering of applause—*maybe*. And I would walk out, I would sit down and start playing. I can remember like yesterday; my first song was 'By the Time I Get to Phoenix.' Because it was recognizable. I would start playing and it was like the crowd went 'Oh no. *No!*' Somewhere in the back of the crowd somebody would say 'rock and *roll!*' Then the whole crowd would start to chant '*rock—and—roll*!' Throwing beer cans onstage—and I'm [up there singing,] 'By the time I get to Phoenix . . .'

Left to right: Dewey, Bill Mumy, Gerry, and Jimmy Webb. *Courtesy of Henry Diltz.*

"By the time America came out, the crowd were like animals. They wanted to hear drums! But it was a wonderful experience, because they just made me part of their band. They let me pretend to be a rock star. They let me be right along there with them." Gerry, Dewey, and Jimmy enjoyed that tour, and Jimmy in particular enjoyed the large-scale, rock-tour element that America brought with them at that time—in 1977. Especially the band's Vickers Viscount tour plane that it used to get from gig to gig. Jimmy was himself a pilot and, like Gerry, an aircraft enthusiast. They even had a near miss one evening, when the not-that-new plane was almost unable to land. Its nose wheel had become stuck. "It was actually my manager William F. Williams who climbed down in the nose wheel, in the machinery down there, and manually cranked the nose gear down," Jimmy remembered. "We were all—you know—'we're going to die!' But it didn't bother us. There's a resiliency to youth. We were laughing and making jokes: 'Well, we're going to hit the ground one way or another, we're going to land nose wheel up or nose wheel down.' Finally it came down and stayed down."

Jimmy Webb's all-time favorite performance with America would be the opening night of the 1977 fall tour, at the Neal S. Blaisdell Center Arena in Honolulu. "It was packed. We were all out there in our Hawaiian shirts; it was sort of like being in the Beach Boys. And we were just having a great time, and got to the end of the show, and they would call me back out onstage. And there would be some kind of good-natured boos from the guys who didn't like the Glen Campbell music.

"But I was happy. I've never been happier. As I stepped off the stage I was given a Ma 'Lei, which is this sort of sweet-smelling vine. That's a very, very special honor in Hawaii. This was put around all of our shoulders. We were just surrounded by these beautiful young island princesses and all of these loving people. And the applause went on and on and on; and America went back up—they didn't really play encores, but they went back up and took another bow and they came off. It was like—*one of those nights*. And I just remember standing there thinking, 'this is one of the nights that I was born to enjoy and to live and to be a part of.'

"Because they were so successful, and they were so surrounded by love, by people who loved them. And I was a part of that family. I can still smell the Ma 'Lei when I think of that moment. And I can always see the lights coming down from the proscenium arch that they carried around with them, with all the lighting on it. And the whole rock show thing—it was just there."

The Last Unicorn project wouldn't quite have the same "rock show thing," but it would exude the same musical magic that seemed to arise whenever America and Jimmy Webb got together.

The film's title track would become its most recognizable song, and come to stand as a musical symbol for the tale's philosophy itself. "The Last Unicorn," the first track of the soundtrack album, was sung by Gerry with a subtle and effective harmony by Dewey. Its melody was mysterious, tender, full of beauty, with orchestration—especially that of the wind instruments—to match. The warmth of the duo's vocals was a match for the unicorn's story, channeling elements of innocence, wonder, and love for the natural world—all qualities inherent in America's artistic character since their group inception. The song's narrative could have almost been a sequel of sorts to "Watership Down" from '76, another nature-forward animated-film soundtrack song. "When the first breath of winter through the flowers is icing / And you look to the north and a pale moon is rising / And it seems like all is dying and would leave the world to mourn / In the distance hear the laughter of the last unicorn," goes the second of three comparable verses. At the end of all things, the song suggests, there will still remain one last unicorn. Given the Christian association with the imagery of unicorns, it is interesting to consider the lyrics here, and the film's story in general, which present the unicorn as a sort of symbol of eternal life or life force. That life itself is indestructible, though many layers and forms of external destruction—including the herding away or extinction of a species—are possible. America's career-long inclusion of nature and the natural world in its catalog's vernacular, kept in the forefront by Dewey's lovely life pact with the reverence of the outdoors and his outdoor songs, finds a welcome place here in Jimmy Webb's title track.

Perhaps the most poignant moment in "The Last Unicorn" arrives in the form of the song's bridge, when there is a buildup in musical drama and a quick reverse resolution of harmonic chords as major switches to minor—all to Gerry's words of "I'm alive." The lines are some of the best vocal deliveries of Gerry's singing career, and they ring with truth. Yes, they speak on behalf of the last unicorn's character in the tale. But they also speak on behalf of every living creature, including Gerry himself. "I'm alive" now, but I will not always be, at least not in my mortal form. To hear these words is to hear a bittersweet paradox. Or, given that energy cannot be created or destroyed because of the law of the conservation of energy, perhaps the "I'm alive" moment is merely stating a pure truth. Beyond this, the fact that Gerry and Dewey—that America—are recording artists, with a literal discography, speaks to the implied immortality of recorded art.

Accompanied by Gerry on vocal harmonies, Dewey provides lead vocals for "Man's Road," another song on the *Last Unicorn* soundtrack. Another "on the road" song fitting for Dewey to sing. Another opportunity for him to revisit the eternal conundrum brought to light by the 1960s counterculture and immortalized in the final shot of the generation-defining film *Easy Rider* (1969)—man's road versus God's road, the pavement versus the soil, societal demands versus nature's way. Which will you choose? The answer will define your life. Basically the predicament that Dewey tackled as a teenager in his own generation-defining song, "A Horse with No Name."

In *Unicorn*, "Man's Road" depicts an incapacitated people who have become victims of fear, here because of loneliness, seemingly acquired due to isolation from nature. "Moon rising, disguising lonely streets in gay displays / The stars fade, the night / shade falls and makes the world afraid / It waits in silence for the sky to explode," Jimmy Webb's song states. "The ocean is a desert with its life underground / And a perfect disguise above / Under the cities lies a heart made of ground / But the humans will give no love," says Dewey's "A Horse with No Name." The ideal that these songs allude to is a morphing of the two, that this would provide utopia: when man decides to walk the road of nature, which is his own true road, is when the universe will regain its balance. "Man's Road" may be the most fitting cover song ever recorded by Dewey—a testament to both Dewey's talent for portraying characters and to Jimmy Webb's songwriting skill and his understanding of what America was (and is) about.

22

THE VIDEO

As a result of America's immense success with *View from the Ground*, spearheaded by the top ten hit single "You Can Do Magic," Capitol Records went all in on Russ Ballard. His composition and production of the single had rendered him a proven commodity for the label, and, in part, a financial savior of the band. So for America's follow-up album, Russ would produce all its songs—and write most of them. Capitol, forever insecure about America's profits-reaping ability since the surprise undersell of their first project together, *Silent Letter*, wanted a sure thing.

"It was 'if a little is good a lot is better,'" Gerry remembered. "We then kind of committed to Russ Ballard to do the entire *Your Move* album, the next one. Which I think was probably a weak decision, because it ended up basically being where Russ played every note on the album, and Dewey and I just kind of had to fly over and sing. We did do some of our own material, but he played the instruments."

Russ was a musical mastermind, a producer's producer. As evidenced by his body of work prior to his time with America, he was capable of harnessing an artist's essence, concentrating it, amping it up with more voltage, and creating a 2.0 version. But this approach would truly work best on an artist who was either new and needed identity definition, or on one who was consistently a covers-only artist and needed to be "produced upon" and given material to perform in order to exist. Of which America was neither. The band had been in existence, without Capitol Records or Russ Ballard, for more than a decade already. The "You Can Do Magic" session had gelled, but it did not necessarily imply a George Martin–America style relationship spanning several albums and years.

Your Move was recorded in Beatle-land, Abbey Road Studios. Ironically it would take this album to offer Gerry and Dewey the opportunity to record in the legendary studio, and not their many years with the fifth Beatle, George Martin, who had recorded nearly all the Beatles' albums there. Six of *Your Move*'s eleven tracks were Ballard tunes, two were Gerry's co-written with Bill Mumy, one was Dewey's song, and one, the title track, was a song by Steve Kipner and Terry Shaddick. The album's ultimate hit, "The Border," was a Russ track that Dewey rewrote lyrics for in an attempt to Americanize it.

All of this wasn't necessarily problematic, except that the Ballard track domination came as a bit of a surprise to Gerry and Dewey, once they arrived to record. *Your Move* had been planned and agreed to on the basis that it would be a collaborative project, with Russ producing. Though the band and their projects had been having a bit of a rough time jibing with Capitol, America was an original artist, a group that mostly penned and played its own material. Gerry and Dewey were easy to work with in part because of their flexibility and talent for compromise, but they were far from being a clueless act that needed to be corralled and told what to do. Although Russ didn't go quite that far, the recording sessions still had a vibe that not much compromise was going to be made. Capitol had steered America toward Russ in the first place, once "Magic" made gold, so it seemed unlikely that it would take America's side in issues that arose, or come to the group's aid in defense of its artistry. Capitol was not looking to take any artistic gambles with its artist. The days of musical risk-taking that had dominated much of pop-rock production in the 1970s now seemed to be a thing of the past. Russ had a clear hold on the sound of '80s pop; America were singer-songwriters who were trying to make the transition into this sound. From a business perspective, the match made sense.

Ballard's compositions on the album are good songs, albeit slightly generic. But America's cuts of them seem to give America a slightly generic quality too. While listening to *Your Move*, it almost seems like any minute Gerry and Dewey will say, "Stop, cut, shut it down. Forget it. We can't do this. This isn't us." But they don't.

"I felt as uninvolved in that album as any album we've ever done, to be honest," reflected Gerry. "Russ cut the tracks we picked, liked just a

THE VIDEO

bunch of things, pushed hard on tracks that he liked that he felt we could really deliver on. We went over to the U.K. and sang it at Abbey Road. And I figured I was a pretty good interpreter of tunes."

Even with all this, *Your Move* is fun to listen to. Gerry does the romantic thing well in the opening two tracks and on "Honey." Dewey's vocals on his tracks, including the interesting, somewhat inspirational, self-improvement track "Cast the Spirit," add a bit of rock edge here and there.

Admirably however, Dewey did step in on the lyrics for "The Border." And the song became a hit, reaching number four on the Adult Contemporary *Billboard* charts and thirty-three on the Hot 100. Russ's original lyrical aim was to go for a dramatic plotline—about a guy trying to meet his love at a vulnerable geographical location: the border. The border could also be viewed as a metaphor for the meeting ground of crossover, where two individuals come together. "If I could make it to the border / If I could make it to the coast / If I could make it to the border / I'd be in the arms of the girl I love the most." The song's plot was slightly thin, with no grand details provided for why the character-narrator was dealing with running away to another country in the first place. Russ's narrative initially attempted to suggest the Southern California–Mexican border aesthetic, using "Pasadena" as the meeting point in question. But it didn't ring true as American, as Californian—a quality that Dewey and his SoCal band most certainly understood. Their cultural legacy and pop discography up until that point were practically sewn into the mythological fabric of the Golden State.

Dewey helped to Americanize Russ's "Border" lyrics, and his talented rock-able voice handled the track well, providing a healthy dose of palpable emotional drama. The orchestral string arrangement made the recording cinematic too.

Dewey's original "My Dear" hearkens back to the surrealist imagery in his earliest lyrics of songs like "Tin Man." "Shall I read you the letter / They sent postmarked from somewhere out here / It's in Latin, I think, I don't know / Can you help me, my dear / Please, can you help me, my dear," went the lyrics. The background musical track is mysterious, ambient, atmospheric, and a bit ambiguous and stand-alone from the rest of the album's regular-love-song ideas: "You can't miss it / A blue forest on a green sky / You must risk it / Don't ignore us if you want us to / If we want us to survive." In his song, Dewey's character narrator wants assistance, guidance, a hand to hold. The track would be the opposite of the album's other Ballard tracks, all of assurance, comfort, and ease. The album's outlier.

The year 1983 would also prove to demand music video accompaniment from America the band, for usage on MTV, which had recently overtaken the world of popular music. If a band wanted a hit song, they would need a successful hit video, too. America had made one for its hit "You Can Do Magic," which consisted mainly of the band playing the song in a heaven-like setting, with intermittent shots of magic tricks—cards, doves, gloves. The music video for "The Border" would be slightly more plot based. Just what the plot was, however, was a bit ambiguous.

"We had nothing to do with the production of that, the scripting of that," Dewey explained. "It was one of their staff video guys, who got a budget from Capitol Records and did it the way he wanted to."

Over the course of the video, Gerry and Dewey take turns delivering a rubber ball—seemingly a McGuffin—to undisclosed locations, all while being trailed by agents in trench coats. There are even vague aesthetic allusions to the colored Chinese checkers pieces featured on *Your Move*'s album cover. And it all ends with a clip of the duo playing the game on the beach, mimicking the cover shot.

"I didn't think it had anything to do with heading for the border," Dewey reflected. "It was like, were those guys immigration men, that were playing with these weird bogus computers? That didn't have anything to do with it. Running around in a subterranean, basement parking garage. We were awkward and uncomfortable. 'Now look at each other from these computers, reach on these two keyboards—okay, look at each other now pensively,' or whatever it was supposed to be."

America had always been an audio more than a visuals group—had always been mellow, understated, and cool performers. They were a cerebral group. So it's not surprising that they would reject the music video medium. It didn't help that Capitol Records didn't quite know what to do with the group and its image, either. Then again, America—like Chicago—was a logo band. The public knew their hits but didn't always know their faces and names. Image had never been their strong suit.

"We missed that boat all the way," detailed Dewey. "I didn't ever embrace [music videos]. I liked MTV a lot: The videos I saw, and I'd watch it probably as much as anybody. I liked MTV videos, the whole concept. But I just didn't see how it applied. I think it was also, for us—

older guys even then—the concept that this song now was going to be given this definitive imagery . . . now that's going to be what the listener, in this case the viewer, is going to take away from that song. So it really narrows what you know. . . . Like Bob Dylan would say, 'You know my lyrics are for the listeners to interpret in their own way and make up their own little movie.' So I think that was a concern."

Gerry also considered music videos for America "a complete and unnecessary diversion."

When asked about what Russ Ballard was like as a person, and how he was to work with in the studio, America would say that he was very nice and polite, maybe a bit reserved. If there were any mild issues during the project, they would never be discussed directly but only through each other's management. No drama. All very clean and concise.

The title track, sung by Gerry, was a catchy tune. It was light pop, and it worked to some degree. But in comparison to the undeniable power of songs like "Ventura Highway" and "Sister Golden Hair," "Your Move" didn't really stand out. America had channeled the sentiments of their generation through its Warner Brothers releases in the '70s. Could they do it in the '80s too?

The album cover featuring Gerry and Dewey playing Chinese checkers on the beach, decked out in clean-cut, light-colored clothing, highlighted the project's overall neatness.

America had done their job; now it was the audience's move.

23

THE CORPORATION

The failure of *Your Move* to re-create the runaway success of its predecessor *View from the Ground* had once again brought the relationship between America and Capitol Records to an uncomfortable place. For this new album, the one-man-show producer approach was out. The multiple-producers approach was in.

"It was decided for us by the label, because the album all done by Russ Ballard hadn't succeeded," Gerry recalled. "By that time it was not unique for an album to have multiple producers. We really came from an era where Peter Asher produced Linda Ronstadt, George Martin produced us for a long run. . . . [T]he label's idea of using different producers for different tracks was really kind of wacky to me. Because I always viewed albums as being a continuum—there should be something, a kind of a thread. You could make the argument that the act itself *is* the thread—even though that might be different producers. And it's gone on to basically become the norm.

"If you look at a lot of the big albums nowadays, virtually every track might be done by different people. But at the time it was a little weird, and it felt disjointed; we actually went from studio to studio, because each producing team used a different studio. And it was the era in which studios were converting to digital. But there were a few competing different formats, and we turned out to be doing that in three different studios, with three different sets of producers. And just as luck would have it, each one had chosen a different digital format. Not that I was too concerned with the technological aspects of it. But I am a producer and so I follow along. Like—'two track Mitsubishi on this track'—it kind of affected your flow."

Perspective, the next album, was produced by Matthew McCauley, who America had worked with on *Alibi*; Richard James Burgess, who had produced Spandau Ballet's first two albums; and Richie Zito, who had toured and worked with Elton John and would ultimately produce thirty-eight chart-hitting singles in his career. As for the instrumentalists, America would once again refrain from utilizing its touring band in the studio and instead opt for L.A. popular session musicians. *Perspective* would be recorded in different L.A. studios—to match its different producers—Amigo Studios in North Hollywood, Larrabee Sound Studios in West Hollywood, United Western Studios in Hollywood, and Oasis in Universal City.

"*Perspective*, we were really run out by then," Dewey recalled. "That was really a low point for me, those songs. They were totally different writers—not even co-writes with us. That was the most un-American album, I think. We were closely monitored by Capitol and their people. It was for the commercialism thing and trying to sell. We were starting to feel a little guilty, I recall."

Perhaps Dewey's and Gerry's hearts, having gone through so much with the evolution of their band, and having lived through the ideological changeover from the '60s to the '70s to the '80s, were no longer as ardently "in it." They had first risen to prominence through the vehicle of an acoustic guitar trio. Now they were dealing with a record company whose sense of respect derived from record sales, not musical artistry. The band had less clout in the record business world of the day. They were taking creative steps to fall in more with the tastes of popular audiences, even if at times on their new record, this effort may have been at temporary costs to their true mellow identity. But ultimately—what was a more artistic action to take, for an artist, than morph, transform, become new? America was trying, fully aware that drum machines had since become a thing.

"My usual response to something like drum machines versus drums is, it's like considering if you used a number two or number three pencil," Gerry reflected. "To me all of the creative elements were still creative elements. But there clearly was a wave of Oberheim, LinnDrum, and [other drum] machines. It did start to take over and, I think, when the machines start to overtake the humans . . ."

America had used drum machines in the studio as far back as "You Can Do Magic." A LinnDrum was used, with one pedal from start to finish, creating the song-defining beat. Artists like Barry Gibb and the Bee Gees, and Peter Gabriel, appreciated and utilized the perfectionist quality that drum machines offered in the recording studio.

"People don't remember," Dewey explained, "it was a huge sort of blasphemous thing—to currently be using these LinnDrum machines, the original machines. You could reproduce a full set of drums, and you could do everything you wanted. It was a tool that was great, and we did use them during that era. Sometimes if I brought the demos we did at Bill Mumy's house, that had used drum machines . . . as part of the process, then we'd try to re-record it with real drums. Not to mention it was really upsetting real drummers, including our own. But it was so convenient. And then suddenly you had a lot of people that were professional drum machine operators, engineers and different guys saying, 'I can work that thing and come up with different beats and different songs.'"

* * *

The eleven-track album would feature five covers, four co-writes, and two Gerry songs. A standout track would be Dewey's "Can't Fall Asleep to a Lullaby," a co-write with Bill Mumy and Robert Haimer, as well as Steve Perry, the talented vocalist of Journey. "The group America I think will be around for a long time," Steve accurately predicted in a 1984 *Cover Story* television interview. "They have been around for a long time. There's gotta be just an honesty about their music I think, that continues to be appreciated by people."[1]

Steve had long been a close friend of Dewey's from their earliest days of living in Marin County. But even before that, Steve had been a fan of America and their music. "I remember the first time I heard 'A Horse with No Name,'" he reflected. "I was driving down the freeway; I was living in Los Angeles at the time. . . . I really liked the song a lot, I was very impressed. And I didn't realize that years would go by—this was before I got into show business—years would go by and I'd end up meeting this guy [Dewey] in San Rafael."[2]

Steve would also provide background vocal harmony on much of the track. Released as a single, "Can't Fall Asleep to a Lullaby" hit number twenty-six on the *Billboard* Adult Contemporary charts. It was a slow and pensive romantic number. A warm-voiced Dewey love song. Steve's notable dramatic vocals complemented Dewey's mellow ones quite well, as though the extreme contrast in their performative attitudes came together in a presentation of totality, of equalizing. The track, as most of *Perspective*'s songs, is of and about loneliness. "'Cause I can't fall asleep to a lullaby / And I miss you so much I don't wanna cry, you are why / I love you, oo-oo-oo, you don't know." Hidden beneath slick production is a version of mature desire.

The opening two tracks, covers by Sue Shifren and Terry Britten called "We Got All Night" and "See How the Love Goes," are catchy enough but serve as obvious attempts by Capitol to get some hits out of the record. Generic love-ish songs, the first sung by Gerry and the second by Dewey, they are a bit literal. Part of America's artistic prowess is rooted in its comprehension of the subtler, milder, cooler flavors of the human emotional scale—in their talent for interpreting musical nuance. These two songs offer little opportunity to showcase this. Gerry's character in "We Got All Night" becomes simplified, super-psyched about having one whole night to spend with this chick: "Feels like we waited a lifetime / To be alone tonight / So make it hard to forget you / 'Cause we don't know when / We can do it again // We got all night / We got from sundown to sunrise / So don't let go, just hold me baby." In "See How the Love Goes," Dewey becomes apathetic yet unendingly hounded by . . . his best friend's girlfriend: "I can hear somebody knockin' / On my bedroom door / I find it rather shockin' / It's my best friend's girl." The tracks render them both as lusty paper dolls. Though the recordings are well executed, with quality vocal performances and interesting instrumentation, they don't quite ring true and so are ultimately unsettling.

"Special Girl" and "Cinderella" are syrupy covers sung by Gerry. As though his character-narrator began the album on too much of a sex-crazed note (for a "nice" group), these tracks seek to even it out with boy-next-door romancing—which is a strong suit of Gerry's performative abilities—so the songs, to a degree, are effective for the listener. The era-appropriate synth-laden production provides sonic drama that contrast the light-leaning lyrics. The plot of "Special Girl" centers on missing a girl he has lost. Gerry's own "Inspector Mills" was a clever version of this trope, providing a specific narrative for a familiar romantic storyline. "Cinderella" tells a similar tale too, but its recognizable fairy tale motif gives it more warmth and identifiability. The tune is pleasant enough, and from a desirous listener's (probably female) perspective, it pretty much seduces.

Again, however, "Cinderella" is a bit too simple of a track when matched with Gerry and Dewey's more intellectually inclined personas.

"Stereo" is different. A song collaboration between Jimmy Webb and Gerry, it—like a traditional songwriter's song—presents ideas for living well, using the motif of the stereo to do so. Only audiophiles—which all musicians are—could have come up with this concept. "We're livin' it in stereo / We fix it so our love is high fidelity / Mix it so we never lose the melody / We try to equalize our lives in stereo." The lyrics are spot-on and ideally placed amid the melodics. And to amp up the song's value, there is a gorgeous and intricate middle-eight section that, as "Horse" does, uses *ooh*s and *yeah*s for its words.

The role of "Stereo" on *Perspective* may be to serve as a meeting place, a middle ground between the technological and corporate future that time seemed to be running toward and the timeless human values that were threatening to slip away, remaining forever locked in the past as a long-ago dream. "We hear both sides / We sympathize / We live our lives in stereo / The left and the right / The dark and the light / We wrestle with the balance / We change our tone / We leave our phone / And tape record our absence / In lovin' memory." Well-done wordplay made the song a strong one, as did its insight into the future: perceiving the important role that technology would continue to play in—and, with the impending arrival of the Internet, smartphones, and Google Glass, would soon dominate—modern life.

Gerry would be one of the only musicians who Jimmy, a notorious solo writer, would regularly cite as someone he could always write with.

"Like Dewey and I, Gerry and me just really like each other," Jimmy said. "We like each other genuinely. The thing is it's easier to stay in a room with somebody you like than someone you're not sure about. Collaboration so often consists of just staying in the same room together. It's like you have to do that first.

"I've always had a pretty clear image of where I wanted to go when I sat down and started writing a song. And letting someone else drive for a while, it's a hard thing for me to do. But Gerry and I would write something ridiculous, like the song 'I Married the World,' and we would laugh. Then all of a sudden he came with this lyric called 'Stereo.' I thought, 'that's a great idea.' Utilizing, citing the medium as a part of the message. Yes it's true that a relationship is like a stereo. A left and a right, but it all has to play together to make this beautiful sound, to be successful. So I thought it was a great idea. That's the first thing. And we've always loved hanging out and laughing at stuff. He's got the best sense of humor. Gerry laughs at everything. And that's our collaboration."

Gerry's own song "Unconditional Love" seems almost like one that escaped and got away from the rest of the album's slightly bland vision. It is piano driven with vocal backgrounds heavily influenced by Beatles recordings, potentially making it the most "American" song on the album. And it may, out of the group's entire catalogue, be the most straightforward articulation of the 1960s "Love Residue" that Gerry had tried to take up the '70s mantle for. "It's a spiritual world / When the darkness comes / But you gotta hold your head up / Hold your head up high / Oo, you got to take a look around / Oo, and listen when you hear the sound / Unconditional love."

Dewey's own song (co-written with Bill Mumy) "Fallin' off the World" closes out the record. It is a fitting farewell to the recording studio for America. The group would not make another record for ten years after *Perspective* was released. And they would not work with a major record label again for twenty-three years. "I'm fallin' off the world / I'm callin' you // All of those who love each other must share in the fight / Nobody knows where their clear spirit goes in the night." The words seem to speak to his fellow, once-hippie-minded folk—the same ones he called to in "Are You There?" "Out of the country it seems so easy / To keep believin' our dream of Fiji / Your image lingers, a faded picture / Your past erased by untold elixir."

Much of the original hippie generation had "grown up" in recent years, choosing to forgo the potential for utopia in exchange for material comforts—which was much easier than trying to save the world. The track's edgy quality of the beat-based production is a glossy translation of Dewey's typical seventh-chords unease.

Given the low-key power of these originals on *Perspective*, it's a wonder why the entire record leaned more in the direction of cover songs, rather than encouraging America's own material. When considering how *Perspective* in some ways falls short of a satisfying listening experience, the reason seems to come down to the songs themselves. Not the slick production, but the compositions—which are good enough as songs, but don't look all that great on Gerry or Dewey. Why?

The absence of the natural world. Nature is so glaringly missing from this record. And from a group who once demanded trees and plants—any kind of living flora or fauna—be present on every stage they graced, *Perspective* seems semi-sacrilege to America's inner core, its identity. The record's vaguely metallic, a perfect release for the ominous implications that 1984 arrived with. *Perspective* is a record company's record. Something about it sounds like it was conceived of, developed, and created within the confines of an artificially lit, air-conditioned office building. The group that had inherently captured *the sound* of early '70s SoCal acoustic rock, had now inherently captured *the sound* of mid-'80s L.A. pop—which shouted "Corporate."

The cover of *Perspective* depicted Dewey and Gerry's somewhat perplexed faces at a skewed angle, sporting sharp blazers and short hair. They stood in front of an office building, 100 Wilshire, the tallest in Santa Monica. Not a tree in sight.

The cover said it all.

24

THE BOWLING ALLEY

The band released one more album with Capitol, a live one recorded at Arlington Theatre in Santa Barbara on June 1, 1985, appropriately titled *In Concert*, which officially ended the mutual contract. Both parties were glad the relationship was over. "The sales had dropped off considerably," Dewey reflected. "There were no hits. We certainly didn't talk to Capitol anymore. With a deal where you really have to recoup, they give you an advance. They paid for the recordings of the albums. But those things come back out of sales before you get dollar one. What pittance of sales those albums made or make—we don't collect anything for those today."

So the band went on temporary hiatus from the recording studio. On the heels of their newest manager's touring game plan, America would become a touring band—which, as many rock/pop bands with the same career demands, it already had plenty of experience in. "I am known as one of the personal managers that is really an expert on touring," Jim Morey reflected. "And anybody that I've ever represented has been heavily involved in touring. Whether it was Mac Davis, the Osmonds, Dolly Parton, Cher, Michael Jackson, or the ultimate tourer, my client Neil Diamond. I knew the touring backwards and forwards, and I knew that Gerry and Dewey could deliver onstage. They just needed some tweaking of their touring machine and how to make it all work."

The thing was—without present-day hit albums to show off, the tour would not have the same sort of promotional pull. The attraction of audiences to America's tours, from 1985 on, would be based on its history. Its catalogue of hits, number ones, top tens, and platinum and gold records was extensive. The band hoped it could carry its fan base through on the basis of its past. It would be, in part, a nostalgia act. And it would need all its band members on board, ready and willing to live their lives on the road in a very determined way.

It was a timely and intelligent move, presupposing the steady decline in record sales that was to come in the impending millennium, focusing on the financial revenue that would come in through touring and determining it to be a main source of income. The concerts would have to do well for the band, be successful, sell out. Towns across the continental U.S., Europe, Asia, and Australasia would be selected carefully. Venues even more so. America would often play gigs in smaller cities and towns, suburbs and outskirts. The band wanted to fill their performance spaces on a consistent basis.

America had tried to make the 1980s recording studio work for them, artistically speaking. It hadn't jibed. Now the band would go back to square one: to its origins, essence, basic data. After more than a decade of behaving as the pop industry accommodators, the band would now have the opportunity to gain what it had always lacked: rock 'n' roll street cred.

Road warriors, rejecting what the '80s seemed to be offering, America would insist upon claiming its '70s cultural legacy's power, reminding listeners of its realness. It would work, but it wouldn't be shiny. But Dewey and Gerry were Air Force kids; they didn't need shine. They had the strength and stamina to rough it, to go lean and mean in their band's operation. They'd always had it. But the opportunity to use it hadn't ever come up—until now. The strength of the band's togetherness would be founded upon the duo's friendship, their faith in each other's talent. The rest of the touring band would sense that, would feed off the good vibes. The touring band would respect them.

"They work together and know what each has to offer, and they try to make the best of what the other one has to offer, and to complement," Wood-z explained. "They know that this is their living. They know how to keep it together. A lot of bands that came from the era that they came from didn't know how to dial it down when they couldn't play bigger places. So they couldn't make any money. So they fell apart. And Gerry and Dewey: it took them a little while, but they figured out how to dial it down and just be humble enough to make the money that made a living for them and the players that played for them. So they could keep doing it and have fun. It was a learning experience for me, to see them be able to do that."

Road lifestyles would have to be toned down. Gone were the days of high-stakes Eagle poker with fellow rock stars, winning and losing thousands of dollars during midtour antics. Gone were the days of the band's private Vickers Viscount airplane. But the '70s had ended anyway. The whole world seemed to be going through a lifestyle adjustment.

"The road is all I really remember, lots of traveling," Dewey expressed. "We were doing well on the road, making money and making ends meet. I'm sure there was a point where we were really down. I know our guarantees had dropped considerably for live performances. If we had strung together a tour of ten dates over the course of three weeks or something, we would be prepared to take considerably lower fees to play a little bridge date between two cities. We were being very creative that way along with the agency. The agency of course books the shows, but they're the ones who have their finger on the pulse of what promoters think of what your chances are of selling out. And that's how they estimate the size of venues and so on."

It was a reverse grassroots campaign. While most artists spent their earliest years building up their fan bases, America would do it during their more mature years. Dues, the same ones that the band's threatened

America's Vickers Viscount private plane, circa 1970s. *Photographer unknown.*

competitors muttered under breath that they had not paid to warrant such a quick number-one hit with "Horse," would now be paid. The balance was outstanding. And Gerry and Dewey had the guts to try and pay. But would they be able to? Could their egos put up with scaling back? After they had been conditioned to luxurious living—the private America plane, the hotel suites, the post-show parties? After the '70s?

How to keep a band alive? Scale down.

"We've been able to carefully keep that very well boiled," Jim Morey explained. "That's how they survived. . . . We've found a way to maximize the income so that they were comfortable enough with what they did and how they did it. We don't have thirty people running around. We found out how to do it lean and mean, and [garner] audiences. As opposed to Michael Jackson who had at some point thirty-eight trucks on the road and a hundred people working at any one time. That was on one end of the scale. In the end, it's all about making sure that the music is driving it, and that's what we've tried to do."

The reverse grassroots campaign they began in the mid-'80s caused the band to experience a learning curve. On their first five-week club tour of North America in 1972, following the mega-success of "Horse," America played high-profile, well-respected music clubs like the Cellar Door in Washington, DC, the Bitter End in New York, and the Whisky a Go Go in Los Angeles. Fans had stood in long lines to see the band play their hit and other songs from their debut album. The Everly Brothers, for whom America served as opening act, had witnessed the band's success and decided to no-show, intimidated by a band of the new rock 'n' roll scene bogarting their performative attention.

Then, once America had relocated to Los Angeles, the band received an instant venue upgrade. For "the next tour we ever did in the U.S, we were in arenas," Dewey remembered. "So we really never had this slow build, as someone like Springsteen, who's had a grassroots career that was built really on pleasing his base, and getting then bigger and bigger and bigger. We just had this splash. We had never worked our way through.

"But now by this point we were trying to find venue sizes that fit us. Like putting on a suit or something. So we were playing some pretty little things, some weird clubs in the South. We played a bowling alley at one point, that doubled as a venue in this small town. That was to sort of 'pay bills' between some other larger shows. It was like that. It'd gotten down to that."

Touring would not be the only source of revenue for America the band in the second half of the '80s. They still had their hits and their albums from the past. People still bought records and therefore still bought America records. As for the sidemen, Willie Leacox, Wood-z, and Bradley Palmer: when not playing on tour with America, they were free to pursue their own projects and to play with other bands.

The regular touring schedule for America, which was extreme and consistent from post-*Perspective* onward, set in motion a connection with the band's fan base all across the world. Instead of being an inaccessible band impossible for fans to experience live, waiting years in between concerts, America would be available. And this would enable them to intensify their relationship to their audience. They had begun as a studio band, able to create a debut master album with nearly just themselves and their guitars. Upon arriving in Los Angeles, they had been driven to assemble a touring band, knowing their new star manager David Geffen was keen to send them out to play for fans. But America had not begun its career on the heels of years of blood, sweat, and tears. The band's ascension had been quick.

"They were real famous all through the '70s, I mean, they couldn't have been more famous," Wood-z recalled. "In the '80s all of a sudden synthesizer music came out. And it was all different. Everybody was into that and there was a new music. But by the end of the '90s there were all these new alternative bands. All of a sudden [America was] real hip. Because the alternative bands always had a really soft acoustic part, and then they'd have a loud grunge part, and then go back to the acoustic part. And a lot of the acoustic stuff was reminiscent of America."

The band's resurgence of relevance that would begin in the late '80s and carry through to the '90s, stemmed from newer genres of grunge, alternative, coffeehouse rock, and the *MTV Unplugged*–style of live performance. America's second wave of relevance was made all the more strong by the fact that they were still performing live, still touring. All the time. During the post-Capitol years America never went on hiatus, they never took a long break to work on a studio album. They had done that already, they had made a name for themselves in music history with their platinum albums and number-one hit singles. They were not a band of the past, though they regularly played many songs that had originated there.

Left to right: Sons Matthew and Joe with Gerry. *Courtesy of the Beckley family.*

They were a band of the present moment, living a continuum of the decade-defining artistic legacy they had established as teenagers. Continuous and accessible live performance from the mid-'80s to mid-'90s, when many bands were hypnotized by new technology of the recording studio, set America apart. Such a choice was a testament to their original hippie and naturalist ideals as well. Proof of their commitment to artistic authenticity.

And by propagating their legacy through live performance and touring, the band received exposure to younger generations of fans as well. Everyone had grown up since America's debut in 1970, and influences could be heard in newer bands. "A lot of those kids in the '90s and 2000s who were coming up," Wood-z reflected, "had listened to America with their parents, and they were replaying or rehashing it, doing acoustic stuff."

The fans were not the only ones who were growing up, who were evolving. Gerry married his longtime girlfriend Kathy in 1988. Their son

Joe was born in 1992. He would grow up to be a photographer, occasionally even shooting live pictures of America's constant performances.

25

THE FARM(HOUSE) AND THE HOME STUDIO

In the early '90s, Rhino Records was successfully taking advantage of sonic tech trends and rereleasing selective pop-rock material on CD. America's *History* album of early hits, first released in 1975, had now been certified "4X platinum." Rhino sensed the potential to hit a high sales mark by releasing another album of America's hits on CD, which would include an alternate array of the '70s material, and the '80s hits as well. As an added incentive for fans and CD buyers, this new hits record—titled *Encore: More Greatest Hits*—would also include four new originals from the group. All via the improved sound quality that the new compact disc format promised. Much of the burgeoning CD culture in the early '90s would revolve around music fans repurchasing albums they'd owned on vinyl, upgrading and staying on trend. Most of America's catalogue, other than the first album, had not yet been released on CD. With the advent of the digital age and its new formats, DATs and CDs, older catalogues of classic rock–era musicians were given new life. Strong classic rock radio stations' frequent airing of America's early hits kept the catalogue selling and the so-called brand "alive." Concertgoers were then very keen to come on out to see the band's live show.

After having tried to update their sound to fit the changing times during the Capitol years—adding drum machines, utilizing cover songs of popular writers—*Encore*'s four new original tracks mark a clear and purposeful return to the band's authentic sound. It was 1991. Enough time had passed since the golden era of 1970s SoCal rock that acoustic guitars and minimally produced music were once again in vogue. The overproduced sounds of the '80s were beginning to move out of fashion as well. Nirvana had released its debut album, *Bleach*, in 1989, the same year MTV's *Unplugged* acoustic concert video series was established.

"The Farm" would be a piano ballad of Gerry's, full of potential for metaphor. The lyrics tell of a farmer's plight in the modern world. But Gerry's story was a set of symbols, too, that articulated changing times and cultural shifts, which America knew very well. The band had now been in the recording industry for more than twenty years. They were familiar with the constant volatility of a product's value in the marketplace. "Daisy I think we must sell the farm / And you know I don't wanna cause alarm / The times are a changin', the money is gone / Where do we go from here?" go the lyrics. Gerry would once again bring in the fictional character of Daisy as a female figure. The concepts of selling the farm and the money being all gone show traces of America coping with its own stature in the music industry. They no longer had ample funds at hand from a record company through which millions of records were sold; such opportunities were getting harder to come by. The band had experienced changing times directly via its toning-down trip in the second half of the '80s.

"Nothing's So Far Away (as Yesterday)" was a Dewey song that exemplified a maturation in songwriting. Bittersweet, melancholy, and moodily reflective on time passed, the track, co-written with pal Bill Mumy, details change, growth, renewal—potentially about a relationship, but also conceivably about life itself and the ongoing saga of America's journey. "Turning the pages / We open the cages / Now I know that / Nothing's so far away as yesterday," the song's chorus articulates. By moving forward, the bonds of the past would be released. The cage of a person's history, including the positive and negative aspects of a life, could be dissipated, its residue left to create something anew. The period was a time of transition for America—who in the interim had since become a real road band. A live band.

The success of Rhino's America release caught the eye of several music industry leads, mainly Chip Davis, the head of Gramaphone Records. In the spring of 1994 he signed America to his record label, which would spawn the band's first studio record in ten years: *Hourglass*. Chip had made a name for himself via his instrumentalist sounds group

Decades of America memorabilia. *Courtesy of the Bunnell family.*

Mannheim Steamroller, releasing a plethora of holiday and atmospheric music. And he sensed success potential via the band America.

In 1975 Chip had co-written the trucker novelty song "Convoy," recorded by C. W. McCall. "It was the days of CB radio then," Dewey recalled. "It was all a craze for a couple of years. People would put CB radios in their cars sort of like truckers did. They would talk to each other—'Breaker breaker.' The song was about CB radioing, trucking, and it was a huge hit." Chip used the financial and industry success he achieved through his hit to start the empire of American Gramaphone, and its studio and production facility, in Nebraska. He was an early pioneer of pre-Internet marketing, creating a list of subscribers to whom he would send regular products—an atmospheric music CD along with an extra thank-you gift of a calendar or mug or something similar, on a scheduled basis.

Chip already possessed a reliable audience base of several thousand subscribers. America hoped that by releasing a brand-new record on his label, it would garner new positive attention for all involved. Gerry and Dewey would record the album— *Hourglass*— and it would be of high quality, a good album, because they were intent upon making it so. America had not recorded a studio album since 1984. The band had attempted to garner a new record deal in the interim but was unable to. Now they had a one-album deal with Gramaphone. Like the George Martin days of old, the band would feel inspired—and pressured—to create and present quality material. And they would make the most of it.

In the cold early months of 1994, Gerry, Dewey, and Hank Linderman, a studio guitarist and producer-engineer the duo had befriended, set out for the Nebraska farmhouse to make their new record. "Primarily we were using Hank as engineer at first," Dewey recalled, "because he really was right on top of the technology of the day, and still is. When digital recording was coming in, and there were a few programs—Pro Tools was the big one. I never got too deep into that stuff but he and Gerry collaborated on that aspect—about the recording process and the studio itself." The record would officially be produced by Gerry and Dewey themselves, with some assistance from Steve Levine in Los Angeles, who would help edit some vocal tracks after the main recording experience was completed.

"Young Moon" would be the album's opening tune as well as its standout track. Wind chimes bring the track in slowly, signaling a beginning. Not only the start of the song and album, but also the start of a new era of America albums. *Hourglass* would establish America as a band of the future, building upon its past triumphs and recording legacy. The sound of a synthesizer rolls in, further setting the cinematic soundscape, and an "America-sounding" guitar riff, with a modern, rawer edge, begins. It is familiar: an old friend who has since grown up, who has shed his skin and become new and improved. The audio experiments of the '80s had been accomplished, the band had had their adventures, and now they were back home—only to know it better than ever.

"Young Moon," a co-write of Dewey and Gerry, is a nature-and-love song, back to the signature realm of America's compositional territory. The idea of a young moon, the moon's form directly after its new moon phase, suggested a fresh, new start, which was what the band was going for. "Fascination with the light in your hair / A celebration, nothing else can compare / An invitation to share my life with you," the lyrics begin. There is optimism here, and positivity, almost as if the band is starting its career all over again—a first love. "Bright lights, long shadows / Tonight, we can handle / All of the doubts we may hold inside / It is a new day, things are different now / We've got each other / We'll keep looking for that young moon // We are here in this moment / Shining twice as bright / We are here for all to see." The track is a testament of intention from the band, a vow from Gerry and Dewey to continue in their artistic quest, to stay in the realm of the new and culturally relevant. The band's togetherness provides them with their strength.

The subsequent track, "Hope," is in the same vein as "Young Moon." The song would soon become a theme of the T.J. Martell Foundation. "There's a clock timing the world as it turns / There's a man marking the candle as it burns / Keeping track of every minute that remains / Still we hope somehow / It's gonna be alright / It's gonna turn out fine."

The track is a composition of Gerry's, and it would demonstrate the all-encompassing worldview he had worked to develop over the past decades of his life. The accompanying music video features Gerry and Dewey singing with a beautiful lake backdrop, with a visual backstory of young boys trying to win at baseball. The video's closing shot articulates the element of support that had driven the band this far: Gerry and Dewey, singing together, walking away with their arms on each other's shoulders. The lifelong friendship feeling was palpable. As was the duo format of the band. It still worked.

"Greenhouse," a Dewey rocker composed with the assistance of Bill Mumy and Robert Haimer, features a wild guitar solo by Wood-z. The song became a live favorite of the band, who would keep it in their nightly setlist for years. "Whole Wide World" shines a light on Dewey's talent for imagery-laden lyrics. Nature and love are once again at the forefront of his focus: "Dragonflies dipped on the swimming pool / By July I had to keep my cool / . . . You were shining like a living jewel / Inside I knew / Time stood still with you."

"After the Capitol years were over and we were going to do something," Dewey recalled, "I remember making a concerted effort to try and reconnect myself with what I was doing. More major seventh chords,

'Whole Wide World' being a good example of that—trying to get that more melodic thing that always inspired me."

Dewey had spent much of his artistic career utilizing the motif of "the road," as a metaphor both for life's journey and the literal experience of his years as a touring musician. *Hourglass* saw the inclusion of his song "Sleeper Train," a co-write with his friends Bill Mumy and Robert Haimer. "We lifted that track, the basic track, from Bill's home recording studio that we recorded it on," remembered Dewey. "Took it out there to Omaha and then built on that and polished it."

The song's melodics are full of forward motion, Dewey's lyric delivery seemingly at odds with the changing rhythmic timings of the song—or rather the words serving as vague homages to Dewey's past connections with the actor's impulsively given monologues. Elements of nature are once again at play: a town, hills, the sagebrush, and "a pink and yellow sky." The character on this sleeper train is "bound for anywhere," like Kerouac's ever-moving story figures. "Ahead now lies another open door / Abandon everything that went before," tells the song's middle eight. Much like the *Hourglass* project on behalf of the band, "Sleeper Train" is a plea for newness, for relinquishing long-held baggage, and for embracing change. Though he would always have one foot firmly in the awareness of history, Dewey was well accustomed to newness and transitions—and their volatile demands.

Hourglass would also introduce a new trend for America albums, in which they would choose to re-record earlier classics of their own. Here, both "You Can Do Magic" and "Everyone I Meet Is from California" are covered, giving a fresher spin to older material.

The album was recorded amid Gerry's ongoing *Like a Brother* project, which inspired him to invite Carl Wilson to the Omaha farmhouse and sit in on some of the *Hourglass* recording. "That was beautiful, because he stayed in the farmhouse with us," Dewey reminisced. "We cooked spaghetti together, talked about the old days. We worked from ten in the morning to six at night. Then we went back to our farmhouse; there was no town around to speak of. We didn't do much but hang out and get ready for the next day, bringing out the notes and what we would pick up the following day. We discussed what we might want to do on that. Maybe some a cappella singing with Carl too."

* * *

America's kinship with Carl, and the realization of such successful collaboration between them, would lead to Carl's involvement on the next America album too. *Human Nature* was recorded at Gerry's Los Angeles home studio of the same name in 1998. "It was a fun project; that was great work," reminisced Dewey. "It felt like Gerry and I [were] doing what we used to do. We were controlling the whole thing." The album would be released through Oxygen Records, a subsidiary label of King Biscuit Flower Hour Records. America's deal had been acquired after King Biscuit released an America concert album in '95. Technically the live recording was of a 1982 King Biscuit radio show episode, on which America had performed. Sales of the live album did moderately well for the label, which led them to sign America with Oxygen in '98, egged on by the promise of high sales.

The new album's track selection was the highest-quality set of songs America had issued in quite a while. "From a Moving Train," the first single, hit number twenty-five on the Radio & Records AC Chart. Though it is a song of movement and travel, Dewey had not composed it. Gerry's song uses the concept of a nonstop train as a metaphor for life, for time that unendingly rushes toward the future. His song "Carousel," which would be released in 2016 on his solo album of the same name, would articulate a similar concern. "From a Moving Train" speaks ardently of the life that Gerry and Dewey had lived since they were born: one of constant relocation. The song's character-narrator details how, although he has a wide and varied realm of experience, he is never home. He is bound to his road life and his fate is unavoidable. "If every venture was / A path to no avail / I'd still be rolling down / This never-ending trail." America, the band that had made themselves into the band always on tour, knew this for their own truth more than most.

"Wednesday Morning" was another Gerry tune heavily influenced by the Beatles' sound. With melodic references to "I'm Looking Through You," the track is at once catchy and unsettling—largely due to the conflict-concerned lyrics. The character-narrator is currently at odds with his lady and unsure about how (and if) elements will resolve themselves, and wonders what he can do. Because he is in a relationship, it doesn't matter who is wrong and who is right in the argument at hand. It doesn't matter who leaves first, because what happens to her happens to him. They are one and the same. When arguing arises, all winners are losers: "Wednesday morning was the last time we talked / I guess she figured it was better if she walked / It could've been me just the same / There's no winner in this game."

"Moment to Moment" marks a mature expression of gained and earned wisdom. "There was a time I knew / All that there was to know / No one could tell me then / I was wrong // I wasn't strong enough / To see where my weakness lay / The world that you hold so tight / Could slip away." The talented teenager who had insisted on taking his band's contest trophy home, who had wowed Dan with the certainty of his own artistic goals and impressed Dewey with musical acumen, had grown up. And he was still as obsessed with music and the making of it as ever.

The song was a co-write with Phil Galdston, who assisted in the track's production and recording as well. "Gerry brought it to me in a very different form," Phil recalled. "We reshaped it, rewrote some of the lyrics. We brought out the 'promise you won't ever change' part. We cut the track in New York. Most of it was Gerry, and then Dewey came into town. So I got to see the magic of these two guys up close."

Once again, Phil, who had produced other legends John Sebastian, Vanessa Williams, and the Temptations, would be wowed by the power of teamwork in pop music. Dewey's contribution blew Phil away.

"I've been fortunate enough to see that kind of thing several times," Phil recalled. "It was almost wordless communication. It took almost no time, because they [Dewey and Gerry] just knew how to work with each other. The most exciting part was when we got to the coda. Gerry had this idea that Dewey should sing those improvs. If ever I've seen a fearless singer, that was it."

The master track that Phil and Gerry had initially laid hadn't taken Dewey's vocal range into account. But it didn't matter. "Sometimes you work in a studio and it's not an environment in which you can rock out." Phil's studio in which the track was recorded "is a large bedroom in . . . [his] apartment. So here Dewey is, singing his lungs out. It was great. We did a few takes, and put it together. That's just visceral talent."

Dewey's own contributions to *Human Nature* seemed to speak to his youngest self, just as Gerry's had done. "Pages" showcased an intricately written set of lyrics, exploring the escapist value offered through stories and the opportunity to inhabit the characters of other people by absorbing their experiences. This was what had first attracted a young Dewey, in his earliest days appearing in his school's rendition of Mary Chase's play *Mrs. McThing*, to the world of theater and his studies at the London

School of Drama. And it was what enabled him to pen what had become the world-famous lyrics of "Tin Man," "Ventura Highway," and "Horse." In "Pages," too, there is movement, there is a river by which to travel: "Drifting down the river of the make believe / We laugh and grieve / Hoping for an ending of our own design / Where all is fine."

"'Pages' was really a lot of intricate lyrical work," Dewey recalled. "It's probably the hardest I've ever worked on a batch of lyrics—just to get the words [to] all fit together and to maintain a theme, which is, of course, reading."

"World Alone" and "Oloololo" were bookend pieces that told the tale of relationship transition. The following year would find Dewey divorced from his wife Vivien after a twenty-five-year marriage. "World Alone,"

Dewey and Penny Bunnell. *Courtesy of the Bunnell family.*

musically alluding to nostalgia and innocence with its malt-shop melody and chordal progression, details the relationship equivalent of an innocence-to-experience journey. When the song begins, the "world alone" is the beautiful, insular universe created by two people when they forge a loving relationship. As the song ends, the "world alone" has become a lonely place in which Dewey's character and his ex-love are in their own worlds, both alone.

"Oloololo," in contrast, would be Dewey's way of expressing an attitude of hope in the wake of despair. The exotic word is Maasai for "zigzagging," a word that Dewey had learned during his African safari in 1981. Going "oloololo" referred to a wild animal zigzagging through a field, straying from the main and direct path—which was what Dewey had done, leaving his marriage and beginning a new era for himself. "I'm going Oloololo / Back to the world where I'm from / Soon I'll be flying solo / On a heading that follows the sun."

"I don't think there're too many cases where you come back as big as you were in the beginning," Dewey reflected, "but at least it's dedicated to history, and I'm glad that stuff's out there for those interested. *Human Nature* might be the last great album we did."

Still, the future looked bright. Dewey married Penny, a fellow nature-enthusiast-animal-lover, in 2002, and, together with Penny's daughter, Destry, they became a new family.

26

THE WORK

Dewey never wanted to make a solo album. Since his days as a teenager in Biloxi, he was inherently in favor of the group aesthetic in music. Singled out in the school's newspaper concert review as "leader of the pack" of his band the Renegades, Dewey had felt perplexed by the dubbing. He didn't want to be a leader of a band. There were too many decisions to make; there was too much pressure. Dewey was a musician who thrived on the principles of nature, a muse-inspired artist. He didn't like to force songwriting when he didn't feel it. Founding and becoming a member of America, of which he was one third of three equal partners, was Dewey's ideal musical career move. But he innately possessed performative charisma, with a recognizable and powerful lead voice and a unique sense of rhythm, timing, and mood.

Gerry, on the other hand, had more songs than he knew what to do with. He couldn't stop writing. He composed to survive. Throughout his tenure in America, he had been involved in countless Los Angeles sessions with a variety of pop and rock musicians. Gerry's natural aptitude as a producer, his confidence in the recording studio, and his ability to hear a recording's "big picture" led him to be valued by other artists. America pal David Cassidy would invite Gerry to participate in his mid-'70s RCA solo recordings; he ended up co-producing and co-writing on both *Home Is Where the Heart Is* and *Getting It in the Street* (both 1976). Gerry also contributed to albums by Dave Mason, Dan Fogelberg, Ricci Martin, several solo projects of assorted Beach Boys, and even the Band's Rick Danko, on whose eponymous 1977 album Gerry made a noticeable, song-defining addition of background vocals to a recording of "Small Town Talk."

Dewey's and Gerry's differences in musical personality and approach and their mutual understanding of and belief in the value of artistic teamwork made for an ideal partnership. They were just different enough to not compete, to give each other the creative and personal space needed for happiness and musical thriving—in whatever way each one saw fit. There was love there, and also respect for their individual freedoms—another example of the band's and their generation's manifestation of the hippie dream. The literal distance between Dewey and Gerry and between their daily lives had been established during the band's earliest days following the relocation to California in '72. Dewey moved to Marin County, while Gerry and Dan remained in Los Angeles. Their minimal time off between tours and recording sessions was spent in different cities, allowing for time spent together to be appreciated. So many bands would crumble and fall under the weight of too much togetherness, allowing resentments—some petty, some major—to completely destroy them. Perhaps because America had been founded by high school friends—they were pals first, band members second—they set an ideal hierarchy of priorities in place from the get-go. In the twenty-first-century edition of America, the distance would grow even larger, with new marriages for each—leading Gerry to spend larger amounts of time in Australia and Dewey in Wisconsin.

"He's the world's greatest partner," Gerry said about Dewey. "It's really more of brothers, I would say. It is built on many things: love and understanding, and an immense amount of respect. And I know that that goes both ways. I think we have a mutual appreciation society." Over the years of their partnership in America, Gerry and Dewey would support each other in their different individual interests, whether it was a charity or organization to get involved with, or a new musical endeavor.

"The contrast between our writing styles is complementary, I think," Dewey said about his work with Gerry. "We know our strengths and weaknesses, so I know that something I'm doing, Gerry probably is not motivated to do or to move in that direction. And I don't play piano—he writes on piano. He owns that department."

In many ways, Gerry and Dewey were completely different people. Gerry moved quickly, thought quickly, created quickly. He liked to consume as much art and knowledge as he possibly could. Time and its

Dewey and Gerry: men at work. *Courtesy of Eric Halvorsen.*

nonstop passage made him uneasy when he thought about it, though he chose to see it as a challenge, rather than an enemy. So much of his solo material would explore the topic too.

Dewey always admired Gerry's style, so unlike his own. "It's hard to keep up with Gerry, for me. Because he is driven to be right on the front end of everything. Aesthetically, creatively, fashion, the latest music. I can't keep up with popular music at all. I try. Gerry is really driven to know all the details, like the make of every airplane we're on. He's driven that way, it's the way he's hardwired. So I don't try to keep up with him in that regard. I don't really get concerned that I haven't done what I could do. Yes, there's stuff I probably should have done or could do better. But I don't lose sleep over it—where I think Gerry might. Sometimes with his own recordings. He can obsess over it, wanting to get back into the studio and finish it. But it's not part of my persona."

Dewey would choose not to cut a solo album, but he would record a couple of tracks with L.A. Renaissance man and industry figure Bobby Woods and the Les Deux Love Orchestra. "The Cool of the Evening," a moody and mature slow-paced track of Dewey's was recorded with Woods and released in 2017. It was a quintessential Dewey song, full of seventh chords and allusions to nature. "Houses in White," cut with Gerry and Bobby, was released in 2019.

Gerry would release seven solo albums between 1995 and 2020, beginning with the strong *Van Go Gan*, the CD of which remained unavailable outside Japan until 1999. In the mid-'90s Gerry had created a home studio on his Sherman Oaks property, a throwback to his '70s-era Buzz Studios in his Kings Road L.A. apartment. The new home studio, dubbed Human Nature Studios, allowed for 24/7 recording access. This encouraged him to record songs that had been backlogged during the post-*Perspective* touring years.

Van Go Gan's track listing offered up a heavily produced selection of Gerry's material that served as satisfying pop fare. Opening track "Emma" was jangly, catchy, and tinged with a vague air of early-'90s guitar rock; "Van Go Gan," a clever take on the complicated path walked by artists and their inspirations. "Playing God" featured old America pal and successful comedian Phil Hartman, via narrative snippets in which he spoke as a televangelical preacher. "Now Sue" would be the most innovative song on the record, showcasing Gerry's studio prowess that had only grown since his earliest days with America. As John Lennon had been inspired toward his melody for "Because" by considering the sound of Beethoven's "Moonlight Sonata" backward, Gerry followed suit with "Now Sue"—but with one of his oldie-but-goodies.

"'Now Sue' is actually my song 'Till the Sun Comes Up Again,' backwards," Gerry explained. "It's the complete song from *Homecoming*. When we were working on *Homecoming*, we used to take home reel-to-reel tapes. And the tape had been spooled the wrong way when I put it on to listen to it. It was all different chords. So I started scribbling down what they were. And I thought, 'one day I'm going to rewrite this thing.' The lyrics were my transcription of what the backwards sounds sounded like. I used the actual backwards tapes of 'Till the Sun' in the middle of 'Now Sue.'"

Carousel, released in 2016, offered up a strong selection of tracks that revolved around the concepts of time passing, maturation, and self-reflection. Similar in album construction to several America records (in its inclusion of several covers), it also provided proof that Gerry's compositional gift had not waned. "Tokyo" was catchy and radio friendly, with ear-pleasing guitar work. "Minutes Count," as well as the album's eponymous track, showed Gerry once more investigating the conundrum of limited time.

The year 2019 would see the release of yet another solo effort, *Five Mile Road*. Though all Gerry's solo albums generated positive responses from America fans as well as online consumer reviews, they were ignored a bit by mainstream audiences and critics. The expansion of the music industry and the world at large, enabled by the powers of evolving technology, had rendered the effects of America's latter-day album and solo project releases a bit lighter than they had been during the band's debut years.

The greatest non-America musical offering of Gerry's came through a collaborative project with two other golden-era pop musicians, both also from well-known L.A. bands. Chicago's Robert Lamm and the Beach Boys' Carl Wilson joined Gerry in the early '90s, recording tracks that would result in the *Like a Brother* album. The project took several years—1992–1997—to complete, in part due to the heavy touring schedules of the three associated bands—Chicago, the Beach Boys, and America. But once the songs had been cut, the project came to a halt upon Carl's devastating news: In early 1997 he was diagnosed with lung cancer, and he passed away on February 6, 1998. For both Beach Boys and America fans, it was a heartbreaking day. The universe had lost a golden voice. Two years later, *Like a Brother* saw its release via the Transparent Music label.

Gerry gave a beautiful eulogy at Carl's wake, sharing with the mourners a practice vocal tape that Carl used to warm up to. It was a recording of fellow pop giant Steve Miller, performing a range of vocal exercises, one of which used the words "It's a beautiful day"—a reminder for the living, and the friends and fans that Carl affected, of Carl's life-affirming and joyful legacy of beauty and spirit.

Like a Brother marked the last recordings that Carl ever made. Today, much like America's discography, the album stands as a legacy to friendship and the power of making music together. Gerry covered his friend Harry Nilsson's "Without You" for the record and contributed two original tracks: another time-awareness piece, "Watching the Time," and the hauntingly beautiful "Sheltering Sky," which would be one of producer Phil Galdston's favorite tracks. "Gerry had recorded a really beautiful demo," Phil recalled. Hearing it, for him, "was an exciting moment."

"Sheltering Sky" borrows its title and its motif of love in foreign lands from the classic Paul Bowles novel. The track creates an eerie musical mood with help from synthesizers, which—in conjunction with the lyrics—alludes to the subtle emotive telepathy that can pass between two people in love, but separated by great physical distances. "It's a long, long way from here to there / Silent shadows over the dateline / We both stare at the same blue moon / Under the sheltering sky." The couple is tied together by the land below them and the sky and stars above them, which could also be seen as a metaphor for two souls who have found commonality with one another. They have discovered that their shared spiritual terrain—here not literal land—also ties them together.

Most of all, Phil was impressed by the camaraderie between Gerry, Robert, and Carl in the studio: "They were a very good team. Very supportive of each other. They were willing to try." Phil, also an accomplished songwriter, had shared his song "Today"—a John Waite co-write—with Robert for the project. Instead of keeping it for himself, Robert insisted that Carl sing lead on the track, feeling that Carl's voice was better suited to it.

The atmosphere of creative teamwork that Phil witnessed in the *Like a Brother* sessions stemmed from the three musicians' abilities honed during their tenure in their respective ensemble-forward bands.

Gerry and Dewey enjoyed their side projects and non-America musical pursuits. But they were only temporary sojourns. The band they had founded together with Dan was their true musical home. The whole was greater than the sum of its parts. "I think in most ways," Gerry reflected, "a lot of the strength of the band itself was the influence that each of us had on the other."

27

THE RELEVANCE

The year 2003 would see another sideman transition for America. Touring bassist Bradley Palmer left the band after twenty-one years, and multitalented musical journeyman Rich Campbell, who had toured with Natalie Cole and Dave Mason, took his place. Rich's ease with a high-harmony, decades-long rock touring experience and his expertise in music technology made him the ideal fit for America in the new millennium. Gerry and Dewey were thrilled to have him aboard, hoping that he would give the live show, which had recently grown somewhat stale from years of sameness, an extra dose of oomph.

"We had a very short audition period," Gerry recalled, "where there were two or three guys [under consideration]. But I knew Rich from his work with Three Dog Night and Dave Mason; we had crossed paths quite a few times, and I'd always really liked Rich. I knew he was a high harmony singer. So when he came, it was really more a confirmation of 'Yeah, I was pretty sure this was the guy . . . and clearly he is.'

"I think that was a real turning point. From then on, everything just started to get better. He had a lovely handle on all of the technologies that were starting to be integrated into the show, things that are behind the scenes—wireless guitars, for instance. So it just all started to move forward."

In 2013 Rich would also become tour manager of America, as the band continued to play hundreds of live shows per year. He was an experienced, gifted musician and talented road warrior. He would become a key fixture and recognizable face of the twenty-first-century incarnation of America.

The band's relevance was palpable through its legacy of recordings and the live touring it had worked to develop a reputation for. But America wanted more: to create newer relevance via the studio album. "We needed to prove some relevance in the modern era," Dewey recalled, "and that was the idea. With management, everybody said we better cross-pollinate with a newer generation. That's definitely what was going on."

The cross-pollination came in the form of Fountains of Wayne musician Adam Schlesinger, a prolific pop writer who seemed to understand America and its compositional strengths. Adam, along with James Iha of the Smashing Pumpkins, were brought in to produce a new studio album for America. It would be recorded at Adam and James's Stratosphere Studios in New York City and—to cement the relevance element of the project—be titled *Here and Now*.

Gerry and Dewey had been fans of Fountains of Wayne since their earliest album releases in the mid-'90s, with 1999's *Utopia Parkway* being a favorite. Upon discovering their mutual fandom, Gerry and Adam began an e-mail correspondence, exchanging new songs they were working on and providing helpful feedback. When Gerry sent over his song "Here and Now," Adam was further impressed, sensing even more the potential that this older rock 'n' roll band possessed for recording studio possibilities. After meeting Adam's producing partner James Iha, America was convinced they wanted to pursue an album project together. It didn't hurt that Adam's consistent output in the past several years—of multiple artistic projects that ranged from film scores to musical theater—had attracted the attention of top industry A&R figures. When word got out that he was working with America, album deals came calling; Burgundy Records, a subsidiary label of Sony's, was chosen. As production began, Gerry and Dewey brought in some of their most recent song ideas. As usual, Gerry had about forty, with more to spare. The tracks that would end up on the album seemed to be a culmination of Dewey's and Gerry's writerly characters, as they had developed, changed, and still remained true to their authentic selves since the 1970s.

Dewey's forever fascination with the road, and with journeying, rendered it a constant motif of his song catalogue, from its first appearance in "A Horse with No Name." He knew that to be alive was to keep moving, and that in the absence of certainty, the best course of action was to continue the journey—to travel. He had been born into a transitory existence with his Air Force family, and constantly relocating had become the most natural thing in the world. Maybe some people traveled the majority of their life journeys metaphorically, living their lives in the same town the whole while. For them the journey was a foundational thing. For Dewey, it could not be more literal.

Dewey's song "Ride On" was co-written with Adam, but it rang out on *Here and Now* as the utmost Dewey song. It was a musically moody tune with a low-key percussive beat, with lyrics that urged continuing: "Once more follow the trail / Long gone into the setting sun / Ride on you must not fail." Its words also rearticulated Dewey's lifelong identification with the peace creed originating in the '60s, a creed that he had tried to keep relevant through much of his canon: "Speak out / Carry the message forth." His teenage lesson learned—by making a go for theater at Corona Academy in London and deciding that it wasn't right for him, that he would move toward music—had also taught him the value of authenticity: "Make sure to speak with a voice loud and true."

Schlesinger and Iha, with Gerry and Dewey, selected a variety of guest artists to contribute to the studio project. Iha aimed to sound timeless, rather than retro—which, with master engineering, would enable America to involve newer, more modern musicians in the project and save it from becoming a "Duets" album. Nada Surf's Ira Elliot, My Morning Jacket's Jim James and Patrick Hallahan, and Maplewood's Mark Rozzo added a dose of modern flavor to America's inherently fresh sound. Ryan Adams did too.

"The first thing from the Schlesinger project that always amazes me is the 'Glass King' song," Dewey recalled, "which was really something, that was a strange left field process. It was a song that came together without any of the norms, or the way I conducted myself writing-wise. When Ryan Adams came in, he was like a tornado that came into the session: 'Hey, what are you guys doing? Let's write a song! You got any titles?' It was really good, it was really strong, a flowing current of energy—like jumping in the stream with Ryan. And just going with it; and we crawled out of the bank on the other side and there was the song. It was really great working with those guys. It was the first time we'd ever worked in New York City."

While "Ride On" seemed to be a culmination of Dewey's road philosophy songs, "Glass King" most definitely spoke to his oeuvre of love songs, which had begun with "Three Roses." The track's vocals find Dewey at his rock 'n' roll-est, raspiest, rawest ever. As the song begins, a simple driving guitar chord progression pulls us into the narrative: "Here within these castle walls / My love is still with you / Watching all the lands below / These stones are always true." The seasoned urgency with which Dewey delivers his vocals coats them in an extra layer of truth—as though he has spent his songwriting lifetime wading through sets of words, verse after verse and chorus after chorus, and "Glass King" has finally enabled him to find the right ones. "As the walls begin to fall / It's not my kingdom anymore / It belongs to me but I, I belong to her." The song is one of surrender: after a lifetime of trying to love and still hold onto the self, here the self is sacrificed upon the altar of big love, the universe. He has everything, but it doesn't matter; he has rediscovered his own mortality, and more, the ego has been harnessed by the heart's inevitable yielding. "She looks through me when she pleases / Breaks me in a million pieces // . . . I'm the glass king," the song concludes. It interestingly chooses to keep hidden its own title line until the very end, as its fact is the last one that needs stating. Nothing comes after.

Gerry's pop-writer brilliance shines shockingly bright in the clever "Look at Me Now," an ear-candy-laden, fun song with incredible wordplay. And his cover of Schlesinger's own "Work to Do" is an ideal album inclusion in the same vein. "Love & Leaving," however, just as "Ride On" and "Glass King" summed up Dewey's writerly character, would seem to encapsulate Gerry's to the utmost. A co-write with Bill Mumy, "Love & Leaving" revisits those very themes and their eternal interweaving that Gerry had explored forty years earlier in "To Each His Own." As Dewey had, Gerry, too, suffered from the scars of continuous displacement as an Air Force child. His inherently romantic nature had often led him to pen songs about loving people and inevitably leaving or being left by them. He knew the routine progression of attachments. Maybe he should've been used to it by now, but he wasn't. Except his decades of experience now rendered it nearly impossible to think positively for long about the honeymoon stage of a relationship. Falling in love or befriending someone now just made him sad; he now knew too much. Even the track's melodics were somber, restrained, painful. "Don't wanna be building walls / Cause everything rising falls / It's darkness here the light's concealing / Love it seems is too revealing." In youth, the bright, revelatory aspects of the romantic love experience are exhilarating, rejuvenating; there is little to hide, the scars are few, the layers to peel away are minimal. A young person in love is proud to have a light shine on him. But an older person knows better; it's happened to him before, only to have the rug pulled out from under him, his soft underbelly pointed to and poked. He's been laughed at. Now he knows there are corners of himself he should hide. To romance a new person is to also romance their old flames, who have left emotional memory stamps behind. Gerry is a romantic, and so he falls again and again. But does he wish to be revealed this time around? When he has the power to stop it before it starts? "The ghosts in here are all competing / Over one more song about love and leaving." Gerry's musical ear is sharp, he can categorize a composition as a love song from its first three notes. But as a lifetime composer of such work, he now finally understands that "love song" is a euphemism. There are no love songs—only love-and-leaving songs.

Here & Now received positive responses from audiences. And it once again brought America to the charts, debuting at number fifty-two. It had been a while since the band had achieved a release with that much commercial impact so quickly. Their visibility was once again raised. "All of a sudden we were on *Letterman* and the *Today Show*, which never would've happened at that time, without *Here & Now*," Gerry explained.

***

The year 2011 found America back in the recording studio, this time to create a quality covers album. Appropriately titled *Back Pages*, it would give Gerry and Dewey the chance to revisit favorite songs of theirs—and their loyal audience's—from the past and also to make use of one of their greatest strengths: performing cover tunes.

It was an album of firsts for America. "Not only were we recording in Nashville for the first time," remembered Gerry, "but it took a lot of the pressure off of us. It was such a unique project from the start because we didn't have to write anything. We removed that whole dynamic of 'You play me your songs and I'll play you mine,' and we could just scan the great works of art and choose."

Produced by their old friend and colleague Fred Mollin, *Back Pages* was partially recorded at Nashville studios and featured guest musicians like Dire Straits' Mark Knopfler. A standout track was Gerry's take on America's close-friend Jimmy Webb's "Crying in My Sleep," which had also been recorded magnificently by Art Garfunkel on his classic '77 album *Watermark*. The song details romantic longing and loneliness in the wake of a painful breakup, and also references familiar L.A. hangouts: the Rainbow Bar and Lucy's El Adobe Café. Both elements made it an ideal fit for Gerry to cover. When Jimmy heard the track, he was pleased. "I thought it was great," he remembered. "I'll tell you exactly what I said. I said, 'there was a time, boys, when that would have been a hit.' Yes, it definitely would have been a hit."

Dewey's choice to cover Joni Mitchell's generation-defining "Woodstock" provided an opportunity to further inhabit the musical character that he had established during his earliest recordings. This character, which Dewey had in part taken up the mantle for since the early '70s, was one who wanted for his society and himself to return to "the garden." To remember humanity's inherent connection to nature and honor its sacred quality. Brian Wilson's "Caroline No," perhaps Dewey's best vocal delivery on the record, also seemed to come from the same vein of the desire to return to innocence. While many musicians shied away from covering a song that possessed such a stellar version in its original recording—with Brian Wilson's hauntingly beautiful voice—Dewey chose to interpret it. "It gives us all a chance to hear Dewey sing something in a register and at a tempo he normally wouldn't write at," reflected Gerry. "He does such an incredible version of it."

The album was released in July 2011, and it would be well received critically. But its impact was affected by a sudden and heartbreaking event that occurred just two days prior to the album's release.

Since his departure from America, Dan had gone on to have a successful career in the Christian music scene. After signing with Pat Boone's record company Lion & Lamb Records, Dan released his first solo album in 1979. Titled *All Things Are Possible*, the record was a testament to the personal transformation Dan had gone through since his departure from America. It reached number one on the Contemporary Christian Music charts and also went on to garner a Grammy nomination for Best Contemporary Gospel Performance. In 1984, Dan recorded "Doer of the Word," and chose to invite Gerry to contribute background vocals. Though fans occasionally expressed desire for a true America reunion, it was not meant to be. That ship had sailed. Dan was not the only band member who had gone through a transformation. Gerry and Dewey had worked hard toward making America successful as a twosome. It had taken band reconfiguring, the hiring of additional players, the redistribution of setlists. America had redefined itself, and it had not been easy. To rejoin with Dan, once all this had happened, had changed—would be to revert back to something from the past, to something that didn't exist anymore. Time and again, when Dewey and Gerry were offered band reunion opportunities from record labels or promoters, they mulled them over but put them on the back burner. "Maybe later. Maybe one day."

After years of quality musical output, and various health problems, Dan passed away on July 24, 2011. "It was totally out of the blue," Dewey remembered. "I had no indication that he had a condition that could be fatal or anything like that. We were really shocked. And we felt the finality of it. Gerry and I spoke that day over the phone; we happened to be home and off the road. And we reached out to Cathie [Peek]."

America fans everywhere and his bandmates Gerry and Dewey mourned the loss of Dan and tried to find comfort in the legacy of quality music, made both in and out of America, that he'd left behind.

28

THE TOUR

Lost and Found, an assortment of Gerry and Dewey tunes that they'd recorded between 2000 and 2011, was released as a studio album in 2015. It began a trend of archival releases that would continue over the following years, as America began to celebrate its own legacy and revisit its own past. Their archivist was California-based musician Jeff Larson, who sometimes collaborated with Gerry on songwriting. In the coming years, older versions, demos, and previously unheard America tracks from as far back as the band's earliest days would be assembled and released. America fans everywhere, many of them intense audiophiles and record collectors, were pleased. When helping to assemble legacy-encompassing track collections of the band, surrounding their fiftieth anniversary, Jeff noted that Dan's role in America's history was "absolutely essential. I'm very conscious of Dan's role, so I make it a point to make sure he's represented. Even recently with the London Palladium 2018 show boxed set, we needed an early Dan song in there. Harmony wise, when you see all three guys at the really early stage of the first year, year and a half, you see that all those roles, all those vocals, all those guitar parts are essential to that sound. Some of the underrated America songs that are beautiful George Martin–strings songs are Dan Peek songs."

A noticeable track on *Lost and Found* was Gerry's catchy rocker "Driving," which would become a setlist favorite in the live act. In recent years America's live show had received several upgrades that only added to the concert appeal, one of which was the tastefully assembled band video clips projected on the background of every stage they graced.

While hearing their favorite songs from America's history, fans were now able to view scenes from the history, too, and to honor and remember fondly the contribution of Dan, who would be featured prominently in the footage. His songs "Lonely People" and "Don't Cross the River," fan favorites, were always included in the setlist too. In this way, Dan's memory was kept alive.

The prestige of the live America show had been building since the mid-1980s, when the band decided to devote itself to touring. In the new millennium, the show—which, to satisfy fans, featured the band's greatest hits plus a few token newer songs—had been honed to near perfection. America's touring operation improved even further when bassist Rich Campbell assumed a dual role and became the band's official tour manager in 2013.

He'd had plenty of road logistics experience. From 1993 until 2003, Rich had served as tour manager to Dave Mason and, on occasion, Three Dog Night, and in 1997 he had tour managed Ringo Starr's All-Star Band. Rich was well acquainted with the various computer software and travel management databases used on the job. And he was used to thinking in terms of 'thirty days out,' the projection of time ahead that rock tour managers planned for during their band's nonstop, multicity tours. "Tour managing comes pretty natural for some reason to me," Rich reflected. "I kind of live naturally in the future anyway; I don't know why that is. I tend to run through scenarios quite a few times over and over again. My dad used to jokingly say that I used to overthink everything, running down different paths. Which really fits the whole tour manager mind-set." America's travel experiences benefited from having a band member as tour manager. By living the band's touring life firsthand, Rich could apply his own normal living standards that he had for himself, on the road, to the entire band. A certain amount of sleep was preferred each night, a functional level of hotel cleanliness too. Rich could provide a realistic approach to scheduling and time constraints, understanding and sometimes anticipating certain travel glitches that commonly arose, like delayed flights.

By 2020, America' fiftieth anniversary year, the band was playing approximately one hundred shows a year, which made for at least two hundred travel days a year. Most shows were stateside, but the band always made sure to play around Australasia and Italy, where their fan base was still huge, as well as select European cities on occasion. By now knowing the types of venues and towns that they were most successful in, they always filled and often sold out the halls in which they played. America was a small operation by now, a tight eight-piece band and crew, so they could easily play intimate venues like the six-hundred-seat Birchmere in Alexandria, Virginia. While large-scale multibus productions with a high staff count were forced to bypass tiny theaters, hardly able to park in the venue parking lot, America could make it work. On the opposite end of the spectrum, America played several large-scale venues every year—typically outdoor festivals in the warmer months—that were in the 20,000-seat range. These events would often be billed alongside other similar acts like Michael McDonald, Chicago, or Boz Scaggs. The ideal venue for the band seemed to be 1,200–2,000-seat performing arts theaters, which tended to be located just outside city centers in the U.S., Europe, and Australasia.

"One of the real beauties with this band is you can basically have a really comfortable ticket price for fans, and a decent-sized theater, and be relatively guaranteed you're going to sell it out. Which is really appealing to those venues that are just outside the downtown of an area, that are outside the city. Some of the performing arts halls used to be the towns' old movie houses back in the 1920s and '30s. America is a decent-priced band comparable to other bands in this era and [of this] genre, and it really sells well. We have a really good track record of being in that 80–100 percent sold-out window, in the slightly outside the urban centers where all the teens and twenty-somethings might go—who we do get some of in our audience, who are more curious of this band that they heard about from another band, or through a video game they played or something like that. Most of the demographic that we have is that forty-, fifty-, sixty , seventy-year-olds who live slightly outside urban centers."

In 2019, America won Live Nation's Pollstar Award for Best Attraction for its reliable and successful live touring. Part of the group's modern success was due to the awareness of its demographic and how best to tour to their satisfaction, geographically. But it was also because the live show was just really, *really* good.

The band's operation was experienced and had earned the right to be confident. America had been on tour for fifty years, and its roster of past crew members was impressive. The '70s-era troupe, who had managed America's largest scale tours, had included Scott Harder, Jim Hoskins, Larry Penny, Ken Warnick, and Doug Suman. Bill Crook spent years as the band's sound engineer, eventually going on to found Crook Custom Guitars, building and selling original guitars. And Doug Kenny, America's high school friend from London Central and an early band member, went on to work on the Rolling Stones' "Steel Wheels" tour in 1989 and was responsible for safely transporting Keith's vast array of guitars from gig to gig.

In 2020, the America crew consisted of Travis Jameson, Eric Halvorsen (who also served as band photographer and social media manager), and Jeff Worrell. Worrell had come aboard around the time when Rich Campbell joined America. A talented musician himself, Jeff soon evolved into the band's house (front of house) engineer, ensuring that the sound of America live sounded as good as possible every night. His son Bill would serve as guitar tech from 2009 through 2011 and was brought back in 2014 to serve as lead guitarist for America through 2016. It began a trend of the band incorporating younger members into the live band—out of necessity, but inadvertently injecting the group with a fresh and different sound. In 2016, when Bill departed to embark upon solo work, Andy Barr of Cobra Starship assumed the role. He too contributed a unique and young sound to the live act—and he stayed for just two years before leaving to pursue his own project, called Formerly Alien.

In 2018, musical journeyman Steve Fekete took up the mantle of America's guitarist. His technical knowhow and performative prowess frequently stole live performance spotlights, as he offered up inventive solos to pieces of "Hollywood," "Sandman," and "Survival." Fans were no doubt reminded of the guitar days of old, in which the onstage antics of wild guitar heroes were a huge part of the rock-show draw. Having worked with both classic and modern pop giants like Jackson Browne and Gwen Stefani, Steve found a real rock refuge through which to wail when he joined America's live band. "The dynamic onstage during the performances is genuine," reflected Steve. "It's not like we're making enthusiastic faces at each other because we know the audience is watching us. I sometimes forget about the audience, and it seems like it's just Gerry and Dewey, and we're having a good time onstage, and it feels really good. It's special when that happens. It doesn't always happen."

The year 2014 had seen the departure of longtime drummer Willie Leacox, who chose to retire after a lifetime on the road with America, and 2016 sadly saw the death of '70s-era America bassist David Dickey.

America lineup in 2019, left to right: Steve Fekete, Gerry Beckley, Ryland Steen, Dewey Bunnell, and Rich Campbell. *Courtesy of Eric Halvorsen.*

Willie was replaced by Ryland Steen, the incomparable drummer of ska band Reel Big Fish from 2005 through 2014. Prior to that, Ryland had been in the power pop band Square, who had also featured James Valentine, eventual guitarist of Maroon 5. The suavity with which Ryland transitioned from the years of playing raucous and rhythmically complex beats that Reel Big Fish demanded, to the nearly polar opposite of soft-and-sensitive classic rock reliability that America did, proved the vastness of his musical abilities. Ryland released a trio of solo albums from 2013 through 2019—the first two under the moniker This Magnificent and the third under his own name—a project that showcased his talent for multi-instrumentalism, elaborate studio production, introspective song composition, and melodic vocals. He would also make frequent appearances on Gerry's later solo albums. "They're great, very supportive bandleaders," Ryland reflected on Dewey and Gerry. "By no means do we feel like the spotlight has to be on them completely. I think if anything, they enjoy having it be the band effort as much as it can be. I mean obviously America *is* Gerry and Dewey. But there've been times in the past where we've done these sort of meet and greets, and they'll say, 'Guys, come to the meet and greets with us,' and they want us as a part of it as well. So they're very, very supportive bandleaders. By no means is it just their faces or does it have to be just them. They're happy to have us [be] a part of it as well. Gerry and Dewey offer a very good example for us younger musicians to follow."

Much like the earliest sidemen of America, this latest touring band had nothing but respect for Dewey and Gerry, with a healthy dose of musical admiration and legacy awareness. Rich understood the subtle achievement of the band's connection to and potential forms of significance of its name: "Their 'America' that they are representative of is the American desert and love, and scenes from the lives of people living in America. Dewey is brilliant at the sort of . . . singing songs about two lazy dogs sitting watching their man. It's really kind of just 'slice of life,' miniature vignettes, little plays that are happening that are just sort of documenting or wondering about that level of American life—not the bigger things, not the politics of specific leaders." Many of America's recent audiences would always be older couples out on date night, frequently instigated by women, who would bring their men along.

"You typically can't have two presidents or two CEOs," Rich reflected. "So when bands do, they find that they all have this equal power, and there's a lot of money and time and creativity. And with all that at stake, of course you're going to fight and probably end up hating each other. So many bands follow that path. It's a fascinating exception to me after so many years that the two of them [Gerry and Dewey] are still friends. There's still a genuine friendship, this mutual respect they have for each other.

"It's sort of this exception showing you can have two presidents, you can actually have two CEOs. They joke around, they make each other laugh, which is just really fascinating to see. Other bands that I've worked with, that's not the case. Which for the rest of us here is really nice, because the tone of the whole organization is always set at the top. If the tone is this real, benevolent friendship—we're on this journey together, and for everybody else who gets to go along on that journey, it's much nicer."

29

THE NEW

America had won a Grammy Award, earned platinum and gold records, and, in 2006, been inducted into the Vocal Hall of Fame. On February 6, 2012, America the band received its star on the Hollywood Walk of Fame. Located at 6786 Hollywood Boulevard, the star proved to be further recognition of the band's illustrious and decades-spanning career. America was now immortalized, Hollywood-style.

The ceremony offered Dewey and Gerry a chance to invite all their past and present cohorts to celebrate right along with them: engineers of the band's classic early records Geoff Emerick and Ken Scott, former

Hollywood star ceremony, left to right: **Billy Bob Thornton, Dewey, Gerry, and John Stamos.** *Photographer unknown.*

managers including John Hartmann, '70s-era bassist David Dickey, Bill Mumy, original crew members, and Henry Diltz, camera in tow to document the proceedings. America's close friends and Hollywood actors John Stamos and Billy Bob Thornton made the presentation. In the band's ceremonial speech, Gerry cited the band's ties to the city of Los Angeles. It was where America had brought their musical dreams, their dreams that had first been established with rampant fanfare and unimaginable success in their second-home city of London. Ushered into the SoCal music scene by David Geffen in 1972, America had learned to call Los Angeles home—the first permanent one the Air Force kids had ever really known.

"The star is a lovely thing, I think," expressed Gerry, "with such an incredible long history. And to me one of the great things about it is that it's across the board. There're people from the great days of radio. There're people acknowledged for their cinematography. So it's really for the creative arts; visual and audio arts, and therefore singers. The great crooners of the '40s, '50s, and '60s are just as valid—as you walk along—as are the great vaudeville comedians or the great directors, the Steven Spielbergs. It really is a very large pool, but a very wonderful pool to be included in."

America's attitude of inclusivity had always been a prime tenet of its creed. Gerry, Dewey, and Dan valued the concept of the group, the team, the ensemble, knowing they were stronger and more creative together. America was a band whose logo the public sometimes found to be more recognizable than its members' names and faces. Like the country from which it borrowed its name, America the band was comprised of different entities that chose to come together as one—exercising democracy, equality, and cooperation with each other in the name of seeking a greater musical good, taking popular music beyond what it had ever been before.

"The emotions, feelings, and drives of youth can certainly be part of trying to reach out and just expand everything," Dewey reminisced. "Expand your mind. You know, Timothy Leary's thing: Don't follow the well-worn, beaten, boring path of life. We are, at any given moment, part of the ongoing evolution of the human experience."

The group's belief in the value of inclusivity didn't mean that they themselves were always included by others. When they had first made it big with the release of "Horse," they quickly rose to the top of the pop music world—where it was exciting to be, but vaguely lonely too. America had arrived at SoCal's musical world in '72, already successful, only to be slightly cold-shouldered by some of the pre-established pop music community there. They would befriend many of them and collaborate with some. But America would come to understand that its own attitude of artistic and personal inclusivity, and respect for mutual individual freedom—a key element of the '60s countercultural philosophy—would thrive best where it was agreed upon the most: in the trio itself. The sense of belonging that eluded Gerry, Dewey, and Dan as children, moving all over the world with their Air Force families, causing them to build emotional walls and blend into backgrounds rather than stand out, was finally found. They had created it themselves, for themselves, in the love-and-peace-themed aural universe of their band.

The year 2020 found Gerry and Dewey still exploring new areas of art and life, and bringing new people into their orbit.

Gerry, a talented photographer who for years had taken daily photographs for his "View from the Hotel Window" series, had his first photography show at the Morrison Hotel Gallery in 2017. In 2019, he collaborated with menswear designer Todd Snyder on a T-shirt line that featured selected images from Gerry's series.

In 2012 Gerry and Kathy divorced after a twenty-four-year marriage. But as was the case with Dewey's personal life, brighter moments lay on the horizon: Gerry married Sally in 2016. He began to spend more time at his home in Sydney, Australia—where Sally was from—a place he felt a lifelong affinity to. "It's a hybrid," Gerry explained. "It's the Beatles and the Beach Boys, England and California, which is what I am. In the case of where do you feel at home, this really feels right." They would still keep a residence in Southern California, setting up camp in the trendy artistic neighborhood of Venice.

Gerry's new marriage had in part worked to redefine his life just as Dewey's had, leading him to a new, streamlined way of being that was fueled by art and artistic friends, travel, and unending newness that seemed to satisfy his naturally curious persona. And he still played an active role in the lives of his sons, Matthew and Joe.

Matthew, who had gone on to become a Grammy-nominated music producer working with pop vocalists Katy Perry, Avril Lavigne, and Camila Cabello, was always inspired by America and their work ethic: "Especially as I get older, I see how difficult it is for everybody to keep it going for three years, let alone fifty. I'm incredibly impressed and awed. I think it's awesome in the literal sense of the word, that these guys who

Gerry and Sally Beckley. *Courtesy of the Beckley family.*

Gerry and Dewey in Italy, 2019. *Courtesy of Eric Halvorsen.*

knew each other since high school—can you imagine being married for fifty years? Most people can't swing that. And they've somehow managed, through ridiculous successes, from arenas to bowling alleys. These two very different people have a lot of love for each other and mutual respect. Just the endurance of that—it's incredible. There're not a lot of people who've been able to do it as long as they have. I don't think we'll see much more of it, in terms of new bands being able to be together for fifty years. I'm grateful that I got to witness it and that my dad, Dewey, and the band, are the people who set my example. As great as the music is, and as impressive [as] their catalogue [is], I really feel lucky for the example they set: of hard work and respect for each other, their fans, and the people that work with and for them.

"I was at my local guitar shop in L.A.; the seller saw my name and asked if I knew Gerry Beckley. I told him that, yes, Gerry was my dad. He said, 'I was an assistant at A&M studios in '74, and he and Dewey were so nice to me.' If I ever have kids, the legacy I want to have is the same. Somehow through all those ups and downs and all of the unbelievably bizarre hurricanes that were his and Dewey's careers. . . . I would want to leave that impression on people. I think that that's far more important than any artistic catalogue."

It seems that now Gerry and Dewey have collectively found happiness in the twenty-first century.

In 2020, Dewey still plays an active role in his children's lives. And he is now a grandfather to young Drake by his son Dylan and his wife, Sasha, who live in Hawaii, and to young Donovan and Alina, by his daughter Lauren and her husband, Dan, who live in Georgia. Dewey now spends a great deal of his time visiting with his grandchildren.

After years of involvement with wild horse rescue projects in the western U.S., lifelong animal lover Dewey—along with his wife Penny—adopted a wild Mustang horse in 2018. She would be the horse with no name, appropriately dubbed "Noname" (pronounced "No-nah-mee"). Their adoption adventure became the cover story of *Peninsula*, the local magazine of Palos Verdes, California: "When you marry a woman who loves horses and the house you move into has a couple of empty horse stalls in the yard, what do you think happens? Well, maybe she makes the case that taking in a wild but endangered horse could be a good thing, and not only because it saves an animal's life but reveals a solidarity with the cause."[1] Dewey's reverence for nature and wild animals, which he had possessed since his days as a woods-loving toddler in England, had been his life's constant companion and his artistic muse. Now it had been brought even further forward with Penny's help and support. They had found kindred spirits in one another and together were fighting for the causes they believed in.

While America's fellow rock and pop artists were slowly beginning to wind down, retire, and wave farewell to a lifetime of road living and live performing, America was not. They had started out as a studio band, a band of young upstarts, a band who—in the eyes of some fellow artists—had not "blood-sweat-and-teared" enough to warrant the massive instant success that first arrived via "A Horse with No Name." But decades had passed. Thousands of gigs had been played and were still being played. The band had paid their dues.

Their star on the Hollywood Walk of Fame was well earned and attested to a history of commercial success in recorded music. It was an honor rooted in the past, in the twentieth century. But like Dewey's many road songs that served as odes to both the present moment and perpetual motion, America's journey was ongoing. The band was still on tour—performing songs of the past to people of the present, with an eye toward the future.

NOTES

3. THE BEATLES AND THE BEACH BOYS

1. Dan Peek, *An American Band: The America Story* (Maitland, FL: Xulon, 2004), 26.

5. THE DAWN

1. Brill Brewester, "Interiew: Jeff Dexter, the Man Who Made England Twist," DJHistory.com, 1998, https://daily.redbullmusicacademy.com/2016/12/jeff-dexter-interview.

6. THE MANOR

1. Dan Peek, *An American Band: The America Story* (Maitland, FL: Xulon, 2004), 89.
2. Ibid.
3. Ibid., 97.

7. THE ALBUM

1. Barbara Schultz, "Ken Scott Mix Interview: A Career of Classic Tracks," *Mix*, February 22, 2010, https://www.mixonline.com/technology/ken-scott-mix-interview-378789.
2. Ibid.
3. Dan Peek, liner notes to *Highway: A Boxed Set*, Rhino, 2000.

8. THE CLIMB

1. Dan Peek, *An American Band: The America Story* (Maitland, FL: Xulon, 2004), 95.

9. THE MOVE

1. Dan Peek, *An American Band: The America Story* (Maitland, FL: Xulon, 2004), 126.

11. THE CALIFORNIA SONGS

1. Peek, liner notes to *Highway: A Boxed Set*, Rhino, 2000.
2. Ibid.

12. THE POLARIZER

1. Henry Diltz, *California Dreaming* (Surrey, UK: Genesis, 2007), 292.

13. THE PRODUCER

1. Rob Sheffield, "The Unheard 'Abbey Road': An Exclusive Preview of Beatles' Expanded Final Masterpiece," *Rolling Stone*, August 8, 2019, https://www.rollingstone.com/music/music-news/beatles-abbey-road-super-deluxe-edition-868805/.

2. Cameron Crowe, "America Starts to Rediscover Itself," *Los Angeles Times*, May 18, 1975.

14. THE IDENTITY

1. Cameron Crowe, "America Starts to Rediscover Itself," *Los Angeles Times*, May 18, 1975.
2. "Concert Review," *Billboard*, May 9, 1975.

16. THE BEAST

1. "America: Harbor Documentary," YouTube, 2016, https://www.youtube.com/watch?v=Gm7hMBvlvHw.
2. Ibid.
3. Leonard Lueras, "America Alone on a Soft Rock Island," *Rolling Stone*, March 10, 1977.
4. "America: Harbor Documentary."

17. THE SPLIT

1. Dan Peek, *An American Band: The America Story* (Maitland, FL: Xulon, 2004), 243.
2. Ibid., 252.
3. Randy Patterson, "Dan Peek's Last Interview—Part Two," Boomerocity.com, 2011, https://www.boomerocity.com/dan-peek-s-last-interview-part-two.html.

20. THE COMEBACK

1. Christopher Connelly, "Apartheid Rock." *Rolling Stone*, June 10, 1982, https://www.rollingstone.com/music/music-news/apartheid-rock-108260/.

23. THE CORPORATION

1. "American the Band on *Cover Story*," YouTube, 1984, https://www.youtube.com/watch?v=qgn4B9qQpJY. All Steve Perry quotes in this chapter are from this source.
2. Ibid.

29. THE NEW

1. Bondo Wyszpolski, "Home on the Range," *Peninsula*, April 2019.

BIBLIOGRAPHY

"14 Hour Technicolor Dream." Concert, April 29, 1967.
"America." Episode. *Musikladen*. Radio Bremen, 1974.
"America: Harbor Documentary." YouTube, 2016. https://www.youtube.com/watch?v=Gm7hMBvlvHw.
"American the Band on *Cover Story*." YouTube, 1984. https://www.youtube.com/watch?v=qgn4B9qQpJY.
Brewster, Bill. "Interview: Jeff Dexter, the Man Who Made England Twist." DJHistory.com, 1998. https://11daily.redbullmusicacademy.com/2016/12/jeff-dexter-interview.
"Concert Review." *Billboard*, May 9, 1975.
Connelly, Christopher. "Apartheid Rock." *Rolling Stone*, June 10, 1982. https://www.rollingstone.com/music/music-news/apartheid-rock-108260/.
Crowe, Cameron. "America Starts to Rediscover Itself." *Los Angeles Times*, May 18, 1975.
Diltz, Henry. *California Dreaming*. Surrey, UK: Genesis, 2007.
Lueras, Leonard. "America Alone on a Soft Rock Island." *Rolling Stone*, March 10, 1977.
Patterson, Randy. "Dan Peek's Last Interview—Part Two." Boomerocity.com, 2011. https://www.boomerocity.com/dan-peek-s-last-interview-part-two.html.
Peek, Dan. *An American Band: The America Story*. Maitland, FL: Xulon, 2004.
Peek, Dan. Liner notes to *Highway: A Boxed Set*. Rhino, 2000.
Schultz, Barbara. "Ken Scott Mix Interview: A Career of Classic Tracks." *Mix*, February 22, 2010. https://www.mixonline.com/technology/ken-scott-mix-interview-378789.
Sheffield, Rob. "The Unheard 'Abbey Road': An Exclusive Preview of Beatles' Expanded Final Masterpiece." *Rolling Stone*, August 8, 2019. https://www.rollingstone.com/music/music-news/beatles-abbey-road-super-deluxe-edition-868805/.
Wyszpolski, Bondo. "Home on the Range." *Peninsula*, April 2019.

INDEX

Abbey Road, 112
Abbey Road Studios, 192
Abramowitz, Howard, 16
accidents, of Peek, D., 71–72, 151–152
Adams, Ryan, 231
addiction, Peek, D., struggling with, 152
adjustments, touring, 172, 205–206, 207, 208–209
admiration, musical, 242
aircraft enthusiasts, 187
Air Force families, xi, xii, 14, 17, 232
AIR Studios, 103, 112
album advances, 78
album covers, 63; *Hat Trick*, 108; *History*, 129–130; *Holiday*, 117; *Homecoming*, 91; *Perspective*, 203; *Your Move*, 194, 195
albums, xiv; as continuums, 197; *See also specific titles*
Alcazar, John, 47
Alibi: cover songs in, 171; McCauley and Mollin duo producing, 169; as non-Martin, George, album, 168; "Our Side" and "Their Side" of, 168; session musicians on, 169
alienation, from authenticity, 144
"All My Life," 166
All Things Are Possible, 234
Aloha Stadium, 137
alternative bands, 209
"Amber Cascades," 135

America, 53, 97, 163, 241; at Hollywood star ceremony, 243; Martin, George, and Hartmann, J., with, 140; Martin, George, with, 116; Roberts, Hartmann, J., and Goodman with, 132; Webb and Mumy with, 186; *See also specific topics*
America, xii, 6, 66, 67
Americana jukebox, 47
An American Band (Peek), xiii, 26
Anderson, Sherwood, xiv
Angel Stadium, 136, 137
Anglophilia, 112
the Animals, 24
anonymity, xiii
"Another Try," 117
apartheid, 175–176
"Apartheid Rock" article, 176
archival releases, 237
"Are You There," 142, 143
Arlington Theatre, 205
arrival, in Los Angeles, 78–79
art enthusiasts, Bunnell family as, 13
artistic ambition, 104
artistic core, Southern California, 44
the art world, 120–122
astrology, 95
Asylum Records, 90
As You Like It, 35
Atkinson, Snake, 28
atmospheric music, 214–216

"Atom Heart Mother," 49
Atwood, Dave, 88–89
auditions, 43, 44, 229
authentic artistry, 58, 68, 144, 210

Back Pages, 233
backstage, 53–54
Ballard, Russ, 171, 178, 195; track domination, 192–193; *Your Move* produced by, 191–192
the Band, 49
bandleaders, supportive, 241–242
band name, inspiration for, 47
banjo, 94
Baptist upbringing, 152
Barnes & Barnes, 179–180
Bass, Charles, 183
Bath Festival of Blues and Progressive Music, 40, 44
Battle of the Bands, 31, 35, 154
the Bay Area, California, 120
Bay Area figurative movement, 121
the Beach Boys, 8, 21, 25, 30, 98, 136–137
the Beatles, 21, 22, 25, 29–30, 57
Beatles vs. Stones debate, 25
the Beatle years, xii
Beckley, Gerry, 15; as aircraft enthusiast, 187; Beckley, M. on, 245–248; Beckley, S., with, 246; bridge writing, 179; Bunnell, Dewey, contrasted with, 224–226; Bunnell, Dewey, co-writing with, 162–163, 170–171, 216–217; Bunnell, Dewey, creative compatibility with, 164–165; Bunnell, Dewey, with, 225, 247; as duo with Bunnell, Dewey, 159, 220; Flicker Way home of, 87–88; Galdston co-writing with, 220; on Gretsch guitars, 161; Harrison, G., meeting, 74; insomnia of, 146; interviews with, xiv, xiv–xv; L.A. fascination of, 83; Martin, George, bonding with, 115–116; on multiple producers approach, 197–198; Mumy co-writing with, 179, 232–233; musical character of, 4; new marriage of, 245; nomadic lifestyle, 17; piano learning of, 15, 15–16; "pop star" intentions, 16; solo albums of, 226; songwriting of, 61, 92–93, 93, 104–105, 117, 122–124, 132–134, 143–145, 167, 169–170, 179, 181–182, 214, 217, 219–220, 223, 232–233; studio session work, 36–37, 37; as supportive bandleader, 241–242; on use of drum machines, 198; vocal talent, 33–34; with the Weags, 29, 30–31, 33; Webb co-writing with, 201–202
Beckley, Joe, 210
Beckley, Matthew, 161, 166, 245–248
Beckley, Raymond, 14, 33
Beckley, Sally, 245; Beckley, G., with, 246
Beckley, Sheila, 14, 15
Beckley family, 210
the Bee Gees, 51, 59–60
"Bell Tree," 124
Bernstein, Elmer, 159–160
Best New Artist, Grammy Awards, 99–100
Beverly Hills home, of Geffen, 79, 83–84
Bickershaw Festival, 72
Billboard charts, 115, 122, 123; "A Horse with No Name" on, 51; *Harbor* on, 147; *Here and Now* on, 233; *History* on, 130; *Live* on, 160; *Silent Letter* on, 166, 167–168; "You Can Do Magic" on, 178
Birchmere (venue), 239
Bird Streets of Los Angeles, 87, 159
Blaine, Hal, 93, 97, 106
Bleeding Hearts Club, 17
the Blue Boar, 49
Bob Hope Special (TV program), 119
Bookends, 40
Boone, Pat, 52
"The Border," 193, 194
Brennan, Daphne, 38
Brewer, Teresa, 11
bridge writing, of Beckley, G., 179
British Invasion music, 25
Brown, Arthur, 50
Browne, Jackson, 84
Bunnell, Dewey, 11, 22; art world appreciation, 120–122; Beckley, G., contrasted with, 224–226; Beckley, G., co-writing with, 162–163, 170–171, 216–217; Beckley, G., creative compatibility with, 164–165; Beckley, G., with, 225, 247; Beckley, M., on, 245–248; Bunnell, Dylan, and Bunnell, L., with, 177; Bunnell, P., with, 221;

INDEX

Cape cobra run-in, 176–177; Clapton and Hillman with, 141; "composerdom" of, 163; compositional talent, 69; Dale with, 23; in the Daze, 37; Diltz and Burden with, 86; dramatic arts study, 35–36, 38; as duo with Beckley, G., 159, 220; Geffen with, 77; as grandfather, 248; Haimer co-writing with, 179–180; hairstyle change, 24; interviews with, xiv, xiv–xv; Kauai reflected on by, 146; Kesey with, 121; as "leader of the pack," 24; Marin County relocation of, 83; Mother Nature connection of, 12, 14; Mumy co-writing with, 179–180, 214; on music videos, 194–195; on *Perspective*, 198; songwriting of, 5–6, 37, 61–63, 65–66, 96–97, 106–107, 114–115, 125, 142–143, 170, 171, 179–181, 220–222, 231, 231–232; as supportive bandleader, 241–242; on symphony shows, 160; on use of drum machines, 199
Bunnell, Dylan, 177
Bunnell, Lauren, 177
Bunnell, Penny, 221, 222
Bunnell, William, 12
Bunnell family, 13
Burden, Gary, 86, 91
Burgundy Records, 230
the Byrds, 142
"By the Time I Get to Phoenix," 186

Cahuilla Indian Reservation, California, 108
"California Dreamin'," 35, 164
California Dreaming (film), 164
California lifestyle, 95
"California Revisited," 95; as rock song, 96
California rock, xii, 5, 214
Calire, Jimmy, 139, 171–172
Campbell, Glen, 184–185
Campbell, Rich, 229–230; as tour manager, 238; tour reflections of, 242
Campbell-Thiebaud Gallery, 121
Campo de Encino estate, of Webb, 184
cancellation, of tour, 142–143

"Can't Fall Asleep to a Lullaby," 199, 199–200
"Can't You See," 135
Cape cobra (snake), 176–177
Capitol Records, 167–168, 191, 192; contract concluded with, 205; Hartmann, J., negotiating with, 160–161
Captain and Tenille, 102
Captain Beefheart, 126
"captive audience," 125–126
Caribou Ranch (studio), 131
"Caroline No," 234
Carousel, 227
Carpenders Park, London, 40
Casey's Shadow (film), 159
Cassidy, David, 223
"Cast the Spirit," 193
catchphrase, of Peek, D., 150
"Catch That Train," 170
CB radio, 215
CDs. *See* compact disc format
Cecil, Malcom, 102
Central Park concert movie, 164
the Centrics, 28
change, xi, 117–118, 172, 173
characteristics: of Dexter, 45; of Peek, D., 4–5
chart bullet, 117–118
chart topping, xii
Chicago, 47, 130
"Children," 38
Children of the Future, 40
Chipperfield, England, 48
"Cinderella," 200
cinematic, *Hideaway* as, 134
Clapton, Eric, 141, 142
"Clarice," 61
Clifton, Peter, 164
clout, 173, 198
"Coastline," 169–170
commercialism, xiii, 185
communes, 7
compact disc format (CDs), 213
"composerdom," of Bunnell, Dewey, 163
composer-performers, 69
compositional talent, of Bunnell, Dewey, 69

compositions: "A Horse with No Name," 8, 66; "All My Life," 166; "Bell Tree," 124; "Can't Fall Asleep to a Lullaby," 199–200; "Daisy Chain," 123; "Don't Cross the River," 94; "Green Monkey," 106–107; "Hat Trick," 108–109; "Hideaway Part I" and "Hideaway Part II," 134; "High in the City," 162–163; "It's Life," 108; "Love on the Vine," 180; "Molten Love," 106; "Monster," 144; "Moon Song," 97; "Now Sue," 226; "Only in Your Heart," 92; "Sergeant Darkness," 146; "She's Gonna Let You Down," 105; "The Last Unicorn," 188–189; "Today's the Day," 136; "Unconditional Love," 202; "Valentine," 171; "Ventura Highway," 98; "Woman Tonight," 122; "You Can Do Magic," 178–179; "Young Moon," 216
concept record, *Hat Trick* as, 104
Continental Hyatt House, 54
continuums, albums as, 197
contract: Capitol Records concluding, 205; Lookout Management disuse of, 78; new, 77–78; Warner Brothers concluding, 160
"Convoy," 215
"The Cool of the Evening," 226
Cooper, Ray, 58–59
Cornwall, England, 96
"Cornwall Blank," 96
Corona Academy of the Dramatic Arts, 38
"Corporate," *Perspective* as, 203
the Corporation, 33
cover songs: in *Alibi*, 171; of "California Dreamin'," 164; in *Perspective*, 199, 200; of "Right Before Your Eyes," 181
Cover Story (TV program), 199
cowman's shed, 48
co-writing: Beckley, G., and Galdston, 220; Beckley, G., and Mumy, 179, 232–233; Beckley, G., and Webb, 201–202; Bunnell, Dewey, and Beckley, G., 162–163, 170–171, 216–217; Bunnell, Dewey, and Mumy, 214; Bunnell, Dewey, Mumy, and Haimer, 179–180; Maberry, and Peek, D., 115, 124–125

creative arts, 244
creative compatibility, Bunnell, Dewey, and Beckley, G., 164–165
Crook, Bill, 239–240
Crook Custom Guitars, 240
Crosby, Stills, Nash & Young (CSNY), 48, 57–58
Crosby, Stills & Nash (CSN), 91, 100, 172
crossroads, for Peek, D., 149
Crowe, Cameron, xiii
"Crying in My Sleep," 233–234
CSN. *See* Crosby, Stills & Nash
CSNY. *See* Crosby, Stills, Nash & Young
cultural boycott, of South Africa, 175
cultural impact, of hits, xiii
cultural legacy, 206, 210
culture shock, 79
the Cyclones, 27

"Daisy Chain," 123
Dale, Dick, 23
Dan Armstrong bass guitar, 52
Darkness on the Edge of Town, xiv
Davis, Chip, 214–216
Davis, Clive, 47
Davis, Gary, 160
Days of Future Passed, 40
the Daze, 33–34, 36; Bunnell, Dewey in, 37; Peek, D., joining, 35
DD Tucker, 89
death, of Peek, D., 235
De Lane Lea Studios, 183
demographics, 239
"Desert Song," 6, 50, 65–66
destination recording, 131, 139
Dexter, Jeff, 6, 41, 42–43, 59; characteristics, 45; management dissolved with, 76, 77; musical connections, 44, 45; Peek, D., attachment to, 75
The Dick Cavett Show (TV program), 52
Dickey, David, 89, 101, 108, 112, 113, 240
Diltz, Henry, 85, 91, 137, 168; banjo playing, 94; Burden and Bunnell, Dewey, with, 86
Dirtpit Manor, 48
documentary film, on *Harbor*, 145, 146, 147
Doe Run, Missouri, 28

INDEX

"Do It Again," 8
"Donkey Jaw," 63
"Don't Cross the River," 94
"Down to Water," 146–147
dragon, 143
dramatic arts, Bunnell, Dewey, studying, 35–36, 38
dreams, of Beckley, 14
"Driving," 237
drum machines, 198, 199; Beckley, G., on use of, 198; Bunnell, Dewey, on use of, 199
duo, Bunnell, Dewey, and Beckley, G., as, 159, 220

Eagle Poker, 141–142
the Eagles, 75
Easy Rider (film), 7, 185
Ed Sullivan Show (TV program), 21, 22, 29
egos, 69, 143, 146, 150
'80s pop, transition to, 192
"Eleanor Rigby," 115
El Mirage, 186
Emerick, Geoff, 119
Encore, 213
English Leather, 24
Erickson, Mark, 120
Europe, touring in, 49, 113
"Even the Score," 180–181
the Everly Brothers, 52
"Everyone I Meet Is from California," 95–96, 218
"Fallin' Off the World," 202

fame, 209
fan base, 209
"The Farm," 214
Fekete, Steve, 240
Felt Forum, 125
Fender Shenandoah guitar, 51–52
"Ferry Cross the Mersey," 34
Fields, W. C., 72
"Fifteen Big Ones," 170
fiftieth anniversary, 238
financial side, of recording industry, 78, 112–113
Five Mile Road, 227
Flicker Way home, of Beckley, G., 87–88
Follow the Buffalo, 41, 43

Ford Country Squire, 88
Ford transit van, 48, 49
formal exit, of Peek, D., 153–154
Fort Worth, Texas, 14
Fountains of Wayne, 230
450SL Mercedes, 84
four-four chords, 170
four-string tenor guitar, 30
the 14-Hour Technicolor Dream (concert), 41
freedom, 3, 6, 48
"From a Moving Train," 219
Fulfillingness' First Finale, 102

Galdston, Phil, 220
"gear guy," 161
Geffen, David, 74–75, 76, 107, 173, 185; Asylum Records founded by, 90; Beverly Hills home of, 79, 83–84; Bunnell, Dewey, with, 77; commission royalties of, 78; Warner Brothers negotiations of, 77–78
Geffen-Roberts team, 75, 76, 111, 117–118
Genesis, 29, 34, 35
George, Lowell, xv
"Glass King," 231–232
the golden-age rock star, xv
"Goodbye," 105–106
Goodman, Harlan, 118, 132
Gramaphone Records, 214, 216
Grammy Awards, 99–100, 243
grandfather, Bunnell, Dewey, as, 248
the Grateful Dead, 72
gratitude, 146
greatest hits. *See Encore*; *History*
Green, Robert, 120
"Greenhouse," 217
"Green Monkey," 106–107
Gretsch guitars, 161
"the group," 164–165
Grundig stereo, 15
guest artists, on *Here and Now*, 231
"Guitarland," 19
guitar playing, of Peek, D., 4, 27, 34, 96
guitars. *See specific models*
guitar tech, Worrell, B., as, 240

Haimer, Robert, 179–180
hairstyles, 24

"Half a Man," 124
Hamptons Way, North London, 43
"Hangover," 171
Harbor, 139–140, 145, 146, 146–147, 150; on *Billboard* charts, 147; documentary film of, 145, 146, 147
A Hard Day's Night, 22
Hard Rock Cafe, 48
harmonies, 8, 39, 57, 59, 92, 237; on "Till the Sun Comes Up Again," 93–94
Harris, Bob, 50
Harrison, George, 74, 127
Harrison, Pattie, 127
Hartmann, John, 117–118, 153, 172; America with, 132, 140; Capitol Records deal negotiated by, 160–161; Geffen-Roberts team and, 117–118; *Holiday* success increased by, 118
Hartmann, Phil, 129–130
Hat Trick, 88, 101–102, 102, 103; album cover, 108; as concept record, 104; session musicians on, 89, 103
"Hat Trick," 108–109
"hat trick" term, 109
Hawaii: Martin, George, on, 139, 140, 145; as touring conclusion, 139
Hayden, Tom, 176
"Head and Heart," 98
health-forward lifestyles, 151
"healthify," 153
"Heart of Gold," 66
Hearts, 119, 122–123, 124–125
helicopters, 140
Henley-on-Thames, London, 127
Hepatitis C, 151
"Here," 61
Here and Now, 230, 231; on *Billboard* charts, 233; guest artists on, 231
"Here and Now," 230
HIC. *See* Honolulu International Center
Hideaway, 131–132; as cinematic, 134; plateauing success of, 136
"Hideaway Part I" and "Hideaway Part II," 134
"High in the City," 162–163
Hillman, Chris, 141, 142
hippie ethos, xii, xiii, 63, 210, 224
History, 213; album cover, 129–130; on *Billboard* charts, 130; Martin, George,

mixing, 129
hits, 213; chart topping, xii; cultural impact of, xiii
H.M.S. Pinafore, 16
Holiday, 103, 112; album cover, 117; Hartmann, J., increasing success of, 118
"Hollywood," 113, 114
Hollywood Bowl, 160
Hollywood star ceremony, 243, 243–244
Hollywood Walk of Fame, 243, 248
Homecoming, 8, 51, 85, 88, 102; album cover, 91; session musicians on, 89
homecoming, from touring, 54–55
"Honey," 193
honing, of tours, 238, 238–239
Honolulu, Hawaii, 187–188
Honolulu International Center (HIC), 139
The Hootenanny (talent show), 34
"Hope," 217
Hopper, Dennis, 7
horse rescue projects, 248
"A Horse with No Name," xi, xii, 11, 50, 66; "A Place with No Name" sampling, 68–69; composition of, 8, 66; as formerly "Desert Song," 6, 50; Grammy nomination of, 99; as number one hit, 54, 58, 66–67, 69, 76; soundtrack use of, 68; themes, 6–8, 68, 69; on U.K. *Billboard* charts, 51; U.K. record award received by, 67
"Hound Dog," 11
Hourglass, 214, 216, 218
house engineer, Worrell, J., as, 240
"House of the Rising Sun," 24
Howson, Dave, 41, 43, 44
Human Nature, 219, 222
Human Nature Studios, 226
"Hurricane," 150

ideological changeovers, 198
identity, 17
ideology: 1960s, 63, 69, 96, 96–97, 99, 245; 1970s, xii, 68; of youths, 7
Iha, James, 230
illnesses, of Peek, D., 19, 29
immigration difficulties, 54–55
"Implosion" (charity event), 45
impressions, 245–248
inclusivity, 244, 244–245

INDEX

In Concert, 205
"I Need You," 3, 4; inspirations for, 59–60; Nilsson loving, 60; as "too British" sounding, 5, 6
Innervisions, 102
insomnia, of Beckley, G., 146
"Inspector Mills," 181, 182
inspirations, 47, 59–60
interviews, with Bunnell, Dewey, and Beckley, G., xiv, xiv–xv
IOU sheets, 142
irreplaceable, Peek, D., as, 155
"I Saw Her Standing There," 26
"It's Life," 108
"I Want to Hold Your Hand," 26

Jackson, Michael, 68–69
Jagger, Mick, 11, 25
Jardine, Al, 136–137
Jenkins, Gordon, 145
J. Frank Wilson and the Cavaliers, 28
Jim, the World's Greatest (film), 124
"Jody," 178
Jolliffe, David, 85–86, 89

Kasem, Casey, 31
Katz-Gallin-Morey, 172–173, 178
Kauai, Hawaii, 139, 146, 150
Kay acoustic guitar, 18
Kellgren, Gary, 126
Kennedy, John F., 22
Kenton, Middlesex, England, 15
Kerouac, Jack, 5
Kesey, Ken, 120, 121
King Biscuit Flower Hour Records, 219
King's Road apartment complex, 87
Kinney Records, 46
Korean War, 13, 14
Kyushu, Japan, 18

Lamm, Robert, 130–131, 227, 228
Larson, Jeff, 237
"The Last Unicorn," 184, 188–189
The Last Unicorn (film), 183, 184, 188, 189
L.A. Times, xiii, 118
Laurel Canyon, California, 84
Leacox, Willie, 89–90, 112, 113, 240
"leader of the pack," 24, 223

Leave It to Beaver (TV program), 17
Lennon, John, xii, 126
Leno, Jay, 52
"Letter," 134–135
Levine, Steve, 216
Lewis, Linda, 43
Like a Brother, 130, 227–228, 228
Linderman, Hank, 216
Lindley, David, 58–59
LinnDrum, 199
Lion & Lamb Records, 234
A Little Touch of Schmilsson in the Night, 145
Live, 160
live album, 159
"Live and Let Die," 111
live performance, xv, 237–238
"logo groups," 130, 244
London, xi, 9
London Central High School, 14, 26, 29, 36
London Symphony Orchestra, 183
"Lonely People," 115, 116
"Longing for You," 11
Lookout Management, 75, 78
Los Angeles, California (L.A.), 74, 76, 244; arrival in, 78–79; Beckley, G., fascinated by, 83; Bird Streets of, 87, 159; Peek, D., unsettled by, 83
Los Angeles Greek Theater, 159
loss, unavoidability of, 92
Lost and Found, 237
lottery drafting system, 72–74
"Love," 180
"Love & Leaving," 232–233
"Love on the Vine," 180
love songs, 94, 97
the Lovin' Spoonful, 115
Lueras, Leonard, 147
Lyceum Ballroom, 42

M1 motorway, 48–49
Maberry, Catherine "Cathie," 36, 63, 71; Peek, D., co-writing with, 115, 124–125
Ma 'Lei, 187
management: change of, 117–118, 172, 173; Dexter, loss of, 76, 77
"Manager of the Month Club," 90
Mannheim Steamroller, 215

"Man's Road," 189
Marcus, Greil, xiv
Marin County, California, 83
marketability comparisons, to CSNY, 57–58
Markovitz, Bob, 102
Martin, George, 103, 111, 131; *Alibi* lacking production of, 168; America with, 116, 140; Beckley, G., bonding with, 115–116; on Hawaii, 139, 140, 145; *History* mixed by, 129; "Inspector Mills" cameo of, 182; as unavailable, 159, 159–160
Martin, Giles, 112
Martyn, John, 98
material success, 141
Mathis, Johnny, 12
maxi-single, 8
McAllister, Eddie, 27
McCartney, Linda, 127
McCartney, Paul, 3, 127
McCauley, Matthew, 169, 183. *See also* McCauley and Mollin duo
McCauley and Mollin duo, 169
McKernan, Ron "Pigpen," 72
melodic line, 39
metered sound, 123
Middle Earth (club), 41
Middle Earth Records, 41
"Midnight," 125
"Miniature," 117
Mitchell, Joni, 84, 234
mobile unit, of the Record Plant, 139–140
modern era, relevance in, 230
Modern Folk Quartet, 180
modus operandi, 153
Mollin, Fred, 169, 233. *See also* McCauley and Mollin duo
"Molten Love," 106
"Moment to Moment," 220
"Monster," 143, 144, 144–145
Moody Blues, 40
"Moon Song," 96–97, 97
Morey, Jim, 172–173, 205, 208
Morgan Studios, 9, 37
Morris Minor, 39
Mother Nature, 12, 14
Mrs. McThing (play), 221
MTV (TV channel), 194, 194–195

multiple producers: Beckley, G., on, 197–198; *Perspective* using, 198
Mumy, Bill, 85–87, 150–151; America with, 186; Beckley, G., co-writing with, 179, 232–233; Bunnell, Dewey, co-writing with, 179–180, 214
musical admiration, 242
musical character, of Beckley, G., 4
musical connections: of Derek Taylor, 74; of Dexter, 44, 45
musical credits, of Samwell, 41–42
musical output, xv
musical personalities, 224
musical variety television programs, 25; *See also specific titles*
music history, 209
music scene: of the Bay Area, 120; of Laurel Canyon, 84
music video: Bunnell, Dewey, on, 194–195; "Hope," 217; "The Border," 194; "You Can Do Magic," 194
Musikladen (radio show), 3
Musikladen (TV program), 113
"Muskrat Candlelight," 101
"Muskrat Love," 101–102, 107
mutual appreciation, 224
"My Dear," 193–194
"My Sweet Lord," 122
mythology, 98

Nashville, Tennessee, 233
nature, xv, 7, 203, 223
Neal, Chris, 37
Neal S. Blaisdell Center Arena, 187
Nebraska farmhouse, 216, 218
"Never Be Lonely," 179
"Never Found the Time," 65
new contract, 77–78
new marriage, of Beckley, G., 245
New Mexico, 65
Nilsson, Harry, 60, 87–88, 126, 165
"1941," 165
1970s: ideology, xii, 68; as remedy, xi; rock-pop scene, 149–150, 154–155
"1960," 165
1960s ideology, 63, 69, 96, 96–97, 99, 245
Nirvana, 214
nomadic lifestyle, of Beckley, G., 17
"Noname" (horse), 248

'Norman, Jim Ed, 103
North America, touring in, 51–53, 71
nostalgia act, 206
"Nothing's So Far Away (as Yesterday)," 214
"Now Sue," 226
number one: "A Horse with No Name" as, 54, 58, 66–67, 69; *America* as, 67

ocean liner, 13, 14
octaves, 116
Old Dominion University, 36
The Old Grey Whistle Test (TV program), 50
"Old Virginia," 124–125
"Oloololo," 222
Omaha, Nebraska, 23
"One Morning," 165
"Only Game in Town," 164
"Only in Your Heart," 92–93
On the Road (Kerouac), 5
origins, returning to, 206
Osborn, Joe, 93
"Our Side" and "Their Side," 168
over-the-counter drugs, 71
overtones, 66
Oxygen Records, 219

Pacific Ocean Blue, 170
"Pages," 220–221
Palmer, Bradley, 229
paraphernalia, 215
Parker, Tom, 161
parties, of McCartney, P., 127
partners, tour, 88–89
Peek, Archie, 28
Peek, Dan, xiii, 18, 26, 73; accidents of, 71–72, 151–152; addiction struggles of, 152; catchphrase of, 150; characteristics of, 4–5; crossroads for, 149; the Daze joined by, 35; death of, 235; Dexter attachment of, 75; formal exit of, 153–154; guitar playing of, 4, 27, 34, 96; illnesses, 19, 29; as irreplaceable, 155; L.A. unsettling to, 83; Maberry co-writing with, 115, 124–125; piano learning, 18; religious focus, 153; songwriting of, 63, 94, 95, 108, 124, 135–136, 150, 154; surgery, 72

Peek, Gerri, 18
Peek, Milton, 17–18, 153–154
Peninsula (magazine), 248
"perpetual virginity of the soul," 105
Perry, Rupert, 160
Perry, Steve, 199–200
Perspective: album cover, 203; Bunnell, Dewey, reflecting on, 198; as "Corporate," 203; cover songs in, 199, 200; multiple producers approach of, 198; nature theme lacking on, 203
Peshawar, Pakistan, 19, 26
Pet Sounds, 184
piano: Beckley, G., learning, 15, 15–16; Peek, D., learning, 18
"Pigeon Song," 62–63
Pink Floyd, 49
"Pipeline," 27
"A Place with No Name," 68–69
Poco, 141
Poipu Beach, Hawaii, 139
Pollstar Award for Best Attraction, 239
pop-ness, of *Silent Letter*, 163
"pop star" intentions, of Beckley, G., 16
popular art, 150
A Postcard from California, 137
pre-Internet marketing, 215–216
Presley, Elvis, 11
pressure, 102, 103, 131
"produced upon," 191
producer, Samwell as, 44, 59
proscenium arch, 187–188
Pro Tools, 216
PSA (airline), 120
Pussycats, 126

Queen Elizabeth I (ship), 13

"Rainbow Song," 107
Ralfini, Ian, 44
Ramsey, Willis Alan, 101
Ramstein, Germany, 30
Rankin/Bass filmmaking team, 183
Ratfields, 41
reassurance song, "Only in Your Heart" as, 92
recording industry, financial side of, 78, 112–113

the Record Plant (studio), 85, 86, 91, 102, 126, 139–140
"record-with-hit," 51
Redgrave, Vanessa, 11
Redwood, 85–86
Reed, Phil, 41
Reel Big Fish, 241
Rehearsal Studios, 153
relevance: modern era, 230; second wave of, 209
religious focus, of Peek, D., 153
remedy, the 1970s as, xi
the Renegades, 24, 223
re-recording: "Everyone I Meet Is from California," 218; "You Can Do Magic," 218
re-releases, 213
respect, 224
returning, to origins, 206
Reuther, Pete, 48
revenue, sources of, 209
reverse grassroots campaign, 207, 208
Rhino Records, 213
"Ride On," 231
"Right Before Your Eyes," 181
"River Deep—Mountain High," 35
"Riverside," 49, 61–62
"the road," 218
roadies, 130
road lifestyles, 207
Roberts, Elliot, 74–75, 90, 111, 132
Rock Machine Turns You On, 47
rock 'n' roll, 4–5, 186
rock-pop scene, 70s, 149–150, 154–155
rock song, "California Revisited" as, 96
Rolling Stone magazine, 3, 147, 176
"Roll Over Beethoven," 27
romantic ballads, 132–133
the Roundhouse in Chalk Farm, 45
royalties, 78, 154
Rubber Soul, 3
"Rudolph Valentino," 181
Ruislip Air Force Base, 33
Russian Romantics, 15

safari, 176
Sailor, 40
Samuels, Calvin, "Fuzzy," 113

Samwell, Ian "Sammy," 6, 42, 58; musical credits, 41–42; as producer, 44, 59
San Angelo, Texas, 28
"Sandman," 61
"San Simeon," 137
Santana, Carlos, 136
"Sarah," 145
"Saturn Nights," 95
Sausalito, California, 119
Sausalito Record Plant, 119–120
Schlesinger, Adam, 230
Schmit, Timothy B., 141, 155
Scott, Ken, 58, 59
scuba diving, 140
Seals and Crofts, 45
Sebastian, John, 115
second wave, of relevance, 209
"See How the Love Goes," 200
segregation, 176
self-producing, 104, 107
"Sergeant Darkness," 145–146, 146
session musicians: on *Alibi*, 169; on *Hat Trick*, 89, 103; on *Homecoming*, 89
700 Club, 152
seventh chords, 5, 37, 161, 202, 217–218
SFMOMA (art museum), 121
Shazam app, 69
"Sheltering Sky," 228
"She's a Liar," 132–133
"She's Gonna Let You Down," 104–105
Silent Letter, 162, 166; on *Billboard* charts, 166, 167–168; pop-ness of, 163; as "Silent Record," 163
"Silent Record," 163
Silvertone electric guitars, 26, 27
SIR. *See* Studio Instrument Rentals
"Sister Golden Hair," 122, 129
"Sleeper Train," 218
Smothers Brothers Show (TV program), 119
societal ties, 8
solo albums, of Beckley, G., 226
solo performer, Webb as, 185
"Sometimes When We Touch," 169
song bridge, 124
songwriting, 5; of Beckley, G., 61, 92–93, 93, 104–105, 117, 122–124, 132–134, 143–145, 167, 169–170, 179, 181–182, 214, 217, 219–220, 223, 232–233; of

Bunnell, Dewey, 5–6, 37, 61–63, 65–66, 96–97, 106–107, 114–115, 125, 142–143, 170, 171, 179–181, 220–222, 231, 231–232; of Maberry, 115, 124–125; of Mumy, 179, 179–180; of Peek, D., 63, 94, 95, 108, 124, 135–136, 150, 154
soundtracks, 68, 188–189
South Africa: cultural boycott of, 175; touring in, 175–176
Southern California, 21, 23, 44, 65
"The Speak," 44
The Speakeasy Club, 45
"Special Girl," 200
Springsteen, Bruce, xiv, 208
Steen, Ryland, 241
"Stereo," 201
the Steve Miller Band, 40
Stevens, Cat, 50
Stewart, Rod, 127
Stone, Mike D., 85, 86
"Story," 124
Story of a Teenager, 119, 124
"straight" crowds, xii
Studio Instrument Rentals (SIR), 90, 153
studio sessions, Beckley, G., working, 36–37, 37
"Submarine Ladies," 105
subscribers, 215–216
substances, 149, 150–151, 152, 154
success: of *Hideaway*, 136; of *Holiday*, 118; material, 141; pressure of, 131
Sun City, South Africa, 175
Sunset Marquis Hotel, 87
supportive bandleaders, 241–242
surfing, 21
Surfin' Safari, 30
"Surfin' Safari," 21
"Surfin' USA," 21
surf music, 21, 22–23
surgery, Peek, D., having, 72
"Survival," 167, 171
Swan Lake, 16
Sweet Baby James, 85
Sweetwater Saloon, 120
Swinging Sixties scene, 26
symphony shows, 160
synthesizer music, 209
Syracuse, New York, 18, 19

"Take It Easy," 7
tax issues, 76
Taylor, Derek, 74
Teaser and the Firecat, 50
technology, 229
television appearances, 50
That's the Way It Is, 60
This Magnificent, 241
"This Note's for You," 185
Thomas, Ian, 181
three-part harmony bands, 153
three-part vocals, 4, 39, 57, 66
"Three Roses," 62
ticket prices, 239
"Till the Sun Comes Up Again," 93, 93–94
time, 224–225
"Tin Man," 114–115
T. J. Martell Foundation, 217
"Today," 228
"Today's the Day," 135, 136
"To Each His Own," 91–92
togetherness, 69, 244
"Tonight's the Night," 127
"too British," 5, 6
Top of the Pops (TV program), 51
Torremolinos, Spain, 71
tour manager, Campbell, R., as, 238
tour opener, Webb as, 186–188
tours, 48–49, 209, 209–210, 229, 248; adjustments made for, 172, 205–206, 207, 208–209; Campbell, R., reflecting on, 242; cancellation of, 142–143; in Europe, 49, 113; Hawaii as conclusion for, 139; homecoming from, 54–55; honing of, 238, 238–239; in North America, 51–53, 71; partners for, 88–89; with Poco, 141; in South Africa, 175–176
track domination, of Ballard, 192–193
Tramp's (club), 45
transition, to '80s pop, 192
Trident Studios, 6, 50, 58
tuning, unique, 65–66
"tuning in," 155
the twist, 13, 42–43, 44

U.K. *See* United Kingdom
U.K. record award, 67
"Unconditional Love," 202

unique tuning, 65–66
United Kingdom (U.K.), 12, 25, 26
United Nations, 175
upgrades, to live performance, 237–238
"Up Up and Away," 185

"Valentine," 171
Van Go Gan, 226
the Vanguards, 30
"Ventura Highway," 90, 98, 99
Vickers Viscount N306 (airplane), 141, 187, 207
Vietnam War, 61, 72
View from the Ground, 177, 178, 191, 197
"View from the Hotel Window" (photographic series), 245
Virgin Records, 184
vocal arrangements, 39
Vocal Hall of Fame, 243
vocal talent, of Beckley, G., 33–34

Wachtel, Waddy, 84–85
Walker, Lew, 29
Walsh, Joe, 107
Walsh, Tom, 139, 152–153
waltz three-quarter time, 144
Warner Brothers, 3, 5, 6, 8; audition for, 43, 44; contract concluded with, 160; Geffen negotiating with, 77–78
Warner Reprise, 44
Watergate Hotel, 142
Waters, Roger, 49
"Watership Down," 133, 133–134, 188
the Weags, 29, 30–31, 33
Webb, Jimmy, 183, 184, 189; as aircraft enthusiast, 187; America with, 186; Beckley, G., co-writing with, 201–202; on Campbell, G., 184–185; Campo de Encino estate of, 184; on commercialism, 185; as solo performer, 185; as tour opener, 186–188
Weber, Dewey, 23
"Wednesday Morning," 219–220
"We Got All Night," 200
Wells, Patricia, 12

West Drayton, England, 39
Whiskey a Go Go (club), 52, 53–54
White Album, 105
"Whole Wide World," 217, 218
"Who Loves You," 133
Williams, Tom, 31
Williams, William F., 187
"Willin'," xv
Wilson, Brian, 21, 88
Wilson, Carl, 218–219, 227, 228
"Wind Wave," 107
"Winning," 178
"Woman Tonight," 122
Women's Movement, 118
Wonder, Stevie, 102
Wood, Ronnie, 88
Woods, Bobby, 226
Woods, Michael "Wood-z," 151, 161–162, 166, 206–207, 210
Woodstock, 3
"Woodstock," 234
"Woodstock generation," 44
"The Word," 3
"World Alone," 221–222
Worrell, Bill, 240
Worrell, Jeff, 240
the Wrecking Crew, 93, 106
Wyatt, Martin, 43–44

Yamaha FG-180 guitars, 48
"You Can Do Magic," 178, 178–179, 191; on *Billboard* charts, 178; music video, 194; re-recording, 218
"You Could've Been the One," 168
Young, Neil, xi, 5, 66
"Young Moon," 216, 216–217
Your Move: album cover, 194, 195; Ballard producing, 191–192; *View from the Ground* compared to, 197
"Your Move," 195
youths, 7

Zappa, Frank, 126
Zevon, Warren, 84–85